THE PRESENCE
OF THE PAST

THE PRESENCE OF THE PAST

Essays on Modern British and American Poetry

Jeremy Hooker

POETRY WALES PRESS
1987

POETRY WALES PRESS
56 PARCAU AVENUE, BRIDGEND, MID GLAMORGAN

© Jeremy Hooker, 1987

British Library Cataloguing in Publication Data

Hooker, Jeremy
The presence of the past : essays on
modern British and American poetry.
1. English poetry – 20th century –
History and criticism
I. Title
821'.914'09   PR601
ISBN 0-907476-71-6

All rights reserved. No part of this publication may be
reproduced stored in a retrieval system, or transmitted in any
form or by any means, electronic, mechanical, photocopying or
otherwise, without the prior permission of the copyright holder.

*The publisher acknowledges the financial assistance of the
Welsh Arts Council*

Cover Illustration by Peter Lord

Cover Design: Jeane Rees

*Printed in Great Britain by
J. W. Arrowsmith Ltd, Bristol*

Contents

Preface	7
1. The Presence of the Past	9
2. Jeffrey Wainwright	33
3. Mary Casey: The Poetry of Aloneness	37
4. T.S. Eliot: Tradition and the 'resident alien'	46
5. Seeing the World: The Poetry of George Oppen	58
6. "The boundaries of our distances": George Oppen's 'Of Being Numerous'	73
7. Crossings and Turns: The Poetry of John Matthias	97
8. John Ormond: The Accessible Song	106
9. The Poetry of Anthony Conran	114
10. John Tripp: *Collected Poems* 1958-78	123
11. R.S. Thomas: Prytherch and After	128
12. Roland Mathias: "The Strong Remembered Words"	141
13. "A Big Sea Running in a Shell": The Poetry of Gillian Clarke	151
14. The Poetry of Nearness: Anglo-Welsh Poetry in the 1960s	156
15. Resistant Voices: Five Young Anglo-Welsh Poets	177
16. Barbarous Reflections	199
Acknowledgements	224
Index	226

Preface

With the exception of the essays on John Ormond and Anthony Conran and the review of John Tripp's *Collected Poems*, all of the essays in this book have been written since the publication of *Poetry of Place* in 1982, and most have been written in the past two years. The exclusion of the pieces on the three Anglo-Welsh poets from my previous book of essays was due to my decision to include them in a book on Anglo-Welsh poetry. That, in part, is what *The Presence of the Past* is. Only in part, however, since it includes essays on English and American poetry as well. The juxtaposition of subjects reflects my belief that different poetries benefit from being seen against or in relation to one another. However, I do not wish to claim for the book the kind of unity that belongs to a pre-determined scheme. I have written about some of the modern poets who interest and move me, and who have, with three or four exceptions, found few advocates or interpreters yet. This is partly what I mean by exploratory criticism, which is the approach adopted in the essays in this book. Except in the more general discussions, my first aim has been to concentrate on and explore the poetry itself, with no thought of illustrating a thesis. If there is no general thesis, however, there are several common concerns. These are urgent concerns, which are woven into experience, and may not be disentangled to form an abstract general pattern. They may be described, briefly, as matters of national and personal identity, of social and individual being, of history, of the relation between history and myth, and between past and present. They are intricate, complex matters, which raise fundamental questions about the nature of reality, especially in the choice or tension between historicist and religious claims. In view of the nature of the book, and of its development from explorations begun in *Poetry of Place*, I had intended to write an introduction which would both bring together the various concerns, and clarify my critical values. On consideration, however, it seemed truer to my exploratory approach to disclose something of the process of thinking and feeling behind the essays. Accordingly, I conclude with a writing, 'Barbarous Reflections', which consists of journal extracts, all arising from reading and thinking in relation to the concerns of the book, and written at the same time as most of it. All critical judgements are vulnerable, but this piece has a special vulnerability. But the element of personal risk is inextricably part of the matter, and it is the only kind of clarification of values that I can, at this time, appropriately make.

The Presence of the Past

I

I want in this essay to discuss work by three modern British poets, David Jones, Basil Bunting and Geoffrey Hill, each with a strong historical sense, and to reflect a little on the relations between poetry and history, especially in England at the present. I am aware that in doing so I am pressing into a bramble-patch of difficulties, since all the keywords of the discussion — 'history', 'myth', 'tradition', 'reality' — bristle with thorny questions. However, instead of trimming these terms to an order that is not found in poems, though it is not infrequently found in critical theories about them, I want rather to show something of the diversity, complexity, and tensions of the historical sense at work in poetry.

With this end in view, I begin with the most famous literary definition of the historical sense, from T.S. Eliot's 'Tradition and the Individual Talent', which gives me my title and also both illuminates and exemplifies some of the difficulties of the subject:

> The historical sense involves a perception, not only of the pastness of the past, but of its presence; the historical sense compels a man to write not merely with his own generation in his bones, but with a feeling that the whole of the literature of Europe from Homer and within it the whole of the literature of his own country has a simultaneous existence and composes a simultaneous order. This historical sense, which is a sense of the timeless as well as of the temporal and of the timeless and of the temporal together, is what makes a poet traditional. And it is at the same time what makes a writer most acutely conscious of his place in time, of his contemporaneity.[1]

The idea of the historical sense means much more in relation to the poet than it would have done had 'Tradition and the Individual Talent' never been written, and perhaps it means more than Eliot makes explicit, since he is concerned not so much with the otherness of the past, let alone with historical facts and movements, but rather with the past as an imaginative order, shaped mainly by works of art. Moreover, what Eliot offers is a statement of faith, not a reasoned argument. The mystical suggestion of "the timeless and of the temporal together" looks forward more than twenty years to *Four Quartets* and 'the pattern of timeless moments'. His England in that work is haunted by the presence of the past, and 'Little Gidding' in particular gives memorable expression to his mystical sense of history.

Although it is in no two cases exactly the same, the historical sense of the other great American, British and Irish Modernists is either mystical or mythic. Thus, W.B. Yeats, Ezra Pound and James Joyce interpret historical events in terms of different mythic patterns. David Jones said of a particular myth that it "proposes for our acceptance a truth more real than the historic facts alone discover".[2] His idea of tradition strongly emphasises history both as a shaping force and as a condition of its mediation, perception, and metamorphosis, but for him, as for Eliot, "the real is sacred and religious".[3] In fact, few if any poets make an absolute distinction between history and myth, or separate history from legend and folklore, and theories which exclusively identify history with reality and myth with fantasy must inevitably reduce poetry to the latter. In any case, historical materialism, which subjects myth to the interrogation of history, has its own mythic history. But this is not to say that all poets treat history equally mythically, or that the different meanings and uses that myth and history have for poets belonging to different times are all equally capable of illuminating reality. Both may either manipulate poets or be manipulated by them, for reasons of state or party propaganda, and their differences may involve radically opposed interpretations of human existence. There is a great difference, for example, between Ted Hughes, who sees all history as the enactment of a stark myth, and Geoffrey Hill, who bears witness to the actuality of specific historical events and deeds. The poles of 'cosmic' and historical awareness attract modern British and American poets, but most exist between them, with an imaginative sense of 'nature', and of history and of myth, which cannot be explained reductively in terms of the polarities.

Some terms of Eliot's definition of the historical sense are more applicable outside his own work than others. For instance, one thing that can be said with confidence is that the presence of the past has been strongly felt by English poets of different periods, from the earliest to the present day. England has been long-settled; even the Anglo-Saxons were awed by the ruins left by their predecessors, and the land and many of the buildings continue to provide what Thomas Hardy called a "past-marked prospect".[4] Both Modernists like Eliot, and poets in the native English tradition, like Edward Thomas and Ivor Gurney, have 'read' the landscape for its historical character, and for both that character has embodied a sense of national identity. For Eliot, the past was present in a mainly literary and religious tradition, and in words which were not literary alone. For it was present for him in speech, too, in words which, on people's tongues as well as in books, were shaped by historical experience, modified or even converted by use, and which 'sounded' their histories. There has never been a period more conscious of the presence of history in words than the present, and while the consciousness owes something to Eliot, it can be developed and used for very different ends. Thus, it is possessed by a poet like David Jones or (in the context of Ireland) Seamus Heaney, who wishes to remember and conserve the past, and by a poet like Tony Harrison, who would like to see "the looms of owned language smashed apart".[5]

'Tradition and the Individual Talent' emphasises tradition, continuity, order. Yet Eliot was writing a year after the end of the First World War, and three years before *The Waste Land*, with its presentation of a state of personal and cultural disintegration. The last three poems of *Four Quartets* were written during the Second World War, and are consciously patriotic. It was in 1942 that Eliot called history "a pattern of timeless moments". It is, of course, no invalidation of Eliot's ideas that they exemplify the relation between ideas of order and times of catastrophic disorder. When if not then are such ideas more urgently needed, and where do constructive principles shine brighter than against the destruction brought about by their violation? By the same token, the concern of recent poets with the presence of the past is not invalidated by the fact that it has been stimulated, in part, by widespread loss of historical memory and of communication with the past. It is present needs that invoke the past, and at the same time demand a sense of responsibility to the future.

Seamus Heaney, in his lecture 'Englands of the Mind' (1976), described certain English poets writing since the Second World War — Ted Hughes, Geoffrey Hill and Philip Larkin — as "afflicted with a sense of history".[6] He ascribed the affliction to the threat to the identity of England, which has possessed the poets of "that defensive love of their territory which was once shared only by those poets whom we might call colonial".[7] At the end of the lecture, Heaney broadened his argument to claim "that English poets are being forced to explore not just the matter of England, but what is the matter with England".[8]

Heaney has, very usefully, isolated a tendency. The sense of history as an affliction felt by English poets is more acute now than it has ever been. But of course, the problematic nature of the poet's involvement with his nation's history is not new. With the rise of the nation state in England under the Tudors, the historical sense of English poets became intimately involved with the sense of national identity, and vulnerable to complication by its vicissitudes. In wartime, or at times of imperial expansion, national identity is felt most widely and intensely as a unifying factor. And the poet may serve it, as Raleigh and Kipling served different phases of British Imperialism, or be caught between conflicting emotions and ideals, as Wordsworth and Coleridge were in the early days of the war against revolutionary France, or as Sassoon and Owen were during the First World War, or reject the national identity, perhaps in the name of a radical alternative, as Blake did.

At times of internal crisis, the national idea or myth will be strained, and even fractured. For example, Roundhead and Cavalier appeal to different histories, different Englands, or at least to different valuations of the same things, but with a difference they are prepared to kill and die for. Especially since the Industrial Revolution, England has had different class histories, too, which both work retrospectively and project different futures, serving the interests of a particular class. Moreover, while political and economic power and the principal means of communication are centred in London, England remains — in spite of the notion of the 'global village' and the fact of Americanisation — a country of distinctive regions and places. While this diversity is a valuable feature, it has to be admitted that the division between areas along lines of privilege, which seemed to blur for a time during the 1960s, has been intensified again since then, and now reflects racial as well as class differences. Class borders are not only geographical, of course, dividing, say, East and West London, or the north and south of England; they may run between members of a family and through individuals too. It isn't difficult to theorise about these things. But there are people who experience class divisions in their inmost being and most sensitive tissue, and for them this is a fact of their 'Englishness' more potent than any national symbol. Awareness of the personal cost of class conflicts has appeared in numerous forms especially among those from working-class homes who have been university educated, and has coincided with the increasing breakdown of political consensus in England. In the work of social and literary critics, as well as of dramatists, novelists and poets, the awareness has produced a radical rereading of the English past. The awareness that language in England is a class issue has also grown parallel to the awareness elsewhere in Britain and Ireland, as well as widely in former colonial lands, that language is a colonial and political issue. The concern of this essay is with poets who, in the main, treat 'the matter of England' with great imaginative sympathy, and even, in the case of David Jones and Basil Bunting, romantically, but each also responds in some significant way to the social and political tensions in modern England, and above all to the sense of national identity fraught with contradictions and uncertainty.

So the phenomenon to which Heaney referred at the end of his lecture is not new. W.H. Auden in *The Orators* summed up a feeling that was fairly prevalent among English writers after the First World War when he asked: "What do you think about England, this country of ours where nobody is well?"[9] To my mind, *Lady Chatterley's Lover* is most interesting and most moving as the culmination of Lawrence's long, passionate quarrel with England and his own Englishness. Earlier, in 'The Spirit of Place' (1924), he had written: "The Island of Great Britain had a wonderful terrestrial magnetism or polarity of its own, which made the British people. For the moment, this polarity seems to be breaking. Can England die? And what if England dies?"[10] Indeed, a quarrel with England, if usually less intense than

Lawrence's, characterises a lot of modern English literature. It may be heard in the great Victorian social critics, too. Earlier, William Blake's question: "Are such things done on Albion's shore?"[11] typified his horror at what the mechanistic philosophy backing industry and empire was doing to his country, and his *Jerusalem* is at the same time a love poem about England and an impassioned and tortured indictment of its present condition. I believe Heaney is right, however, in his perception of a new, troubled exploration of England by poets "afflicted with a sense of history", though I see it as a new phase of the long and often difficult relationship between English poets and the national idea. I am aware, too, that this essay is a symptom as well as an examination of the problem. Yet neither before nor after the Second World War do English poets bear their sense of history only as an affliction. In what follows I shall be speaking of praise and celebration, too.

2

"We have been forced to live history as Tennyson's generation had not."[12] David Jones, writing in 1948, and as a man who had fought in the First World War, was speaking for his generation, but his words are generally applicable to this century. *In Parenthesis* (1937), the writing which he started ten years after the war, shows how the war made the past present for him:

> My companions in the war were mostly Londoners with an admixture of Welshmen, so that the mind and folk-life of those two differing racial groups are an essential ingredient to my theme. Nothing could be more representative. These came from London. Those from Wales. Together they bore in their bodies the genuine tradition of the Island of Britain, from Bendigeid Vran to Jingle and Marie Lloyd....
> I suppose at no time did one so much live with a consciousness of the past, the very remote, and the more immediate and trivial past, both superficially and more subtly.... Every man's speech and habit of mind were a perpetual showing: now of Napier's expedition, now of the Legions at the Wall, now of 'train-band captain', now of Jack Cade, of John Ball, of the commons in arms....[13]

For David Jones, the war called up "the genuine tradition of the Island of Britain": the men bore it in their bodies, and showed it in their speech and minds. *In Parenthesis* shows the horror and pity of war, but it is unmistakably a patriotic work, which also shows the past living in the present, and recreates an ancient traditional unity among the men. Its initial difficulties for the reader are the result of richness — richness of mythological, historical and literary allusions, and richness of language, in the combination of literary English with technical jargon and the vernacular. In the following passage two stretcher bearers are handling a casualty under shell fire; they flatten themselves to the ground in a desperate attempt to avoid a shell, but are hit, and the remains of men and stretcher shower down on the back of the Forward Observation Officer who is trying to use a field telephone:

> Lower you lower you prize Maria Hunt, an' gammy fingered upland Gamalin — down cantcher — low — hands away me ducky — down on hands on hands down and flattened belly and face pressed and curroodle mother earth
>
> she's kind:
> Pray her hide you in her deeps
> she's only refuge against
> this ferocious pursuer
> terribly questing.
> Maiden of the digged places
>   let our cry come unto thee.
> *Mam*, moder, mother of me
> Mother of Christ under the tree
> reduce our dimensional vulnerability to the minimum –
> cover the spines of us
> let us creep back dark-bellied where he can't see
> don't let it.
> There, there, it can't, won't hurt — nothing
> shall harm my beautiful.
>   But on its screaming passage
> their numbers writ
> and stout canvas tatters drop as if they'd salvoed grape to the mizzen-sheets
> and the shaped ash grip rocket-sticks out of the evening sky right back by
> Bright Trench
> and clots and a twisted clout
> on the bowed back of the F.O.O. bent to his instrument.[14]

The words correspond to the extremity of terror being experienced, which they communicate in a palpable form. The men's voices, their dialects and accents, are sounded in the writing, which is both active, participating in their extreme emotions, and provides a larger perspective. The physicality of "cover the spines of us/let us creep back dark-bellied" presents the soldier become a child again, close to the earth, crying his primal cry. The range of the language between extremes of "*mam*" on the one hand and "dimensional vulnerability" and "F.O.O." on the other, and between the barely articulate cry and the language of a developed religion, at once embodies what the war does to human beings, the dehumanizing jargon that facilitates its continuation, and the perspective that explains and judges it. The range is also between the modern form of certain words and their roots, as in "*mam, moder, mother*", where both the infancy of an individual and the past of his people buried in the word "work up" into the present. And the whole passage shifts subtly between subjective experience and overview, between this 'now' and its historical context. Here, the most basic human needs and fears cry out in the nightmare of technological war, and all the elements working together have their reality against the ground of the "sacred and religious".

David Jones chose epigraphs for the seven parts of *In Parenthesis* from *Y Gododdin*, the sixth century Welsh epic, attributed to Aneirin, which commemorates the three hundred Welsh princes who died fighting the English at Catraeth. It is a choice which, on the face of it, would seem hardly appropriate to the comradeship of Welsh and English in the trenches. But he made the choice because *Y Gododdin* "connects us with a very ancient unity and mingling of races; with the Island as a corporate inheritance, with the remembrance of Rome as a European unity. The drunken 300 at Catraeth fell as representatives of the Island of Britain."[15] It is this ancient unity underlying the British People which the men in the trenches recover, as *In Parenthesis* presents them. The English are part of the unity, but they neither impose nor dominate it.

The political and cultural implications of the idea of unity embodied in *In Parenthesis* were to have far-reaching significance for David Jones's art. He was part Welsh, part English, and it was as much his love of England as his love of Wales that opposed him to English ascendancy over Britain. Although his thinking was close to that of members of the early Welsh Nationalist party who saw Wales as part of Europe, and especially to the thinking of his friend and fellow Catholic Saunders Lewis, whose ideal was the diversity of independent nation states united by the order of medieval Catholic Europe, he was not a Welsh or an English separatist, but sought to recover a tradition in which all the peoples of the Island of Britain participated. The irony and apparent paradox of this aim is that in his later work it led him increasingly to stress the opposition between Wales, seen as the main repository of the ancient unifying tradition, and England, seen as the agent of a false unity based on secular material powers.

The Anathemata (1952) is about the making of Britain, from the geological foundations through the arrivals, interactions, and cultural formations of different peoples. It was written partly during and partly in response to the Second World War, and is as consciously patriotic as *Four Quartets*. However Eliot's mysticism reconciles opposing factions, which "Accept the constitution of silence/And are folded in a single party".[16] David Jones, on the other hand, observes the integrity of differences. Thus, the Lady of the Pool, a personification of London, speaks of the regenerative potential of the ancient British traditions buried in the city, and kept under by the English ascendancy:

> For should these stir, then would our Engle-raum in this
> Brut's Albion be like to come to some confusion!
>   You never know, captain:
> What's under works up.[17]

"Engle-raum", especially in the context of the Second World War, carries a charge of bitter scorn, which in fact is a measure of David Jones's patriotic feeling for "the Island as a corporate inheritance", as opposed to the English ascendancy. "Albion", the earliest recorded name of the Island, recalls — among many echoes — Blake's "All things Begin & End in Albion's Ancient Druid Rocky Shore".[18] David Jones's love of his country, like Blake's, envisages it as a great creative force imprisoned by a false ideology, but capable of release: "What's under works up". He, too, working from the same mythological sources that inspired Blake, personifies the dormant underlying powers in a form which also identifies them with the land. Of course, it is not difficult to see the limitations and even contradictions in his sense of the past considered as a strictly *historical* sense, since he brings together historical and mythic elements and is hostile to the main forces shaping the world since the Reformation. What is more important to observe, however, is that he is one of the very few poets to have responded, in depth, to the historical crisis of his time, considered as the conflict and interaction of diverse cultures and the forces of Empire, and, more fundamentally, as the clash between the religious and materialist ideas of reality. More specifically, his Brut's Albion subverts the English national idea of his time. The positive effects of this are that he unearths treasures of common memory, releases the energies of language, and apprehends place in depth.

David Jones's commemorative and regenerative intentions both involve the sense of the past, which he brings into the present through his '*data*', through words and names in which the past has been deposited, and through the metamorphic qualities of his language and symbols. Language as he uses it embodies the realities, the 'things', of a people of mixed descent, and is metamorphic because he is concerned with the things in the process of adaptation, fusion and change. His places are always firmly located in a physical landscape, but the overall effect is of place as a specific cultural formation, adapted to its terrain but unmistakably the creation of a particular people or mixture of peoples. The following passage from 'The Sleeping Lord' (1967) represents an abandoned Roman port as seen from the vantage-point of Dark Age, Arthurian Britain:

> ...the stone-built *eglwys* (its gapped roofing repaired, more or less, with thatch, its broken walling patched with unmortared rubble) that stands by the narrowing and silted estuary where the great heaped ruins are, that tell of vanished wharves and emporia and cement bonded brick & dressed-stone store-*cellae* for bonded goods and where walk the ghosts of customs officials and where mildewed scraps of sight drafts, shards of tesseratallies and fragile as tinder fragmented papyri, that are wraiths of filed bills of lading, litter here and there the great sandstone blocks of fallen vaulting... where also, if you chance to be as lettered as the Irish eremite up stream, you can read, freely & lightly scratched in the plaster of a shattered pilaster,

in *mercatores*' Greek, what seems to mean: Kallistratos loves Julia and so does Henben and so do I

. and a bit more
that you can't decipher....[19]

Clearly, this is not a romanticized and sentimental description of ruins in neo-Gothic style: the picturesque as a way of seeing was totally alien to David Jones. For one thing, the details are far too precise in their depiction of the commercial function of the place, and the buildings are known almost by touch, as the masons knew them. For another, the cultural 'deposits' are mixed. In a few words the Greek and Egyptian influences on the Roman world and different peoples brought together by the *imperium* are recalled, while the patched-up church and the lettered Irish eremite living up stream are also connected with that world, yet represent another phase, and another order. Other images emerge from the depths: of ruined temples in the Indian or South American jungle, of the Anglo-Saxons peering in fearful awe at what they take to be the work of giants. But this is nevertheless a specific historical location, a Roman 'thing' abandoned to the Celtic wilderness, but in which the relationship between the "*eglwys*" and the traffic which once used the now silted estuary reveals the connections between Church and Empire. If a few other writers have both the requisite historical sense and the craftsman's feeling for the materials, no one but David Jones could have written this passage, or added the tender and humorous detail of the lover's inscription, "freely & lightly scratched in the plaster of a shattered pilaster". The latter may however recall how, in Homer or in Virgil, a detail of human action, feeling or expression will produce a shock of recognition across the distance between cultures and ages, although it belongs exactly where it occurs in time and place.

It is the depth to which David Jones descends into the British 'mythus' that affects his creative subversion. Thus, the language of his writings — not only the cockney of *In Parenthesis* and 'The Lady of the Pool', and the other dialects and 'foreign' words used liberally throughout, but also the cultural and etymological histories which he habitually makes words recall — subverts the standardization of English, with its diminishing power to signify diverse traditions, and the cultural poverty it voices. In his words themselves, the diverse traditions of the Island — but especially of Wales, London, the southern and eastern English regions, and to a lesser extent Scotland — "work up" in opposition to an uniform "Engle-raum". In this respect, despite his anti-democratic views, David Jones is practically our most radical modern British poet. Not only formally, but in restoring roots to the language. The practical effect of deepening the humanity of words, by recalling their burden of place and time, is the achievement against which we should see the exclusions of his sympathies, and such contradictions as his romanticization of Wales in terms implicitly hostile to a large part of its modern social experience.

3

Basil Bunting wrote *Briggflatts* in 1965, after returning to his native Northumbria after an adventurous life spent mainly abroad. Like *Four Quartets* and *The Anathemata*, it is, in several senses, a poem of recovery. It is apparently more romantic than either, however, in Bunting's recovery of first, childhood love. But his poetic 'objectivity' — his concern to make the poem an object, in accordance with the principles he shared with — and partly learnt from — Louis Zukofsky and his fellow American Objectivists — is hardly less rigorous than David Jones's. It is interesting to note that while David Jones developed his artistic objectivity in accordance with his Catholicism, integrating post-Impressionist theory and the neo-Thomist philosophy of form, the Objectivism which Basil Bunting shared with the Americans also had — largely through the Jewish influence — a strong religious element, as well as owing much to the same post-Impressionist theory, and something to Marxist ideas. In both cases the attitude towards form is inseparable from an attitude towards life, which involves both a religious apprehension of the material world and a sense of the self which defines it in terms of the order to which it belongs, instead of in exclusively subjective terms. There are differences at all levels between the two kinds of artistic objectivity, as well as differences between the Objectivists themselves, but the important common ground is the belief that the poet both makes a form of order in his work, and reveals the order of the world. Without an understanding of this fundamental difference between poetic objectivity and romantic subjectivism, it is not possible to grasp how *Briggflatts* is at once intimately personal and highly ordered. As Bunting says, it is "an autobiography, but not a record of fact".[20] It is an autobiography because it sounds, in words, images and musical structure, the movements of a life in all its emotional turbulence and ultimate acceptance, and in relation to the ordered rhythms of the world.

Bunting locates his imagination in the history and geography of Northumbria, making it both personal and representative: an embodiment of the spirit of place. Here, history is a physical and speaking presence:

> Copper-wire moustache,
> sea-reflecting eyes
> and Baltic plainsong speech
> declare: By such rocks
> men killed Bloodaxe.
>
> Fierce blood throbs in his tongue,

lean words.
Skulls cropped for steel caps
huddle round Stainmore.
Their becks ring on limestone,
whisper to peat.
The clogged cart pushes the horse downhill.
In such soft air
they trudge and sing,
laying the tune frankly on the air.
All sounds fall still,
fellside bleat,
hide-and-seek peewit.[21]

The man's eyes and speech "declare" the presence of the past, as for David Jones "every man's speech and habit of mind were a perpetual showing". Of course, it is in fact the poet who makes the declaration, as when he juxtaposes word and name to state that the blood throbbing in the man's tongue is Bloodaxe's blood. But what he makes clear is what he sees and hears: the long-dead Scandinavian king living in the living Northumbrian. Speech, physiology, landscape, wild creatures, and human generations and occupations, all work together to form the continuity of human existence, and the continuity between man and world, which is enacted by the natural and human musical sounds and rhythms. We may doubt that the same effect would be possible in a less elemental setting: in Bunting's Northumbria as in Jones's Wales, it is not the cities but the natural world which forms the ground of a traditional culture and gives rise to the spirit of place. But here, in this passage, the past is present, in the man and in the landscape, as the "becks ring on limestone" and the children sing. The poet sees the continuity between the living and the dead, and between man and world, in the Northumbrian's "sea-reflecting eyes". But the rhythmic order is in his own eyes, too: Bunting sees himself in what he sees, and what he sees is what has made him what he is. And at the same time that he sees the order, he hears it, in speech, in song, in natural sounds, and what he hears he recreates, in the poem's corresponding form.

Bunting's tradition is that of the Old North, which differs greatly from "the Saxon south of England", and includes strong Celtic and Scandinavian elements. "Southrons", Bunting maintains, "would maul the music of many lines in *Briggflatts*."[22] He finds the tradition in music and design, in the tongue and in the landscape, which is patterned like the native medieval tracery and sculpture. Like David Jones, he invokes Aneurin and Taliesin, the first-known poets of ancient Celtic Britain:

I hear Aneurin number the dead and rejoice,
being adult male of a merciless species.
Today's posts are piles to drive into the quaggy past

> on which impermanent palaces balance.
> I see Aneurin's pectoral muscle swell under his shirt,
> pacing between the game Ida left to rat and raven,
> young men, tall yesterday, with cabled thighs.
> Red deer move less warily since their bows dropped.
> Girls in Teesdale and Wensleydale wake discontent.
> Clear Cymric voices carry well this autumn night,
> Aneurin and Taliesin, cruel owls
> for whom it is never altogether dark, crying
> before the rules made poetry a pedant's game.
> Columba, Columbanus, as the soil shifts its vest,
> Aidan and Cuthbert put on daylight,
> wires of sharp western metal entangled in its soft
> web, many shuttles as midges darting;
> not for bodily welfare nor pauper theorems
> but splendour to splendour, excepting nothing that is.[23]

It is as if the ancient poets are present, physically and audibly, together with Bunting in the passage. "I hear Aneurin"; "I see Aneurin's pectoral muscle"; "Aneurin and Taliesin... crying": these are no more disembodied spirits than Bunting is a ghost haunting his own poem. The tongue is his, but their fierce blood throbs in it.

This may seem a romantic view of what Bunting achieves in *Briggflatts*, but the 'incarnational' quality of the poem, the way in which it gives flesh to the past in the present, justifies it. It is necessary, however, to make an important distinction between Bunting and the ancient Celtic poets, while further examining their affinities. The presence of Aneurin and Taliesin in *Briggflatts* gives it a certain bardic quality. The poem is a tribal boast and Bunting is a singer of deeds. He is also a poet of large acceptance, with something of that more pagan than Christian attitude towards fate that we find in most poets of the Old North, whether Celtic or Norse or Anglo-Saxon. Yet Bunting is not altogether bard, and could not be. Aneurin and Taliesin had a specific function to praise and commemorate the princes of an aristocratic society. Bunting, as his life has amply testified, is an extreme instance of the poet without a given 'place', who is the type rather than the exception in most modern Western societies. Therefore the 'tribe' of which he boasts is not an entity whose existence he can take for granted, but rather one he has to recover, and even, in a sense, recreate. There is, in fact, a tension in the poem between the poet as bard and the poet as bohemian, as landless, anti-social adventurer.

Bunting resolves this tension through his sense of poetic 'mission' and the objectivist techniques through which he accomplishes it. Thus, at the beginning of the second movement, the poet is seen as a social outcast and a sponger. But he is "appointed", with "nothing to authenticate/the mission imposed", while those who despise and betray him are "toadies, confidence men, kept boys", and "whores".[24] To be sure, this is sufficiently

Rimbaudian, and has an air of self-justification which is not an attractive feature of Bunting's art. The point is, however, that he has a mission, which in this passage he authenticates by gauging, counting, scanning, feeling, even in the apparent chaos of the modern city, a rhythmic order outside himself. And what he sees and hears in London he sees and hears on a much greater scale in his original Northumbrian home. However I do not want to gloss over the fact in the case of Bunting, any more than in that of Jones, that the cultural identity of place is not given by prevailing circumstances — or at least not entirely — but is a formation of the individual imagination, although from the actual things of place. If any English poet, even the most 'rooted' in a particular place, could take for granted the existence of a sustaining society and culture, English poetry today would be completely different from what it in fact is.

The effect of the tension between ideas of the poet in *Briggflatts* is that — to paraphrase a Coleridgean definition — it contains a great deal of strong and disorderly emotion within a highly ordered form. Yet it should also be said that while Bunting submits his bohemian experience to Objectivist and bardic discipline, his view of the bards is coloured by his adventures as an outsider. Hence, in his presentation of Aneurin and Taliesin, his emphasis on numbering the dead and on killing. Hence the "cruel owls", and "being adult male of a merciless species" — all of which names notable features of the poets of the Old North, but at the expense of their social function and even of their civilization. In other words, Bunting, for his own purposes, presents them as more 'primitive' than they were. Essentially, though, like bard or epic poet, Bunting does not measure the cosmos by his ego, but celebrates an order he is part of and has to accept. He invokes early missionaries and saints, as well as the poets with their pagan traditions. The light weaves a great pattern: "not for bodily welfare nor pauper theorems/ but splendour to splendour, excepting nothing that is". But there is no abstract message or design: "Follow the clue patiently and you will understand nothing".[25] Nevertheless *Briggflatts*, with its musical and imagistic techniques, and its metaphors drawn from music, art and nature, *sounds* a great order. A cosmic harmony recalling the medieval music of the spheres sounds through — and sometimes against — the betrayal and remorse, the sensuality, love and generosity of one man's life. There is no systematic symbolism, let alone religious philosophy, as in *Four Quartets*. Yet, despite all differences, Bunting's imagination is as incarnational as Eliot's or Jones's. For Bunting, "Starlight is almost flesh".[26]

4

It is well known that Aristotle and Sir Philip Sidney accord poetry the precedence over history. To Aristotle, the poet brings out the universal in events and situations, irrespective of whether his account of them is historically true or not. Sidney in *An Apology for Poetry* (1595) describes poetry as "a speaking picture". The poet "yeeldeth to the powers of the minde an image", which is able to "possesse the sight of the soule". His great model is Christ, who with a "divine narration" inhabits "both the memory and judgement", and makes us seek what is morally right by making us see and feel it. For Aristotle and Sidney, the universal and the ideal are not revealed by the historian's fidelity to what actually happened.

In Romantic and Modernist thought, there is a strong current running in the opposite direction. Poets, in particular, give precedence to history, to what really happens or has happened, as the measure of reality. In extreme forms of this view, poetry is not only sometimes guilty of falsehood; it is constitutionally inclined to deceive. It substitutes art for life, dream for reality; idealization is not its virtue but its vice. Crabbe offered a fairly mild example of the view when he wrote: "I paint the cot,/As Truth will paint it, and as bards will not".[27] After all, he was boasting of his veracity, whereas, more often, poets who take this view accuse themselves. Keats in 'The Fall of Hyperion' makes the prophetess address him scornfully: "What benefit cans't thou do, or all thy tribe,/To the great world? Thou art a dreaming thing,/A fever of thyself." A similar spirit animated Wilfred Owen when in the unfinished Preface to his war poems he wrote: "Above all I am not concerned with Poetry". Such things as this, from 'Insensibility', makes his meaning clearer: "they are troops who fade, not flowers/For poets' tearful fooling". He has identified Poetry with dreaming, and even with "The old Lie: Dulce et decorum est/Pro patria mori". The English poet's traditional, if often unadvertised, grounding on love of country has been shivered by the split in the nation between combatants and non-combatants; now, the patriots are the likes of Jessie Pope. Poetry fools with life and tells lies about death. Paradoxically, while some poets have developed a suspicion of poetry, most modern historians would agree with R.G. Collingwood[28] in stressing the historian's need for imagination — traditionally the poet's greatest faculty – in interpreting the past, and deny the possibility of the task described by Ranke in the 1830s: "simply to show how it really was". But, as Geoffrey Hill says in 'Poetry as "Menace" and "Atonement"': "Romantic art is thoroughly familiar with the reproaches of life".[29]

Geoffrey Hill's own poetry struggles to escape from the context he defines: "that obsessive self-critical Romantic monologue in which eloquence and guilt are intertwined, and for which the appropriate epigraph would be one abrupt entry in Coleridge's 1796 Notebook: 'Poetry — excites us to artificial feelings — makes us callous to real ones'."[30]

Blake's Albion revives an ancient image: of the Island as a giant's body. Bunting's Northumbria and Jones's Brut's Albion both identify history and myth with the physical structure of the Island. The past lives in the rocks and trees and waters, and in the bodies and speech and minds of the people.

Geoffrey Hill's powerful poetic sequences about England — 'Funeral Music' (1968), *Mercian Hymns* (1971) and 'An Apology for the Revival of Christian Architecture in England' (1978) — occupy some of the same ground. But Hill's mind is much more sceptical and his emotions more guarded than either Bunting's or Jones's, and he reads the romance of the Matter of Britain much more critically. Yet his mind is, in a phrase from his essay on 'Funeral Music', also "vulnerable alike to admiration and scepticism",[31] and it is possible to overemphasise his scepticism at the expense of his admiration.

There is something Shakespearian about Geoffrey Hill's imaginative brooding on the violence of English history:

> They bespoke doomsday and they meant it by
> God, their curved metal rimming the low ridge.
> But few appearances are like this. Once
> Every five hundred years a comet's
> Over-riding stillness might reveal men
> In such array, livid and featureless,
> With England crouched beastwise beneath it all.
> 'Oh, that old northern business...' A field
> After battle utters its own sound
> Which is like nothing on earth, but is earth.
> Blindly the questing snail, vulnerable
> Mole emerge, blindly we lie down, blindly
> Among carnage the most delicate souls
> Tup in their marriage-blood, gasping 'Jesus'.[32]

'Imaginatively, the Battle of Towton', 1461, in the Wars of the Roses, commands Hill's "belated witness".[33] But to witness 'imaginatively' is also to know what we cannot see. Thus, Hill witnesses what appears to be the absolute seriousness of the leaders: "They bespoke doomsday and they meant it by/God". These men believed in the divine justice of their cause, and called on the Last Judgement. But the weak meaning of "by God", as an automatic oath, casts a shadow of doubt on its original strong meaning. What we see is "appearances". Yet, "Once/Every five hundred years a comet's/Over-riding stillness *might reveal* men...." The poet, standing at a distance in time from the men, sees both appearances and the possibility of revelation, which together show the impossibility of knowing with absolute certainty what is real. Reality, as in Plato's myth of the cave, and in the Christian Last Judgement, (both of which Hill images in this sequence, as well as widely elsewhere in his work), is hidden from men. It is hidden from the witness, but it was also hidden from the actors in the event. Hill shares with both the ancient philosophers and Christian theologians a profound sense of man's blindness. What we see in looking at the men at Towton is not "that old northern business" but our human condition. The image of "England crouched beastwise beneath it all", the sound of the field after battle, "which is like nothing on earth, but is earth", the blindness of the creatures and of "the most delicate souls" alike, all powerfully display man's condition: bestial, mysterious, violent, blind. Hill's image of "England crouched beastwise beneath it all" measures the distance of his imagination, which is essentially moral and historical, from the mythic Albion of Blake and the 'Sleeping Lord' of David Jones.

In the image of 'Annunciations',[34] the Word subsists in "the stiffening-mire". Christ, the Logos or the Word, also, in traditional Christian thought, justifies the poetic imagination. The poet's word, by analogy with the Word, is creative: it brings a world into being in accordance with the forms of the original creation; it reveals and illuminates spiritual truth; it moves us to see. For Hill, though, the poet is a seer only in so far as he sees man's blindness, which includes his own. Even the Word exists in the world through man's violent and sexually voracious, mortal nature; which is not to discount divine revelation, but to acknowledge its subsistence in language. Blackstone's view, quoted from C.H. Sisson as epigraph to *Mercian Hymns*, was that upon "the law of nature and the law of revelation depend all human laws".[35] Hill, though, is acutely aware of the duality of nature and revelation. It seems that for him they are opposing laws, which language habitually conflates, binding revelation to man's blind natural passions. His sense of duality — body and soul, beast and angel, appearance and reality, nature and revelation — is Dostoyevskian in its intensity, but, sceptical of the Christian order, which his mind nevertheless persistently circles, he emphasises the clash or the conflation of opposites in man. Coleridge's great definition of imagination, the esemplastic or unifying power, stresses its "balance or reconcilement of opposite or discordant qualities".[36] Hill, on the other hand, shows the irreconcilability of opposites, or their deliberate confusion by man's self-interest, and the absence of a transcendental order in the human sphere. It is not that he refuses the authority of revelation, but that he shows how in this world we invariably find God's word being manipulated by the natural man. The historical and moral witness of Hill's poetry keeps open the difference between opposites, refusing to sink evil in good, or merge the actual with the ideal, or call reality by the name of appearance; or else it shows how reconcilement serves man's blindness.

It is in this perspective that we should understand the conflation of the poet in childhood with the bloody, luxurious, cunning, semi-barbaric King Offa of Mercia in *Mercian Hymns*. Hill's Offa is "the presiding genius of the West Midlands, his dominion enduring from the middle of the eighth century until the middle of the twentieth (and possibly beyond)".[37] Like Jones and Bunting, Hill identifies the source of his imagination with native ground, with a part of England rich in history and myth. His more sceptical mind manifests itself partly through irony and sardonic humour.

In Mercia, as in much of midland and northern England, industry coexists with the natural world, and is now being reabsorbed by it. Hill depicts this process, showing a nature which, with its sexual energy and strange, menacing forms, is equally potent and dangerously unpredictable in man: in the child who is not innocent, but subject to dark, murderous impulses. The child, like the autocratic Anglo-Saxon king, may turn viciously upon a friend:

> After school he lured Ceolred, who was sniggering with fright, down to the old quarries, and flayed him. Then, leaving Ceolred, he journeyed for hours, calm and alone, in his private derelict sandlorry named *Albion*.[38]

The humour is partly in the disparity within continuity — schoolboys in the early 1940s acting like warring Anglo-Saxons — and partly in the image of the boy-poet, "alone, in his private derelict sandlorry named *Albion*".

'Albion' was the name of a make of lorry, common at that time, and the image of the young Hill sitting at the wheel of the abandoned vehicle and taking long, imaginary journeys is amusing and attractive. But the image has uncomfortable implications, too. Is Blake's Albion, the Albion of the poets, carrier of a potent myth or romance of national identity, now at most only a "private derelict sandlorry", only useful for an imaginative child's private game? Has the public myth of the Tudors, which for all Blake's isolation he kept in currency though in a radically altered form, become so cast out from the common world that it can only be privatized by the poet's individual imagination? And if so, what does that tell us about the poet's relation to his 'people' and any common stock of images or shared values?

Mercian Hymns offers no reassuring traditional continuities, nor a Coleridgean or Eliotic reconcilement or transcendence of discordant elements. Yet the book is marked by admiration as well as scepticism, and manifests a commemorative and even celebratory impulse. This is evident in the imaginative savouring of landscape and made things, and in the feeling for the people who made them — the 'Opus Anglicanum', a term which Hill, like Nikolaus Pevsner in *The Englishness of English Art* (1956), extends from its original application to English embroidery of the period AD 1250-1350 to other works, including (in Hill's case) medieval sculpture and nineteenth century utilitarian metal-work. These things have helped to give Mercia its distinctive character, and Hill's feeling for their makers, and especially for his grandmother who is commemorated in Hymn XXV, bears witness to the human cost of labour. The admiration is also evident in images compact with history and myth, which help to counteract the mordant humour in the work. For example: "crepitant oak forest where the boar furrowed black mould"; "Christ's mass: in the thick of a snowy forest the flickering evergreen fissured with light"; and "the shire-tree dripped red in the arena of its uprooting".

Geoffrey Hill's Mercia, dense with history and myth, becomes a microcosm of England:

> Primeval heathland, spattered with the bones of mice and birds; where adders basked and bees made provision, mantling the inner walls of their burh:

> Coiled entrenched England: brickwork and paintwork stalwart above hacked marl. The clashing primary colours — 'Ethandune', 'Catraeth', 'Maldon', 'Pengwern'. Steel against yew and privet. Fresh dynasties of smiths.[39]

The intimacy with the ground shows a "child's-eye view, close to the common earth, the hoard of history",[40] which Seamus Heaney has observed in *Mercian Hymns*: a child's-eye view which recalls Hardy's, and above all his closeness to Egdon Heath in *The Return of the Native*. By formal positioning and syntax, "coiled entrenched England" looks, as it were, in two directions: towards a nature whose creatures share both their mortality and their arts of provision and building with man, and towards the works of man's hands, "brickwork and paintwork stalwart above hacked marl". It is a concentrated, rich phrase, suggesting coiled earthworks, coiled adder, coiled spring, involuted; entrenched armies, entrenched privileges and politicians. These things do not exhaust the deep image, in which history and nature interact and different meanings clash, generating a pent-up, volcanic force. We have a glimpse of England, personified in mythic terms, not as a giant, but as the ancient dragon, coiled and dug into the very land. But, such is Hill's humour for punning, more mundane associations also gather about the image, and, looking back, we may suspect that 'heathland' is not only 'primeval' but also the land of Mr. Edward Heath. Yet, even as scepticism sounds at this violent, backward, involuted land, this land riddled with privilege, admiration rings out for the deep-rooted and long-enduring, the concentrated and contained. Then 'Catraeth' is named, together with other British battles: and these, ironically, are also house names now. But who in the suburbs hears the echoes of a violent, exotic past, or sees "the clashing primary colours" as anything but mismatched paint? "Steel" may rest "against yew and privet", or clash with them. Few may care for the difference, or be conscious of any of these things. But the past is present in people's names, in "fresh dynasties of smiths". Again, in the link between the royal word, with its echo of Hardy, and the common family name, a complex tension between admiration and scepticism is held.

"There is no document of civilization which is not at the same time a document of barbarism".[41] Walter Benjamin's words are apt to Geoffrey Hill's English 'histories', in which admiration of English civilisation is constantly subjected to awareness of its barbarism. Thus, in 'An Apology for the Revival of Christian Architecture in England', Hill takes as a motif Coleridge's "the spiritual, Platonic old England" and shows its barbaric embodiments in an imperial and exploitative history. His method in the sequence is to employ versions of English Pastoral, and suggest the relation between the rhetoric of idealising nostalgia and the reality of power. His genius for concentrating meanings in a line, image or single word, and charging it with ambivalent feeling, is well represented by the sequence. For example, in the seventh sonnet, 'Loss and Gain': "Platonic England grasps its tenantry".[42] Those who traditionally hold the land — the tenantry — are in fact held; not just held, they are grasped. The implied cliché — grasping landlords — is reanimated: it is "Platonic England" that "grasps", the spiritual ideal disguising social and economic power.

It would be wrong, however, to suggest that Geoffrey Hill's complex art can be reduced to a simple political moral. I do not mean, either, that he is not concerned with the morality of politics. Far from it. But Hill is a sensuous, passionate poet, and the strength of his poetic intelligence both derives, in part, from feeling, and controls and questions what he feels. This should be borne in mind when treating him as a subtly diagnostic poet. Hill's diagnosis of England's ills takes the form of acute sensitivity to poetic rhetoric and verbal ambiguity, and to the relations between ideal and reality. But his feelings are implicated in what he diagnoses, and while this may give some reason to those who think he equivocates, for example, by both using Pastoral as a diagnostic tool and savouring its poetic pleasures, I think it a strength. 'An Apology for the Revival of Christian Architecture in England' might almost have been written to disprove the contention of John Barrell and John Bull in *The Penguin Book of English Pastoral Verse* (1974), that: "now and in England, the Pastoral, occasional twitches notwithstanding, is a lifeless form, of service only to decorate the shelves of tasteful cottages, 'modernised to a high standard'".[43] Evidently, this is a knock at Eliot, and while Hill's pastoral England is far from Eliot's, his historical sense owes something to Eliot's. It is more important to observe, however, that Hill's feeling for the past, even his nostalgia, is essential to the authenticity of his poems about England. In other words, his feeling for the *romance* of English history works together with his realism and his diagnostic sense, giving his apprehension of England emotional depth and complexity, as well as a sharp critical edge.

In the ninth sonnet of the sequence, 'The Laurel Axe', Hill writes:

Platonic England, house of solitudes,
rests in its laurels and its injured stone,
replete with complex fortunes that are gone,
beset by dynasties of moods and clouds.[44]

The sonnet takes its title from John Cowper Powys's *Autobiography* (1934), from the incident in which Powys's father fashioned a laurel axe for the child.⁴⁵ The object became identified with the great subjectivist's sense of childhood as a magic Arcadia and the source of imagination, by which the man could repossess it through memories of such objects of fetish-worship. Powys represents an extreme of Romanticism, which by denying the reality of the external world in fact internalises it, creating a magical inner world which seems to be an escape from outer pressures. But Hill is aware that the laurel axe — symbol of the gift of poetry — may cut both ways, hurting the hand that wields it and harming others: the faculty which is the poet's greatest gift is also his greatest danger. In this sequence, as in *Mercian Hymns*, Hill is returning to imaginative sources in childhood, and to the "house of solitudes" in which dreams and ideals stand in equivocal relation to the social and historical world. The difficult love, the overrich sense impressions revealing inner decay, the pastoral dreams raised on a history of exploitation, injustice and hypocrisy, the ironic yet tributary stylistic allusions, even the pastiche Romanticism of the sequence, all locate what it means to be 'English' at a time when it is perhaps impossible for the person of integrity, whose affections and judgement are equally engaged, to disentangle scepticism from admiration. In a number of his poems about England, Hill is akin to Bunting and Jones in returning to historical beginnings which are closely associated with his childhood. He differs from them, as he also differs from Eliot, in subjecting poetry to history's scrutiny. But he writes with a sense of the mutual intrication of poetry and history, and in the knowledge that both may serve to deepen or partially enlighten man's blindness, while neither contains the final judgement to which both are subject.

5

Neal Ascherson, writing in *The Observer*⁴⁶ recently, quoted the Welsh philosopher J.R. Jones on the "experience equally agonising and more irreversible" than the pain of exile: "the experience of knowing, not that you are leaving your country, but that your country is leaving you, being sucked away from you, as it were by a consuming, swallowing wind into the hands and the possession of another country and civilization". He quoted the words to apply them, not to Wales, but to England. He quoted Raymond Williams too: "Many of the things that happened, over the centuries, to the Welsh are now happening, in decades, to the English". I believe this loss of identity has been apparent for some time, or rather that it has been, at different levels and in various ways, a widespread fact of experience, a confusing, irritating, more or less obscured fact, affecting feelings and ideas. As Ascherson notes, it accompanies a feeling that 'change' no longer means change for the better, but loss. It is my impression that a few intellectuals began to reflect on the loss of a sense of English identity in the 1970s, or perhaps somewhat earlier, which was when it began to be felt in an acute form, although its beginnings may be detected among a minority much earlier, even with the rise of industrialism which radically transformed English society, and with painfully confusing manifestations among the most sensitive patriots — such as Edward Thomas, Ivor Gurney and D.H. Lawrence — during and — for those who survived – after the First World War. What is particularly interesting about Ascherson's thoughtful article is that its prominence backs up other signs that the loss of identity is now beginning to appear more widely in the open, and to be discussed by more individuals if not generally yet. The fact that the subject is beginning to be discussed in England is especially noteworthy, although while the feelings which the loss engenders have been powerfully, if usually obliquely, expressed in poetry, most of those who have openly reflected on the subject, even in England, are not English, but Scottish, Irish or Welsh. Indeed, it is a peculiarly difficult, and even painful, subject for the English to talk about. And in one sense, of course, the difficulty is general, since for many older people any mention of 'nationalism' produces the same reaction as the word 'Europe' did in Sartre: they hear the march of jackboots. Yet there are elementary differences between a racist ideology that seeks to conquer or destroy all that is not itself, and the love of cultural diversity which starts from the experience of having our own 'country and civilization' under our feet. But perhaps the difficulty in England is that the sense of national identity was taken for granted for so long — with whatever justification, in that it subsumed the identities of other peoples within the British Isles — that we have never learnt how to think about it. And thinking about it now is hard because of the complications of the situation, and because it is very much a matter of feeling, too.

In 'The Sound of England', an essay which appeared in *PN Review* in 1978, David Martin distinguishes several elements constituting what he calls 'the myth of England'. These include religion, nature and music, and "the sea, the Empire, London Town and — eventually — the sorrows of war and the craving for peace".[47] He finds that in recent times listening to the music of Benjamin Britten is "one way of sharing in the sound of England".[48] To my way of thinking and feeling, this eloquent, affirmative essay is exquisitely sad, with the plangency of wishfulness. Martin experiences 'the myth of England' mainly through literature and music, and the myth either subsumes history or is abstracted from the particular historical difficulties — arising not least from class and the aftermath of Empire — which form the context in which most poets experience their Englishness. Even in the case of David Jones, who unites more of the elements named by Martin than any other modern British poet, the relations between Empire and war on the one hand, and "the Island as a corporate inheritance" on the other, are exceptionally problematic. Moreover, they are developed — and sometimes stumbled over — painfully. Martin's essay, by contrast, reads too smoothly — it gets to its destination by avoiding the discontinuous road-surface and massive bumps, but the quest he is on cannot be accomplished without going over them. The pity is all the greater in that he is sensitively aware that it is a spiritual quest.

Tom Nairn, on the other hand, in his book *The Break-Up of Britain* (1977), writes incisively, from an historical materialist point of view, about the crisis of the British state following the end of Empire. He describes what he sees as the need for a 'progressive' English nationalism, which would include an idea of the people as an active force. He sees a healthy sign in 'history from below', as opposed to history in which the people are assigned their part by the ideology of the ruling class, and he links certain thinkers, including Raymond Williams and E.P. Thompson, and movements like Raphael Samuel's History Workshops, which in his view are contributing to "a left-nationalist popular culture". The influence of what Nairn calls "this progressive and generous cultural movement"[49] is evident on a number of younger poets, including Jeffrey Wainwright and Tony Harrison, who began publishing their work in the 1960s or early 70s. It is possible to sympathise substantially with this movement, but to feel that while poetry provides some evidence for Nairn's overall thesis, it also reveals its inadequacy to dissect experience. I believe — and hope I have demonstrated in this essay — that poetry which concerns itself — in Heaney's words — with both the matter of England and the question of what is the matter with England shows that feelings are much more complicated than Nairn allows. The poets differ in their interpretations of the history they have lived, or are living, but what all show is that the historical sense is rooted in the poet by the forces making him what he is: it may be diagnostic, or provide an overview, but it always works through primary attachments and emotions. While Nairn's kind of incisiveness is necessary, I doubt whether the situation could possibly be that clear for any poet — which is not to say that poets should be unclear, but that there is a certain kind of mental cutting-edge that makes poetry impossible. It is significant that the only poets whose evidence Nairn calls on are Enoch Powell and, to a lesser extent, Kipling, Housman, and certain unspecified romantics and Georgians — had he called on others, as I have here, he would have had to complicate his argument. True, he does not write as a literary critic, and he wants revolutionary change, not to explore the English literary heritage. But the history which does not consider the witness of the best poetry, especially to such an emotive thing as a sense of national identity, must inevitably simplify. One emerges from reading Tom Nairn and David Martin with opposed ideas, but what they have in common is that they are much more clear-cut — and abstract — in their conceptions of England than David Jones, or Basil Bunting, or Geoffrey Hill, or any other serious contemporary English poet. And if we simplify experience, instead of trying to understand it as it is most livingly dramatised or recorded, we shall not know our "place in time" or any other.

Notes

1. *The Sacred Wood*, University Paperbacks, (1960), p. 49.
2. *The Anathemata*, Faber, (1952), p. 124.
3. 'Art and Sacrament', *Epoch and Artist*, Faber, (1959), p. 158.
4. *The Mayor of Casterbridge*, (1886), Chapter XIII.
5. 'On Not Being Milton', *Selected Poems*, Penguin Books, (1984), p. 112.
6. *Preoccupations*, Faber, (1980), p. 150.
7. *Ibid.*, pp. 150-151.
8. *Ibid.*, p. 169.
9. *The Orators*, Faber, (1932), p. 14.
10. *Studies in Classic American Literature*, Penguin Books, (1971), p. 12.
11. 'A Little Boy Lost', *Songs of Experience*, (1794).
12. 'The Arthurian Legend', *Epoch and Artist*, p. 205.
13. *In Parenthesis*, Faber, (1937), Preface, pp. x-xi.
14. *Ibid.*, pp. 176-177.
15. *Ibid.*, General Notes, pp. 191-192.
16. 'Little Gidding', *Four Quartets*, Faber, (1944).
17. *The Anathemata*, p. 164.
18. *Jerusalem*, 27, 'To the Jews', (1804-1820).
19. *The Sleeping Lord*, Faber, (1974), p. 81.
20. *Briggflatts*, Fulcrum Press, (1966), p. 43.
21. *Ibid.*, p. 13.
22. *Ibid.*, p. 43.
23. *Ibid.*, pp. 31-32.
24. *Ibid.*, p. 17.
25. *Ibid.*, p. 32.
26. *Ibid.*, p. 37.
27. *The Village*, Book I, (1783).
28. *Cf.*, *The Idea of History*, (1946), especially Part V, 2, 'The Historical Imagination'.
29. *The Lords of Limit*, Andre Deutsch, (1984). p. 3.
30. *Ibid.*, pp. 3-4.
31. Geoffrey Hill, *Collected Poems*, Penguin Books, (1985), p. 200.
32. *Ibid.*, 'Funeral Music, 3', p. 72.
33. *Ibid.*, p. 200.
34. *Ibid.*, p. 62.
35. *Mercian Hymns*, Andre Deutsch, (1971).
36. *Biographia Literaria*, (1817), Chapter XIV.
37. *Collected Poems*, p. 201.
38. *Ibid.*, p. 111.
39. *Ibid.*, p. 124.
40. *Preoccupations*, p. 159.
41. 'Theses on the Philosophy of History', *Illuminations*, Fontana Books, (1970), p. 258.
42. *Collected Poems*, p. 158.
43. *The Penguin Book of English Pastoral Verse*, (1982), p. 433.
44. *Collected Poems*, p. 160.

45. John Cowper Powys, *Autobiography*, Macdonald, (1967), pp. 2-3.
46. 'Chords of Identity in a Minor Key', *The Observer*, 12 December 1985, p. 7.
47. 'The Sound of England', *PN Review*, number 8, p. 8.
48. *Ibid.*, p. 10.
49. *The Break-Up of Britain*, Verso, (new, expanded edition, 1981), p. 304.

Jeffrey Wainwright

Acute suspicion of language is a feature of some of the best modern poetry. This may be explained, briefly, by reference to the lesson Coleridge read, when in 'Fears in Solitude' he spoke of "all our dainty terms of fratricide". Modern history has greatly reinforced the lesson, and consequently poets have increasingly come to share Coleridge's knowledge of the corruptibility of language which enables it to be used as a means of distorting or concealing reality. This knowledge is not confined to modern poets, of course, but its pressure has led to their refinement of two closely related faculties: the historical sense, which is a perception of history in words and words in history, and the moral imagination, which sees the gap between language and reality and attempts to bridge it.

For Jeffrey Wainwright, a poet who remembers the lives destroyed by industrial society or expended in its wars, poetry involves scrupulous testing of language against the history which it reflects, or is used to manipulate or evade. This testing goes beyond the care for meaning of all good poetry, and manifests a suspicion of poetic artifice which Wainwright shares with a number of important modern poets, including the Polish poet Tadeusz Różewicz, and the American George Oppen. In England its most notable representative is Geoffrey Hill, who has developed the tradition of moral imagination descending from Coleridge through the poets of both world wars and applied it to the witness of historical atrocities. Their sense of the poet's responsibility is the measure of the suspicion of artifice which such poets have, and they meet it with an art which, in historical awareness and moral integrity, tests itself against reality. Jeffrey Wainwright is a student of modern European and American poetry; he is also one of the best critics of Geoffrey Hill. But what he has learned from other poets (and his greatest debt is to Hill) obviates superficial notions of influence, since the historical sense and the moral imagination are usually refined by reading, but are exercised only by one with an equivalent independence.

Broadly speaking, Jeffrey Wainwright belongs to the post-war generation of British poets who are working class in origin or sympathy, and whose recovery of 'history from below' shares in the spirit of social historians such as E.P. Thompson to whom it is also indebted. This characterization is broad indeed, however, for Jeffrey Wainwright is anything but a populist claiming to speak for the people, or as one of them. Nor is he like Tony Harrison, a poet who writes from a fully developed sense of himself, as autobiographical subject, divided between the love and pain of his original working-class home and the world into which academic and literary success has introduced him. Harrison's is one, interesting, response of a poet highly conscious of his 'place' in society and history; but Wainwright's is very different. There is, for example, little sense of self in his poetry, and he deploys modernist techniques of obliquity, irony, adoption of personae, fragmentary narrative, and lyric sequence instead of continuous long poem, and with the modernist sense of difficulty — the difficulty of saying 'I', the greater difficulty of saying 'we', together with the difficulty of writing poetry true to his subject, in a language heavily influenced by the ideology of a dominant class, and in forms affected by the isolation and self-regard of the aesthetic sensibility. The result of his struggle, however, has been both a continuing concern with the oppressed in the toils of history, and an increasingly subtle exploration of the inter-relationship of nature and society. From the early poems in *Heart's Desire* (Carcanet, 1978), to the later 'The Mad Talk of George III *and* A Hymn to Liberty', and 'Transitive', his perception of the connections within society which determine apparently disparate actions and experiences has deepened to the point at which he has become a genuinely philosophical poet, asking fundamental questions about the nature of love and power.

'1815', the first poem in *Heart's Desire*, is an early example of how Jeffrey Wainwright reveals the realities which clichés and propaganda conceal. The poem with its sequential structure shows his art of exposing connections within the social 'field', here, among industry, war, and the land, and of setting the human cost of action against murderous contemporary rhetoric. Some of his most powerful effects are achieved, here and in other poems, when his juxtapositions of nature and the human reveal the inversion of natural order implicit in the language of the ruling ideology, as when the 'fallen' — the dead — lie under apple trees "stripped about their heads". This example also shows his sensitivity to religious language, to its power, and its capacity for abuse in the hands of social managers. The sources of man's power, in nature and in faith, are turned against him; water, the primary element, is made to flow uphill. The image of dead roach staring above the face of the dead mill- girl in the canal, with which '1815' opens, is effectively an iconographic representation of this recurring theme.

The aesthetic sensibility, with its arts of evading reality and inverting values, is the subject of several poems in *Heart's Desire*, most notably 'Sentimental Education'. The aesthete, hearing of 'revolution', pictures it in his mind, and compares it unfavourably with the life he enjoys with his *amour*:

> One can conjure whole suburbs, postmen,
> Plumbers, flushed inelegant shopgirls

> Ardent to be tearing up cobble stones.
>
> What is all that compared with an eel stew,
> Chicken, hard bread, and wine sharp on the tongue?
> We eat ravenously, honest jagged knives
> In our hands, the light of candles
> Surrendering to your eyes.

Confusion of political and personal emotions, resulting in the perversion of both, is shown by their depiction in terms of each other, for example, "ardent" revolutionaries and *bon vivants* eating "ravenously" with "honest jagged knives". The confusion arises, however, not from the bringing together of private and public concerns, but from their divorce, from the failure of the educated 'heart' to make connections, and to see feelingly outside a narrow, privileged circle. Jeffrey Wainwright is adept at finding formal and linguistic means to present the divorce, but his main concern is to explore possibilities of integration. Thus, the love poems in the the third part of *Heart's Desire* seek to free the form and its emotions from the kind of confusion dramatised in 'Sentimental Education', while his 'historical' poems show the connection or disconnection between man's desire for a better world and his individual life.

A moment of self-deception is wittily shown in 'Thomas Müntzer' when the eponymous hero speaks of "The very poorest, those I fancy most/ Blessed...": the emphatic "fancy most", followed by the pause before "blessed", reveals his confusion of sanctity and sexual desire. But Müntzer at once recognizes it, and continues "I am in love with a girl". He is the most integrated of Wainwright's personae, and his way of seeing is close to the poet's, as when he imagines his learned opponents "pleading now for/*Mercy* a new sweet thing they've found a taste for". This does not reduce the poem's historical veracity, however. 'Thomas Müntzer', one of the finest English poetic sequences of recent years, convincingly embodies the experience of the sixteenth century Protestant reformer, so that when at the end of the poem he says "Stately tearful/Progress... you've seen how I have wept for it", the reader assents, for he has indeed *seen*. But Wainwright is able to enter into Müntzer's world of thought and feeling because it is at the roots of the revolutionary tradition to which he himself belongs.

The main theme of 'Thomas Müntzer' is the integration of "religious thought and experience... with ideas and movements towards social revolution" to which Jeffrey Wainwright refers in his prefatory note. In the second section, Müntzer's shock of recognition (*"This is not/A vision"*) at seeing "my brother crawling in the woods/To gather snails' shells" is followed by his subversive perception of the traditional tree metaphor for the 'organic' hierarchical social order. "I feel the very earth is against me," he says at the beginning of the next section, and we see that the ruling ideology, invested in language, determines even man's apprehension of nature.

Müntzer's struggle is to release natural instincts in accordance with his understanding of the gospel, and to act with an integrated vision. One strength of the poem is that Wainwright does not simplify or force the integration, and although he seems to endorse (through Müntzer's words) the modern substitution of History for God, he recognizes the claims of Christian ambiguity and paradox.

The words composing the verbal tableau of 'Heart's Desire' — "heart", "sleep", "desire", "dream", "breath", "light" — occur again and again in Jeffrey Wainwright's poetry. They are words of primary importance, and they are daily words; men live and die for or by them, and their many possible combinations, whether unifying or contradictory or dialectical, define the human world and its possibilities. Jeffrey Wainwright's explorations in this field show both his historical sense and his moral imagination. He is a politically committed writer who reclaims for poetry the desire for liberation and an integrated 'common' world which moves through the radical tradition to which he belongs, but in his awareness of the corruptibility of all language, and his measuring of ideals against the reality of flesh and blood, he is the opposite of a propagandist. The pleasure of reading his poetry is inseparable from the challenge to think and to see which it poses, and which he uses his art to meet.

Mary Casey: The Poetry of Aloneness

Mary Casey neither published nor sought to publish more than a few poems during her lifetime. Now, two years after her death, in 1980, *Full Circle* and *Christophoros* have been published. Each book has a foreword by Charles Lock, and together, they comprise a selection from her three hundred or so poems.

Posthumous publication is always poignant, but in this instance there is something about it that is awesome, which accords with the nature of the poetry. Here, the poet asks nothing for herself of the reader, but the gift of poetry is absolute, with no special pleading, no self-display, no other compromise of its integrity, nothing but intense concentration. Concentration of the poet on the act of writing and shaping each poem, on discovering what she must say and how to say it; concentration of word and image in the poem; concentration of a life in the poetry. Her editors have, then, worked in her spirit in concentrating her essential poetic achievement into these two books.

Mary Casey's poetry is instinct with her being, but not overtly autobiographical. She wrote from experience, not about it, and used her poetry to see, not to be seen. The places in which she lived — Hampshire, Dorset, Kenya — are vivid presences in her poetry. But although they are seen and felt as she lived in them, they lived in her too, providing imagery for a range of emotions and perceptions, whether presented personally or dramatized in her religious poems, so that in the latter, for example, African mountain and desert landscapes make spiritual dryness and biblical wilderness as palpable as they are in T.S. Eliot. Mary Casey did not transform the world into the matter of her subjectivity, but saw it in the light of her Christianity. She was, like David Jones, an incarnational poet — one for whom the natural image is always an adequate supernatural symbol because it is part of the divine order, and transfiguration reveals the true nature of things.

The mill on the Test in Hampshire where Mary Casey spent her childhood is brought to life in these lines from her poem 'Water-wheel':

> this is not a pose
> he stands at ease as do those

> who ponder while the sack fills
> and the chills of the river mingle
> with the smell of hot barley meal
> headier than pollen
> while the leaning willows feel for
> and finger the face of the river

The poem opens with a quotation: "the day of country milling is over". But nothing once known is ever over for the person who loves it, and it can live for others too, if the imagination can recreate it. Here, different sense impressions combine through a pattern of images, sounds, rhymes and half rhymes to reform a first world, known as intimately as willow and river touch. Mill and miller are so alive in the poem that it would be easy to overlook the consummate but unobtrusive art that presents them, concealing its means of showing in what is shown. An even hastier glance at Mary Casey's poems might lead one to think her sensuous notations and lack of punctuation artless, instead of what they are: elements of a poetry of exceptional purity and concentration.

Of course, all poets begin — and most continue — as readers, and the purity of Mary Casey's poetry has nothing to do with naive ideas of originality or spontaneity. She is traditional in being unconventional, alien in spirit and form to the fashions of contemporary English poetry, but having absorbed lessons from poetry of the past, including modern poets with great apparent differences but common vitalizing principles — the Imagists, Ezra Pound, T.S. Eliot, D.H. Lawrence and Edward Thomas. She could be as strongminded as Eliot and Pound in naming what was, for her, a living European tradition, and the 'aloneness' which her poetry expresses is not isolation, but exists in harmony with a community transcending the confines of past and present:

> there is truth and the poet
>
> Wyat Surrey Emily Brontë
> Old English laments the bearers of ballads
> Homer and Pindar and Sappho
> who touch gold in the living vein
> in this dazzling sorrow
> hold hands
> in this Alone
> there is a fellowship
>
> ('In This Alone')

It is significant that Mary Casey was closely related, through her mother, to the remarkable Powys family, which produced the writers John Cowper, Llewelyn and T.F. Powys: a major source, as yet insufficiently appreciated or explored, of the energy of tradition in its opposition to convention in this century. But just as each brother is distinct from the others, so Mary Casey does not lose definition against a background of inherited characteristics and common values, but stands out with the independence and unique individuality which family and literary tradition do not reduce, but nourish and confirm.

The excellence of her art is as modern as only that of a poet with a sense of tradition can be. The following short poem, written in 1970, might be seen as a fine, late fruit of imagism:

>   all day by my door bowed
>   two black men break stones
>   a dull rhythm beats upon the sun
>
>   the shining drum drops behind the hills
>   the river gleams with another light
>   an arrowy wake
>
>   > pursues the black duck
>   > circling a single rock
>   > this for her silent pleasure
>   > in the shadow of the western hills
>   > ('The Pool')

Spare, hard and clear, the poem has the virtues of the best imagist poetry. It also has virtues rarely found in predominantly imagist poems: in its sound patterns vivifying the actions seen and heard in almost every line, and enacting the rhythm or beat which is its theme. These in turn are strengthened by a correspondence between the images of the "dull rhythm" of the men breaking stones and "the shining drum" of the sun, on which the rhythm beats, and an imagery of circles linking the human and planetary rhythms. Everything in the poem combines to show and sound more than can be said, and its action is surprisingly and sharply quickened by the "arrowy wake" cutting across the circular movement and reversing cause and effect by pursuing the black duck, while "the river gleams with another light". Crosscurrents of feeling have been subtly captured, and even the sense of the numinous is not single, but appropriately an awe in which peace and apprehension contend. 'The Pool' reveals the correspondences and reversals possible in a Creation that is one, real and miraculous, but as something seen and felt, without a hint of the complacency or rhetoric that too often accompanies a symbolism of absolutes.

The division between *Full Circle* and *Christophoros* has been made in order to separate poems of a personal nature from religious poems, and is justified by emphasis. But reading Mary Casey brings home the artificiality of the division when applied to a religion held not as part of life but as its ground and medium, blood and breath, so that the personal lives in the religious and the religious is personal. In her words,

> God giving himself incarnate
> to immolation
> is the root being of all men
> who fall into the hands of the living God...
> ('Christophoros')

Words which, abstracted from the poem, and isolated from the work as a whole, may wrongly suggest a poetry of theological concepts rather than a religious poetry. But in this instance that would be only another artificial distinction, for in Mary Casey's integrated vision the language of faith and the truth of experience interpenetrate.

Charles Lock in his Foreword to *Christophoros* writes interestingly of Mary Casey's search "both within and beyond the Christian tradition for the redeeming comprehension, the universal sacrament". He says that her poetry "will hold an important place in a vital corrective movement within that tradition, that long, humble, vibrant apology to paganism on which the future energy of Christianity may depend." The inclusiveness of Mary Casey's Christianity is reminiscent of David Jones's, since for her, too, living myth is sap of the Tree of Life.

As I understand it, the "apology to paganism" is partly a matter of recognizing vital connections between Christ and Dionysos or Adonis, for example, and complementary illuminations in mysticisms and philosophies other than the Christian. It is also a relaxation of the Christian will to subdue nature, allowing a marriage of Romantic feeling with sacramental theology, imagination with doctrine and devotion, so that we find Mary Casey, like David Jones, not only responsive to the delicate and sensitive tissue of nature, but willingly moved by elemental forces, and recognizing in both the order of Christian signs. The images of light and flowing water filling her poetry are at once natural and numinous, not manifestations of a beauty to be resisted. Not for her Job's sense of an iniquity to be punished when he kissed his hand to sun or moon; she could honour paganism without succumbing to it, because she saw in the nature she loved, not distraction from faith, but life springing from "the root being of all men".

This metaphor carried the literal truth for Mary Casey. 'Good Friday', one of several major sequences in *Christophoros*, (a book which may also be read as one long sequence comprising several movements), shows her development of the metaphor of Christ as the Tree of Life, and is a fine example of her embodied vision. There is at once something simple and solid about this, and an exceptional care in the intelligence shaping it.

In the part of 'Good Friday' called "him of the tree" it is her empathy with natural processes that makes the metaphor live:

> I am the life of the tree
> cool ichor secret juice
> stealing sharper more potent than dew
> within my rugged sheath upwards
> spreading abroad in arms
> in tentative fingers
> finally fostering butterfly wings in
> clear green in fine-sawn fringes
> that flutter and fall at my withdrawal
> mottled and golden.

While this imaginative projection into a tree's seasonal cycle embodies her sense of living myth, in the next part, 'dithyramb', beginning "I am the tree of life", there is a fine example of the intelligence and care with which she uses words. When Christ says

> I hang on the dead tree
> they take my life the fluid forms
> water and blood flow down

"they take my life" is so simply and quietly spoken that it may take another reading to see what is being shown — that it means both 'they kill me' and 'they have their life from me', and the meanings are mutually dependent. No crucifixion, no redemption; no sacrifical God, no essential human life. Christ the tree of life is the life of the tree.

Time and eternity, tradition and immediacy, the universal and the personal: these were necessary conjunctions for Mary Casey, as they are for every Christian poet. Their necessity is the measure of a great responsibility, of the care and technical skill needed to give a valid contemporary embodiment to truth, in the language of a culture in which it is now either widely assumed that eternity, tradition and the universal are meaningless concepts, or, at least, that there is no living relation between them and our time-bound, immediate, personal circumstances. Such care and skill are evident everywhere in Mary Casey's poetry, as in this passage from a poem in *Christophoros*:

> Now my dear comrade in invisible arms
> I who have kept close to you from youth
> am outwardly old and all the harms
> and thorns in the flesh we have shared
> have lost point but the inmost pains
> pierce to the heart of truth —
> without your word for this sharpness
> I could not stand
>   (' "It is hard for thee" ')

This is unmistakably a voice of feeling, modern in its expressive movements, in which the emotional force and dynamic rhythm work together with a quick, painstaking intelligence, alert to every nuance of meaning in the words, and not above punning. The reader is simultaneously moved by strong emotional currents and made to think, or, more often, to see — as in this instance by the relation between suffering and truth, shown by the extremely subtle use of the central image "thorns in the flesh", which is transferred from the physical to the spiritual realm, but to depict the whole being in its total dependence on "your word for this sharpness". The imagery could be translated into specifically Christian terms — but the poem would then be destroyed as a poem, since it is not a translation of doctrine into experience, but an embodiment of experience in which the truth lives.

There are rare occasions in the poems when I could wish Mary Casey had used conventional punctuation or adopted a different lineation, but her method is clearly meant to define meaning, not to merge all in a vaguely suggestive cloud. And, in the main, it succeeds, because her rhythmic and syntactic skills enforce a reading pace which prevents the reader from smoothly over-riding the subtler movements of meaning — a pace which, in making us follow the movements, is a means of making us see.

The extreme concentration and precision of her writing owes something to imagist techniques, and perhaps to the later Pound, too, and the Eliot of 'Marina' and 'Ash Wednesday'. These qualities also correspond to a spiritual discipline, and are poetic equivalents of Plotinus's doctrine of mystical purification, which involves the soul cutting away all externals in order to approach the One, in the depths of its own essential being. But this does not mean that she is either puritanical in any crude, 'anti-life' sense, or solipsistic.

The need for purification, which Mary Casey often expresses in elemental images, especially of starlight and moonlight, together with her independence of spirit and her strong attachment to life, recall Emily Brontë. An equivalent lack of compromise makes Mary Casey's poetry no less awesome than Emily Brontë's. But the latter's intensely prized solitude, and ambivalent passion for a freedom possible only in death, are countered in Mary Casey by her warm and tender feelings for people, and a mysticism which, in life and death, is founded on union. Her passion for elemental purity and what she calls "the much-worshipped moon" do not signify morbid isolation, but "the poetry of aloneness" which must not be confused with it.

This may be understood in terms of the Plotinian mysticism subsumed by her Christianity. The potent word 'alone' in her poetry usually refers to Plotinus's famous "the flight of the alone to the Alone", to which her frequent use of a traditional bird imagery for the soul is also related. The communion of the consciousness turned towards an inner life is not with the ego, but with the Alone in which, through an incomprehensible enlargement of being, the soul is at one with a creation in which neither itself nor any other is lost. Aloneness, in this sense, is at-one-ness. This is, at any rate, how I interpret the ground of her living tradition, whether a Plotinian mysticism whose tendency to abstract idealism is countered by sacramental Christianity, or a spirit kept alive by certain writers through the centuries, or her awareness of not being a self-contained ego, belonging exclusively to herself:

> this is the night I know
> I am nothing of my own
> long bones brown eyes
> the scarlet tree of life
> are no more mine
> than is the child within
>
> I am of those in the graves
> with all the lives before me
> in this mystery of ancestry
>   ('Centenary')

'The Scarlet Swan' is a mysterious poem of visionary happiness, which images a union of souls (particular persons, not a vaporous abstract collective) and merges her childhood river with a vision of light. There is a fine example in the second of its three stanzas of her ability to link the homely and the visionary, or rather to see the latter in the former:

> the wooden footbridge waiting
> here and not here
> a simple preparation
> a means of crossing
> the vision's intolerable brilliance.

Here the footbridge is actual, a means of crossing the Test, and also, surely, a symbol for the cross, a means of crossing (the serious pun is characteristic) a vision that would otherwise be too brilliant for mortal eyes, the conjunction (in Christ, the shining river) of human and divine love, time and eternity. Yet perhaps all is also based, primarily, on childhood images — it is not always possible to be sure; in poetry arising from a life of such consistency, earliest impressions often generate the latest glimpse of truth.

'The Scarlet Swan' is one of a number of poems which triumphantly envision reunion of the beloved after death, and show what Charles Lock calls Mary Casey's "medieval attention". "She uses," he says, "symbols to bridge the divide between her eyes, captured by the natural, and her mind, absorbed in the religious ideal." This is a happy metaphor, in view of 'The Scarlet Swan' and her frequent recourse to imagery of running water. I am uneasy with the word 'ideal' in this context, however, and feel that Mary

Casey shows an intimacy between the natural and the religious — in fact, an immanence of the religious in the organic world — that makes even the metaphor of a bridge between them too divisive. The trouble is, of course, that both Charles Lock and I are writing prose, which is at best a partially sighted guide to what the incarnational imagination shows.

It is at least clear that Mary Casey's power as a poet derives, not from a versification of doctrine or a general symbolism of the absolute or even an assured faith, but from the concentration in her poems of an intensely feeling and acutely seeing life — her own life, but with an embodiment in the life of each poem, which only a high degree of art can achieve. It should also be evident, though I have dwelt on it little here, that the movements of this life include spiritual dryness, suffering, pain which only a strong spirit could bear. This is another awesome feature of the poetry, which is reminiscent of Emily Brontë and Frances Bellerby. In 'The Chariot', for example, the pull towards life and acceptance of approaching death are held in almost unbearable tension, and the knowledge of suffering in her poems is a suffered knowledge.

It may seem odd to conclude that it was right that such poetry should have remained unpublished until now. To begin with, however, there is no way in which it could have fitted in to any poetry 'scene' or to the specialized 'world of poetry' in which reputations are sought, and sometimes made. Nor could it very well be taught, unless in a context — and I do not know of any – in which supreme value is placed on reading as an act of attention, and a meeting — with the text, yes, but also with the spirit of the poet in the text – that makes the reader question himself. On the other hand, we have not been able to grow with Mary Casey, poem by poem, book by book, as we have with R.S. Thomas, for example, but have now to meet her challenge all at once, or not at all. But it seems to me that her aloneness was necessary to her achievement. I use the word now in a commoner sense than her special meaning, not to suggest isolation from family and friends, but an extreme concentration on the matter in hand, as serious as prayer or what Keats called soul-making, without regard to literary reputation or any other ghost that comes back to haunt and distract the poet from the existence of his poems and extension of his ego in the literary world. Her aloneness does not ultimately exclude the reader, as other extreme poetries, whose admission is only to the poet's enclosed ego, may, but admits them to the whole movement of her search:

> my freedom   since I have fallen
> into the power of the living God
> to explore the unsearchable riches of Christ
> in the given light of his knowledge and love
> in the company of so great a cloud of witnesses

and for he went to the mountain apart to pray
in the poetry of aloneness.
                    ('Atonement')

T.S. Eliot: Tradition and the "resident alien"

To Ezra Pound, writing in July 1922, *The Waste Land* was "the justification of the 'movement' of our modern experiment since 1900."[1] To William Carlos Williams, it was "the great catastrophe to our letters".[2] More than sixty sixty years later, *The Waste Land* is no longer a shock (unless to readers coming to modern poetry for the first time), but more a monument in the institution of English Studies, with a familiarity and a largely taken-for-granted authority which make it difficult for us to see it anew. But while this may be the institutional fate of the poem, and indeed of Eliot's body of poetry, his achievement is still as divisive for many poets in England and America today as it was for Pound and Williams in 1922. The division is sometimes, but not always, conscious and it occurs within individual poets as well as between opposing factions. I have no doubt that Eliot is a great poet, with the capacity to form minds and influence lives, which monuments do not have. The divisiveness of his poetry is an aspect of its life. It is my intention to approach the poetry from some angles which are particularly awkward for the person who both acknowledges and questions Eliot's influence, in the hope that the resulting reflections may be useful to those who are similarly divided, and usefully provocative to those who are not.

I

It is perfectly understandable that Pound should have been so excited by *The Waste Land*. Setting aside his own part in its shaping, which generosity would prevent him from making a proprietorial claim, the poem was in form and style a great vindication of Imagist and Vorticist principles, and conceived on a scale to compare with the new art and the new prose. As for what it actually said, in its showing of cultural disintegration, Pound shared enough with Eliot not to question the poem's vision. As Americans remaking themselves as Europeans, and with strong English affiliations which in Eliot's case extended to his adoption of (or at least disguise in) an English social identity, they were concerned with renewal among the ruins of an old civilization. But for Williams in America, what mattered was very different.

He recognized Eliot's genius, but maintained that with *The Waste Land* it "gave the poem back to the academics".[3] Years later, he was still regretting that "Eliot had turned his back on the possibility of reviving my world" and thinking that "he might have become our adviser, even our hero".[4] Williams's sense of Eliot's defection from America, from his rightful place in the vanguard of those who were rediscovering "a primary impetus, the elementary principle of all art, in the local conditions",[5] had far-reaching implications. It referred explicitly to a language, to what Williams called "the western dialect",[6] and it implied a different way of seeing and feeling, a different apprehension of reality. Eliot, who remained more of an American than Williams allowed — they were, after all, different kinds of American, and would have remained so whatever their choices — said in later life of his poetry that "in its sources, in its emotional springs, it comes from America".[7] The America in Eliot's poetry is the Missouri, the sea, his childhood and his childhood landscapes; these were a source of his mysticism, and provided the most haunting images and elemental rhythms of his poetry, in *The Waste Land*, 'Marina', *Ash-Wednesday* and 'The Dry Salvages', but they did not mean history to him, or the grounds of a civilization and a social order. An exception to this must be made for the Puritanism of his American forebears, but Eliot went back to its source in English history. History, when it appears in his poetry, is English and his 'tradition' has European roots and branches and the poetic accents and intellectual and spiritual authority of the English Church in the seventeenth century. The exploration of which Eliot wrote in East Coker, remembering Andrew Eliot's voyage from England in 1667, "for a further union, a deeper communion/Through the dark cold and empty desolation," is a search not for America but God. But of course, Williams's language, his talk of "a primary impetus, the elementary principle of all art, in the local conditions", looks back to Whitman and would have been quite alien to Eliot. Where Williams found reality, in the human and phenomenal world, Eliot found unreality; the reality of which human kind cannot bear very much, which Eliot found in his Christianity, was heaven and damnation.

Nevertheless, thinking briefly of what Eliot might have become, as an American *or* an English poet, if he had been concerned to rediscover "a primary impetus... in the local conditions", we may see that there are passages in *The Waste Land* which suggest the possibilities of a very different kind of poem from what it actually is. There is this, for example:

> The river sweats
> Oil and tar
> The barges drift
> With the turning tide
> Red sails
> Wide
> To leeward, swing on the heavy spar.

> The barges wash
> Drifting logs
> Down Greenwich reach
> Past the Isle of Dogs.

Out of context, this is a good imagist poem, but with obvious limitations compared to the formal and thematic scope of *The Waste Land*, which both uses and transcends imagist techniques. Yet it might have worked in the poem as an 'opening' — an opening onto the reality of the squalid, beautiful, historic river, and an opening of wonder in the reader's mind. It does both to some degree, of course, but to a degree that is strictly limited by the poet's design. The passage itself is haunted by Conrad's river leading into "the heart of an immense darkness", and the lament, the image of Elizabeth and Leicester, and the voices of the Thames daughters which follow it, shut the mind back into the poem's narrow and predictable emotional world, and its rigidly determined historical perspective and mythic framework. Of course, *The Waste Land* has great poetic authority. What it has also is a way of deliberately killing wonder, and of turning moments of release into glimpses of underlying horror. Its greatness is in the suffering which it proves on our nerves and emotions. The suffering is in the poem by virtue of the mastery with which it projects a world that is a mental and emotional prison, and the suffering may be interpreted as the consequence rather of restricted sympathies determining what is seen and felt than of a land that is truly waste. If, for example, we do not know whether the "white bodies naked on the low damp ground" are corpses or naked lovers, the reason is because the 'love' in the poem is a kind of death; the ambiguity tells us something about the emotional pattern of the poem, but nothing about love or death, or the relationship between them, which Shakespeare and the Metaphysical poets explored. The only promise of real release comes as the structure containing the pattern breaks down, the voice of the thunder sounding from another order of reality, as the imprisoning mental and emotional world fragments. If the poem itself is made of fragments shored against ruins, then it is a construction which, by holding the ruins together, keeps out the hope of reintegration until its collapse. The tension between will maintaining a false order, and desire to let go so that another and possibly destructive principle of reality may enter from the outside, is characteristic of Eliot's poetry before the 'release' of 'Marina' and *Ash-Wednesday*.

2

Seen against the darkness of the year in which it was written, 1919, and in the context of Eliot's poetry before and for some years after it, 'Tradition and the Individual Talent' is at first sight a very surprising essay. Not surprising in its authoritative tone, for Eliot's voice in his major writings always has authority, or in being less a coherent argument than it is a series of assertions, for this too is not uncommon in his criticism and discursive verse, but for its strong affirmation of order. "The historical sense", we are told, "involves a perception, not only of the pastness of the past, but of its presence; the historical sense compels a man to write not merely with his own generation in his bones, but with a feeling that the whole of the literature of Europe from Homer and within it the whole of the literature of his own country has a simultaneous existence and composes a simultaneous order". 'Gerontion', written in the same year, is sometimes described by critics as a reflection of 'the mind of Europe'. But the persona voices a state of loss, guilt, impotence, of complete separation, in which physical disintegration complements total loss of contact with any existence outside the self, while the mind of Europe is identified with the order which the poet with the historical sense perceives. It is surprising in any case that such an idea should have been arrived at in 1919, in an existing Europe left exhausted, divided, perhaps irreparably damaged by the worst war in its history, but it is the more surprising that its author should have been the poet of 'Gerontion' and *Prufrock and Other Observations*, which are fraught with an acute sense of disorder. Or perhaps the idea is surprising only if we fail to see it as the expression of a desperate need, in Eliot and in the post-war world, and of the human response to need which constructs an image of the desired object in the mind. Certainly the need was strong in Eliot's world as well as in him personally, and it would be wrong to overemphasise his isolation. Eliot understood that there is a relationship between individual and communal sickness, and his preoccupation in later years with the 'common' language of a 'people' developed from the concern with 'tradition' which is explicit in his writings after the First World War. He was to find that there are many who need his idea of order as badly as he needed it himself.

Peter Ackroyd in his fine biography, *T.S. Eliot*, makes much of Eliot's references to himself, settled and established in England, as "resident alien".[8] Towards the end of the book, after he has shown the establishment of Eliot's enormous influence upon the literary, academic and intellectual life of England, Ackroyd offers a view of him near the end of his life as a man whose "extraordinary authority was based on that sense of a cultural order which he had once sought and which, by the strange alchemy of his career, he now embodied. He had become the representative of a tradition which, without his presence, might finally disappear".[9] This is a touching view of the aged eagle in his isolation, but the suggestion of a 'tradition' of *one* can hardly be entertained, except at the risk of emptying the word of meaning. Nor does it need to be, since Ackroyd exaggerates when he claims that Eliot had "no real predecessors or successors".[10] Eliot's creation of a tradition, and of himself as its representative, was the most successful instance of what almost all important modern writers in English have sought to do.

When Eliot in the first part of *Ash Wednesday* writes:

> Because I cannot hope to turn again
> Consequently I rejoice, having to construct something
> Upon which to rejoice

the possibility of rejoicing is fresh in his poetry (it appears first in 'Marina') but the idea of construction is not. The poet always constructs, of course; but this obvious sense is complicated in Eliot's case by his construction of personae that have an anxious awareness of the need for self- making and its difficulty. Eliot has made us hypersensitive to the peril of assuming that we can find the poet's self in his poems. Nevertheless, there is clearly a connection between the concern with identity in his poems and his construction for himself of the image of a certain kind of Englishman, which was remarked on by many of his friends and acquaintances, and perhaps most memorably by Edmund Wilson's reference to him, in 1933, as "a completely artificial, or, rather, self-invented character".[11]

Eliot was not alone among modern 'English' writers in his self-invention. Most have had to remake themselves, though not always into Englishmen and women: it is the inevitable response of the writer to a society in which he does not have a clearly defined role, and in which, therefore, he is to some degree an alien. America failed to provide a sustaining tradition, as far as Eliot was concerned; and in England, even before the First World War, the idea that there was a tradition uniting the 'best minds', let alone common to all, could not bear scrutiny. Of course, Eliot was under no illusion that what he called "the main current" of the past could be plucked out of the air in England in the early twentieth century, and he maintained that tradition "cannot be inherited, and if you want it you must obtain it by great labour". It is not always, or perhaps ever, possible to make a clear distinction between invention and discovery, and Eliot's idea of the historical sense maintains a dialectic between creative newness and recovery. At any rate, the tradition he came to represent brought to life an English aware of its past, especially in Shakespeare and the seventeenth century, with their memory of the integrated vision of the Middle Ages, and aware of its connections with Europe. In doing so, the tradition fulfilled a need in many of his English readers which was similar to his own, and for the same reason, that he created it at a time of acute disorder. And in the historical sense Eliot gave to his successors — as the work of David Jones and Geoffrey Hill shows — an imaginative faculty which can extend to a 'matter' of England (and Britain) which transcends his own limitations in this direction.

3

The poetic image can be a means of connection on many levels; traditionally, it has been used to present the image of man made in the image of God. While it is rarely found in this form in modern poetry, there was, as Peter Jones has pointed out in the introduction to his Penguin anthology, *Imagist Poetry*, "an element of mysticism"[12] in the poetry of the Imagists. Hulme's thought was religious; the mysticism is evident in H.D.; and Pound's idea of the image as "the word beyond formulated language"[13] implies a faith in the poet's contact with reality, as does Williams's "no ideas but in things".[14] Holding in mind Pound's definition of the image as "that which presents an intellectual and emotional complex in an instant of time", Peter Jones reminds us that the period of the Imagists was also the period of the exploration of the subconscious, when seekers such as Frazer, Jessie Weston, Freud, Jung, Croce and Whitehead "contributed to make the complex deep enough to reach the very Word, the Logos, the Divine — to be held in the word, the phrase, the analogy, the image".[15]

From his later explorations of the relationship between words and the Word, we might expect Eliot's early poetry to have at least a shadow of this mysticism, even though he was not directly associated with Imagism. There is such a shadow, in 'Preludes', for example:

> I am moved by fancies that are curled
> Around these images, and cling:
> The notion of some infinitely gentle
> Infinitely suffering thing.

The "fancies" are undercut by irony, however, and the moments of transfiguration in the early poems, such as the "vision of the street/As the street hardly understands", in 'Preludes', and "the heart of light, the silence", in *The Waste Land*, are circumscribed by a consciousness which sees the world's unreality, not its penetration by another order. In his words in 'The Metaphysical Poets', Eliot uses the image, or conceit, to transform "an observation into a state of mind". Perception in the early poems cannot make contact with reality because it reflects only the perceiver's mind. This solipsism is inherent in F.H. Bradley's philosophy, which Eliot quotes revealingly in his note on 'the key' passage in *The Waste Land*: "My external sensations are no less private to my self than are my thoughts or my feelings. In either case my experience falls within my own circle, a circle closed on the outside; and, with all its elements alike, every sphere is opaque to the others which surround it.... In brief, regarded as an existence which appears in a soul, the whole world for each is peculiar and private to that soul." The result of his closure in this philosophy is that, in Eliot's hands, the power of the Metaphysical image implodes in "a circle closed on the outside", which is the world of the consciousness of each poem. But in Donne and the other Metaphysical poets, the image is a means both of defining relationships, either between lovers or between the poet and God, and of relating and humanising different areas of knowledge. A poetry of relationship was not possible for Eliot until the circle was broken, and the word, released from its prison in an individual mind, was grounded on the Word.

As well as being a means of connection, the image can present disconnection – the discrete 'things' of a meaningless world, or the fragments of a world which has disintegrated:

> 'On Margate Sands.
> I can connect
> Nothing with nothing.
> The broken fingernails of dirty hands.'

This is as perfect an image in its way as 'In a Station of the Metro'; but Pound characteristically presents an instant of connection between mind and world, while in Eliot the only coherence is of fragments within a state of mind. With its mythic framework, and its echoes and allusions and recurring images, *The Waste Land* is much more than "a heap of broken images"; but it is also the most extreme and ambitious example of Eliot's method of fragmenting the human image and presenting a world seen and experienced by the broken parts.

One evidence of fragmentation often adduced in the early poems is the obsessive imaging of parts of the body — eyes, hands, hair, legs, fingers, and so on. It is these, not a complete bodily image, that Eliot's 'characters' see when they look at each other or at themselves. This physical dismemberment corresponds with an inner division whose most ambitious projection is Tiresias, who is both male and female, and suffers the lust and mutual fear or indifference of the sexes, and with a 'world' obscured in fog or seen as fragmentary or dissolving images. What holds the personae together is style — most obviously, Eliot's styles, but also style in the sense of discourse and social behaviour, or disguise. Prufrock prepares a face to meet the faces that he meets; the young man in 'Portrait of a Lady' "must borrow every changing shape/To find expression"; Gerontion, like Tiresias, is a master rhetorician in the poetic style of another age; and all have lives like the lady's, "composed... of odds and ends", in which 'composed' means both the composition of self-invention, and the composure of false self-possession. The disguises are their only means of saving themselves from the demands and formulations of others, since they are without a centre.

There are alternative apprehensions of reality and unreality to that which we find in Eliot's early (or later) poetry, but I do not believe their assumption is a legitimate ground for criticising him for 'defeatism' or lack of 'human' sympathy. Eliot had a different sense of 'self' and 'world' than many of his contemporaries, and suffered a terrible knowledge of their unreality and emptiness. The images in his early poetry are 'hard', but with the hardness of empty shells; they are like the broken spring in 'Rhapsody on a Windy

Night', a "form that the strength has left/Hard and curled and ready to snap". Their emptiness reflects the disintegration of the human image, by which men and women are separated from each other and divided inwardly, with no centre. The images in the poems are simultaneously hard and soluble, as in Prufrock's mind:

> Shall I say, I have gone at dusk through narrow streets
> And watched the smoke that rises from the pipes
> Of lonely men in shirt-sleeves, leaning out of windows?...
>
> I should have been a pair of ragged claws
> Scuttling across the floors of silent seas.

Perception moves from the surface of a world composed of disconnected, obscurely threatening gestures to inner depths in which the confused, yearning self transforms its fragmented image into parts of the non-human creation. Both surface and interior are equally subjective: points on a closed circle.

Eliot in the early poems is already a religious poet: the emptiness is haunted by absent meaning, the disintegration remembers an integration. A language that once had significance has been corrupted by the broken human image, as in Gerontion's confusion of the Passion with adultery, or dissolved in romantic atmosphere, as when, in 'Portrait of a Lady', 'soul' and 'resurrected' are the vocabulary of a self-regarding emotionalism. The language of religious integration is moribund, though its rhythms and images haunt the poems. And in the disintegration of the human image, the forces of love and fear which its traditional order contained have flowed back amorphously to the elements, to the sea in particular, which waits at the end of 'Prufrock' and 'Gerontion' to swallow the human atoms. Seen from this angle, the greatness of *The Waste Land* is that it builds up a storm which is comparable in magnitude to Lear's, revealing the disintegration of order at every level.

4

> What seas what shores what grey rocks and what islands
> What water lapping the bow
> And scent of pine and the woodthrush singing through the fog
> What images return
> O my daughter.

The voice of 'Marina' is poised between question and exclamation. It is a voice conflating Pericles', the king who has voyaged in his ship to a miraculous recovery of his daughter, and Eliot's, the poet whose construction has brought him a vision of wonder under the form of his earliest images: a woman and the sea coast. The poem itself is a kind of boat, made "unknowing, half conscious, unknown, my own", and its voyage is a release from the closure of the early poems, bringing Eliot to

> This form, this face, this life
> Living to live in a world of time beyond me; let me
> Resign my life for this life, my speech for that unspoken,
> The awakened, lips parted, the hope, the new ships.

'Marina' is a "word beyond formulated language", a word beyond Eliot's own formulations, and its mysticism is perhaps the farthest reach of Imagism in that direction, or, rather, of Eliot's independent development of techniques common to Imagism. Eliot's epigraph from Seneca's *Hercules Furens* invites us to see a possibility of horror 'crossing' the mysterious revelation. The poem is plangent, but to me, there is no horror in it; the horror is a shadow from the past upon Eliot's mind, which cannot fully accept the vision his poem has brought him.

If there is any deception in 'Marina', it does not succeed in disguising a new directness in Eliot's poetry. This comes with the return of primary images which are allowed a fresh exploratory freedom, and it continues, in *Ash-Wednesday*, with the construction, not of another closure, but of stages of self-abandonment. In the stage at the beginning of the second part, based on Ezekiel's vision of the valley of dry bones, in one of the finest sustained passages in all Eliot's poetry, he does to himself what his poems have habitually done with the human figure. The dismemberment is a form of disguise ("And I who am here dissembled"), until completed as an act of self-unmaking, with the proffering of "my deeds to oblivion, and my love/To the posterity of the desert and the fruit of the gourd". The construction of "something/Upon which to rejoice" involves total destruction of the false self, and in submission to the reality which it has closed out, through the guidance of the Lady, restoration of the human in the image of the divine. The 'I' of *Ash-Wednesday* receives its integral strength from willingly undergoing the breakdown which makes possible the recovery. The most poignant line in the poem, "Suffer me not to be separated", is a plea for integration at every level, and the positive equivalent of the lament, "I can connect/Nothing with nothing", which arose from the whirlpool of disintegration. *Ash-Wednesday* contains passages whose meaning seems to remain just beyond the reader's reach (and perhaps Eliot's, too,) but its Christianity is strongly stated. This at first seems to make the connection between construction and rejoicing paradoxical, since the biblical and liturgical elements in the poem make the ground for rejoicing clear. These elements are not Eliot's construction, unless in the sense that he has built them into his poem, which contains the first completed personal prayers in his poetry. But it is the combination of tentativeness and authority, directness and subtlety, beautifully cadenced articulation and hard images with a dreamlike indeterminacy, which makes *Ash-Wednesday* one of his two or three greatest poems.

Eliot's vision of reality was transfigured rather than changed. That is to say, it seems doubtful whether he ever lost the atomized and dismembered vision of the early poems, although it came to have a different meaning. "You must not deny the body", he wrote in 'Choruses from *The Rock*'. But Eliot had no belief "That we are sound, substantial flesh and blood". Moreover, the eye which in 'Morning at the Window' sees "brown waves of fog toss up to me/Twisted faces from the bottom of the street", as if the faces are relics of the non-human world at the bottom of the sea, and "an aimless smile" vanishing along the roofs, belongs to the same man who sees the "hints of earlier and other creation" thrown up on the beach, and the endless "trailing/Consequence of further days and hours", in 'The Dry Salvages'. Eliot's dismemberment of the human image may be seen in 'East Coker', too, in the resonant 'open field' passage, in which the villagers are glimpsed dancing:

> Round and round the fire
> Leaping through the flames, or joined in circles,
> Rustically solemn or in rustic laughter
> Lifting heavy feet in clumsy shoes,
> Earth feet, loam feet, lifted in country mirth
> Mirth of those long since under earth
> Nourishing the corn.

The whole passage has been a focus of indignant discussion, mainly by English critics who feel that Eliot, American and patrician, looks down on the people he has evoked, and shows no understanding of the cultural and labouring conditions of rural England. Questions, reservations, and objections cluster round every passage in Eliot's poetry in which he reveals his perception of the 'common' people — and with good reason. Here, for example, as well as the characteristic dismemberment we may observe a curious dichotomy between Sir Thomas Elyot's courtly language invoking medieval order in his description of the marriage dance, and T.S. Eliot's "the coupling of man and woman/And that of beasts". What does the juxtaposition of these two languages achieve? Are both views equally true? How could they be? In any case, the emphasis upon the ultimate reduction of human harmony, in "dung and death", places the weight upon the poet's deliberately crude diction. Yet still the whole passage evokes a 'presence' of the long-dead, which belies reduction and dismemberment.

Still point and timeless moment might be atoms in a vision of disintegration. In Eliot's philosophy they are, of course, the opposite: the centre which, through the Incarnation, alone gives meaning to man and the world.

The theology of *Four Quartets* is incarnational — but Eliot's imagination is not. He is a Christian poet who gives, not a restored body to the world, but the world to a refining fire. His theme is transfiguration, and only through this does he find meaning in the flux of phenomena and ideals:

> This is the use of memory:
> For liberation — not less of love but expanding
> Of love beyond desire, and so liberation
> From the future as well as the past. Thus, love of a country
> Begins as attachment to our own field of action
> And comes to find that action of little importance
> Though never indifferent. History may be servitude,
> History may be freedom. See, now they vanish,
> The faces and places, with the self which, as it could, loved them,
> To become renewed, transfigured, in another pattern.

"See, now they vanish,/The faces and places, with the self..." As they have vanished in the fog and city streets and on the waters of the early poems, as they have melted or fragmented in the mind or the dissolving "floors of memory"; but at last vanishing itself is a condition of their renewal, "transfigured, in another pattern". Symbols hint at the pattern, but no image can hold

> a lifetime burning in every moment
> And not the lifetime of one man only
> But of old stones that cannot be deciphered.

Robert Jay Lifton, in his book about the survivors of Hiroshima, *Death in Life*, quotes from his interview with a Japanese professor of English. The professor refers to the lines from 'Little Gidding': "They can tell you, being dead: the communication/Of the dead is tongued with fire beyond the language of the living". Remembering the lines, he misquotes them, but as Lifton notes, he "had retained Eliot's psychological message if not his exact words". The professor continues (the ellipses are in the text): "When I read these words, I felt very moved... I thought of the fires of Hiroshima.... These days... we are losing our faith in language... but when I read these lines in T.S. Eliot, I returned to my former naive faith in language — in its ability to express what we feel.... The voice of those who died — that is the important question."[16] Although it arose in an extreme situation, I do not think this an extreme example of the psychological and moral value of great poetry, or of its trans-personal value to human communities. The Japanese professor's experience of the lines from *Four Quartets* is not different in kind from the effect that the poem has had on many English readers since its publication during the Second World War. It is significant, of course, that the last three quartets were written and appeared in wartime, followed by the publication of the complete poem in 1944. The last three quartets are consciously 'patriotic' poems, and their continuing appeal at this level has much to do with the value a national identity is felt to have when it is threatened or begins to erode, as it has increasingly in England since the last world war. What is involved in this erosion is not only a greater divisiveness between people who are physically neighbours, but also separation between present and past, in effect, a silencing of the dead which tears language from its roots, and encapsulates the living in a ghostly isolation. Eliot's sense of Englishness, and his construction of an English tradition grounded upon seventeenth-century Anglicanism, were both highly selective, as has often been pointed out. Certainly, a great writer whose ways of seeing and feeling influence several generations may also help to deaden and blind them to what he did not see and feel. But to my mind, it is more important than any quarrel with Eliot to recognize that, in giving his tradition a voice, he helped to restore a sense of community in and across time, "now and in England". It is a paradox that a "resident alien" should have achieved this, but a familiar paradox in a century in which 'tradition' has usually been partly created and partly recovered by writers beginning with an acute sense of its absence or loss.

Notes

1. Quoted by Peter Ackroyd in *T.S. Eliot* (1984), p. 127.
2. *The Autobiography of William Carlos Williams* (1948. New Directions Paperback, 1967), p. 146.
3. *Ibid.*, p. 146.
4. *Ibid.*, p. 174.
5. *Ibid.*, p. 146.
6. *Ibid.*, p. 175.
7. Quoted by Peter Ackroyd in *T.S. Eliot*, p. 311.
8. *Cf. Ibid.*, pp. 24-25.
9. *Ibid.*, p. 317.
10. *Ibid.*, p. 355.
11. Quoted in *Ibid.*, p. 199.
12. *Imagist Poetry* (1972), p. 38.
13. Quoted in *Ibid.*, p. 33.
14. *The Autobiography of William Carlos Williams*, p. 390.
15. *Imagist Poetry*, p. 40.
16. *Death in Life*: The Survivors of Hiroshima, (Penguin Books, 1971), p. 217.

Seeing the World: The Poetry of George Oppen

The sense of awe, I suppose, is all I manage to talk about. I had written that 'virtue of the mind is that emotion which causes to see,' and I think that perhaps that is the best statement of it.

George Oppen

We awake in the same moment to ourselves and to things.

Jacques Maritain

"Some of us are writing to say things simply so that they will affect us as new again."[1] Louis Zukofsky's comment to Harriet Monroe, at the time of the 'objectivist' number of *Poetry*, in 1931, is relevant to George Oppen's first book, *Discrete Series*. Saying things simply, however, is unlikely to be what any reader finds at a first reading of *Discrete Series*, or, for that matter, of much of George Oppen's poetry. But, as with any poet who says things "so that they will affect us as new again", our initial difficulty in understanding will be due largely to what we bring to the poems — expectations formed by poetic conventions, and their way of structuring the world, from which the poet has freed himself, and from which the poems can free us. Understanding George Oppen means coming alive to his way of seeing.

George Oppen himself has said of *Discrete Series*: "What I felt I was doing was beginning from imagism as a position of honesty. The first question at that time in poetry was simply the question of honesty, of sincerity".[2] I doubt whether any poet has ever been as conscious as George Oppen of the need for honesty in the poem, and of what it actually requires in the act of writing. He is faithful in all his poetry to his perception of the essential lesson of imagism and tests each word to see whether it holds meaning, and whether in using it he is being true to his experience. As he said in the same interview, he is "really concerned with the substantive, with the subject of the sentence, with what we are talking about, and not rushing over the subject-matter in order to make a comment about it". The result in his poems is an extraordinary attention to the primary unit of meaning, the word, and to the relations between words which both articulate meaning and form the poem as an object. With *The Materials* and his later books, he extends "the position of honesty" from the instance of perception to complex processes of thought. His achievement is a philosophical poetry which retains what he has called "the imagist intensity of vision".[3]

Starting with *Discrete Series* George Oppen has steadily refused to let any conventional poetic or commonsense or ideological order represent the world for him; he has done his own seeing. The strangeness of *Discrete Series* — its initially estranging effect upon the reader, and its enactment of the author's estrangement from conventional modes of perception — is not a subjective remaking of the familiar but the effect of a mind which is uncompromising in its truth to what it sees. We learn with these poems to trust George Open not to say more than he means. As he said later, "what I couldn't write I scratched out. I wrote what I could be sure of, what I could write... what I could think, could say, could do."[4] The empirical attitude denotes a radical scepticism about the world — specifically, urban America in the late Twenties and early Thirties — as seen, explained, interpreted, taught to see itself, in terms of conditioned images. George Oppen, from the beginning, is a breaker of false images in the tradition of William Blake, with a scepticism towards the received world equal to Blake's scepticism towards the values handed down in *his* time. There are obvious considerable differences between, say, Blake's 'London' and the following poem from *Discrete Series*:

> Bad times:
> The cars pass
> By the elevated posts
> And the movie sign.
> A man sells post-cards.[5]

In Blake's poem a rich metaphorical language connects one human action and instrument of state power with another, exposing "the mind-forg'd manacles" with which all are shackled together. George Oppen's language is stark, but in its scrupulous attention to the relationships between words and images and things, no less capable of exposing man's plight in the web of a false system. These "bad times" are not a condition of nature but of a society with false values, in which a word of great value — "elevated" — has been so devalued as to be associated only with posts, which "the cars pass", as if their mechanism had taken over the city from human agency. The only human action is a complete reduction of the human being: "A man sells post-cards". What George Oppen shows is that in the value-system of these bad times a man is less than a post or a machine.

To alter our perception of things and enable us to grasp them anew, poetry must change our sense and valuation of the words naming them. This is what

George Oppen does in *Discrete Series*. There he begins his work of *slowing down* the mind, concentrating it on words and things one at a time, and so *quickening* it to a new sense of the relations between them.

Before the reader's attention adapts itself to George Oppen's care, most of the poems in *Discrete Series* are easy to read *over*. For example:

> The edge of the ocean,
> The shore: here
> Somebody's lawn,
> By the water.

This might be shrugged off with a careless 'so what?' except that *Discrete Series* establishes a way of seeing, and a pitch of attention, which enable the mind to grasp the non-human otherness of 'ocean', and the shore as its 'edge'. "Here/ Somebody's lawn" then comes as an astonishing fact: something human, a possession, a piece of cultivated wilderness, alongside everything that it is not. In this, as in many poems, George Oppen takes us to the roots of America and relates the peopled, settled world to elemental conditions, and to the forces and processes by which they were converted to serve human need. His words name the things of an interaction between man and nature and he restores meaning to each word and to the relations between them. Consequently, in the first line of the next poem in the series, "Tug against the river", 'against' carries the effort of the tug's struggle with the current and we see a thing — the tug — made by man for use, and able to move with or against the forces of nature. This is not the poetry of a man who cares nothing for the rich resources of language, but of a man for whom language and the world are deeply involved in each other.

George Oppen's awe at the things of the world is the measure of his scepticism about what man makes of them, socially and mentally, with his ideas and forms of order. For him, there can be only one response to awe:

> Clarity, clarity, surely clarity is the most beautiful
>   thing in the world,
> A limited, limiting clarity
>
> I have not and never did have any motive of poetry
> But to achieve clarity
>   ('Route', 1)

The motive ensures that at times his poems seem to be a kind of pointing at things, as if things can be seen *through* words:

> Not to reduce the thing to nothing —

> I might at the top of my ability stand at a window
> and say, look out; out there is the world.
>
> ('Route', 3)

But the transparency of words is an illusion, as George Oppen knows. Man is in a world which his language orders or disorders, and he sees with words or is blinded by them.

In 'Psalm', George Oppen's awe at the deer is not conveyed by gesture or by a simple act of naming alone — even the exclamation "That they are there!" is an emotive verbal action. He conveys the otherness of the deer by imaging them "in the strange woods", in their bodily activities, and in their relationship with the things of their world — grass, roots, earth, woods, fields, leaves, sun. He juxtaposes their world with the words naming it:

> Their paths
> Nibbled thru the fields, the leaves that shade them
> Hang in the distances
> Of sun
>
> The small nouns
> Crying faith
> In this in which the wild deer
> Startle, and stare out.

"This in which" is wholly other, and at once local and cosmic, but it is an order of existence, not life as a blind force. The faith is in language and in the world, or in language *in* the world; in the relationship between the language man has made, and the world he has not made, but shares with the creatures.

George Oppen's awe belongs, in part, to a specifically American tradition, which arose from the experience of the pioneers and settlers, and found literary expression in Emerson, Thoreau and Whitman among others. The tradition apprehends nature with conflicting emotions of wonder and fear. Nature is absolutely other than the human world, a fearful barrier to be overcome, and a savage wilderness, but also the ground which man must tend with care if he is to exist on it; the ground supplying materials which man may adapt with his skills to make a harmonious settlement, and which in misusing he will destroy, and destroy himself. To the latter perception, as well as to his experience as a craftsman, we owe George Oppen's contactual knowledge of the practical crafts by which men and women make their world, and a poetry that recognises, as fully as any poetry can, the impermanence of human order, and the threat of universal destruction posed by our misuse of knowledge. If there are poems that are equal to the nuclear threat, in the sense of seeing what it means, then George Oppen has written them, in 'Time of the Missile' and 'The Crowded Countries of the Bomb'. The recognition is less a matter of particular poems, however, than of the knowledge of the complete vulnerability uniting us from which George Oppen always writes, and of his understanding that man *cannot live* without a sense of the future.

Clearly, George Oppen is in no way a naive explorer or celebrant of American 'roots'. The distinctive character of his thought comes from his combination of crosscurrents within the American tradition arising from the making of a new world out of the wild, by diverse peoples, with an existentialist philosophy — owing something to Buber and Kierkegaard as well as much to Heidegger — which apprehends the difficulties of achieving meaning and authentic being in the world.

Wonder and fear are equally present in 'The Building of the Skyscraper':

> O, the tree, growing from the sidewalk –
> It has a little life, sprouting
> Little green buds
> Into the culture of the streets.
> We look back
> Three hundred years and see bare land.
> And suffer vertigo.

Here, in the last verse, there is awe at the continuing process of nature in "the culture of the streets", and vertigo at the distance travelled in three hundred years from the 'bare land' to the city superimposed upon it. Yet to isolate these meanings, germane to the American experience, is to simplify the poem. For 'The Building of the Skyscraper' is also concerned with the poet's work in a world where

> There are words that mean nothing
> But there is something to mean.
> Not a declaration which is truth
> But a thing
> Which is. It is the business of the poet
> 'To suffer the things of the world
> And to speak them and himself out'.

The concerns are one. Vertigo is at the meaninglessness of some words, wonder at the fact of meaning. (Neither is a natural phenomenon, of course, any more than the skyscraper is. Meaning for George Oppen depends upon what a man *intends*.) George Oppen has lived a life in which questions of personal integrity have been inseparable from his relationship with the people, and his roots are entangled with the roots of cities raised in the wild.

"The data of experience", George Oppen has said, "is the core of what modernism restored to poetry, the sense of the poet's self among things."[6] This is a statement of relationship, and George Oppen is above all a poet who looks for meaning in relationships and interactions, between the self and others, the self and things, people and the world they make, man and nature. He knows, in the words of 'Of Being Numerous', 10, that "the isolated man is dead, his world around him exhausted". This is not a didactic gesture indicating a poetic stance to which he opposes himself as a poet at home in a sustaining community. On the contrary, George Oppen's sense of other people, let alone of 'the people', always implies his need of them, as a man who knows isolation and what it means. In 'World, World — ' he writes:

> Soul-searchings, these prescriptions,
>
> Are a medical faddism, an attempt to escape,
> To lose oneself in the self.
>
> The self is no mystery, the mystery is
> That there is something for us to stand on.

His poetry is an attempt not to lose himself in the self but to find himself in the world. He faces the difficulties inherent in the aim with complete honesty, and neither denies that being a poet increases isolation, nor accepts the fact complacently. He is certainly a metaphysical poet, and may even be described as mystical, if we take the full force of "the mystery is/That there is something for us to stand on". The poem continues, and ends:

> We want to be here.
>
> The act of being, the act of being
> More than oneself.

He may be called mystical not by virtue of any transcendentalism but because of the intensity with which he regards "the act of being", seeing the 'world' and the relationships in and by which 'we' and 'the self' exist anew.

There are times when the purity and intensity of George Oppen's vision recall Simone Weil and the desire for self-effacement which led her to write: "May I disappear in order that those things that I see may become perfect in their beauty from the very fact that they are no longer things that I see", and "If I go, then the creator and the creature will exchange their secrets".[7] There are, indeed, affinities between George Oppen and Simone Weil in respect of their integrity and the uncompromising truthfulness with which they follow through and face up to ultimate intellectual consequences. The parallel between them might be developed further on the basis of their Jewishness, and if we were to make much of George Oppen's remark to Charles Tomlinson during a visit to Wells Cathedral: 'I guess I'm a Christian, but with all the heresies'.[8] Personally I think it would be as wrong to dismiss this remark as insignificant as it would be to build on it a theory of specific Christian orientation to apply to the religious sense which is everywhere present in his poetry. Nor must the observation of the mystic in George Oppen be allowed to obscure his humanism, which is as fundamental and all pervasive in his work as it is in William Carlos Williams's and Charles Reznikoff's too. It is a humanism which shares Simone Weil's concern for the spiritual and material welfare of people but also has a dimension which is not only absent from her thought but is alien to the desire for self-effacement which was temperamentally hers. This may be seen in his fine 'Birthplace: New Rochelle':

> Returning to that house
> And the rounded rocks of childhood — They have lasted
>   well.
>
> A world of things.
>
> An aging man,
> The knuckles of my hand
> So jointed! I am this?
>
>   The house
> My father's once, and the ground. There is a color of his
>   times
> In the sun's light.
>
> A generation's mark.
> It intervenes. My child,
> Not now a child, our child
> Not altogether lone in a lone universe that suffers time
> Like stones in sun. For we do not.

Here we see the metaphysical sense of human continuity which is very strong in George Oppen, and which he knows to be precarious and increasingly vulnerable in the modern world — which is indeed widely distinguished by loss of the sense. It is, of course, a sense of relationship, linking past and future and experienced in the present, and in this instance connnecting three generations, his father, himself, and his and Mary's child, and also his childhood and his manhood. I have described this sense as alien to the desire for self-effacement because it is totally dependent upon the existence and agency of the self and of other selves, and upon the relationship between self and world. Returning to his childhood home George Oppen perceives "a world of things", and seeing this he sees himself with wonder and surprise: "An aging man,/The knuckles of my hand/So jointed! I am this?" The wondering self- recognition comes with a recognition of all that is involved in the place: the people with their own impenetrable and irrevocable lives — for his father has gone, and though "there is a color of his times/In the sun's light" he belonged, as all do, to time, *his* time — yet who are people who leave "a generation's mark", which "intervenes", and who are "I", "my father", "my child,/Not now a child, our child", people who have lived or are living in the relationships which brought them into being, and in the love which is implicit in the poem. This is a human world which George Oppen shows, where we do not suffer time "like stones in sun", and are "not altogether lone in a lone universe". The poem, like all George Oppen's, is itself an "act of being more than oneself". Discovering the self in the world, and among others, makes the self-recognition a necessary act of *being there*, and the opposite of an egotistic gesture.

George Oppen's differences from William Carlos Williams are instructive. Williams, though as skilful a maker as any poet, spoke in his *Autobiography* of the poem as the "underlying meaning" in the lives of the people. "It is actually there", he wrote, "in the life before us, every minute that we are listening, a rarest element — not in our imaginations, but there, there in fact. It is that essence which is hidden in the very words which are going in at our ears and from which we must recover underlying meaning as realistically as we recover metal out of ore".[9] For George Oppen, on the other hand, the poem is to be found not in recovering meaning from what people say but in meaning which is made by the poet living in the world, in relationships, in personal authenticity. He shares Williams's openness towards experiencing America, but the ground is less firm under his feet than it was under Williams's, and he is more philosophical, more sceptical, much less certain of what and where he is, and therefore more exploratory in his attitude towards self and world. Perception is more complicated in George Oppen's world than in Williams's, because his mind is more questioning of both the self which sees and the nature of that which is seen.

For all the continuity between *Discrete Series* and George Oppen's subsequent books, a major obvious difference between them is that the latter contain another thirty years of experience. These were years when George and Mary Oppen, as political activists on the streets and in the tenements of New York, were closely involved with the lives of people suffering the injustice and hard conditions of their time. These years also saw George Oppen's war experience in Europe and the Oppens' exile in Mexico during the McCarthy era. All were experiences that evidently strengthened George Oppen's sense of the impermanence and precariousness of human order, especially in the city itself, which is a current within the American tradition, and which in his case, no doubt, also owed something to his break with his original home and class. At any rate, it is easy to understand why Charles Reznikoff's line "a girder, still itself among the rubble" should have come to mean so much to George and Mary Oppen,[10] who found themselves and kept their integrity among the rubble of their time.

Mary Oppen has said that Charles Reznikoff's poetry "really is what's happening on the streets".[11] Reznikoff's strength is different from George

Oppen's in this respect. He developed the imagist technique, in poems like *Jerusalem the Golden*, to present the life of the streets as he saw and heard it, and he himself is there alongside the rest, a man keenly alive, but little troubled by questions of the reality of self and world. There are vivid passages in George Oppen's poetry, which justify the claim that he shares with Williams and Reznikoff and a few others, the great distinction of opening modern American poetry to the urban experience. George Oppen, however, is much less an observer than Reznikoff, and, in the act of seeing, much more self-questioning. The self-questioning intensifies as the tensions inherent in his way of seeing increasingly manifest themselves in experience. In experience, not theory — for it is apparent that he was aware of the tensions when writing *Discrete Series*. For George Oppen, the 'I' of the poem is never a dramatic convention or the eye of a camera but always his experiencing self. In his poetry, therefore, some terms of Louis Zukofsky's definition of the 'objective' — writing "which is the detail, not mirage, of seeing, of thinking with the things as they exist"[12] — combine with an 'I' that is integrally personal. 'Honesty' and 'sincerity' are among the words which George Oppen revalues by his use of them: so, too, are 'honour' and 'companionship' (see, for example, 'Pro Nobis' and 'To C.T.'). Such revaluation of debased words is a distinguishing feature of all important modern poets, and in George Oppen's case it is a consequence of the necessary relationship between personal integrity and the integrity of the poem. Or, in short, of meaning, as Oppen handles it. He has spoken in these terms of his reason for giving up poetry, an abstinence which lasted twenty-five years: "when the crisis occurred we knew we didn't know what the world was and we knew we had to find out so it was a poetic exploration at the same time that it was an action of conscience, of feeling that one was worth something or other. And I thought most of the poets didn't know about the world as a life."[13]

"The world as a life": this is the "position of honesty", in which being true to experience and the truth of the poem cannot be separated. By this, the clarity of the original imagist perception becomes the aim of every thought; the integrity of the person and the integrity of the poem are interdependent, as they must be when the poet uses the poem to *see*; the poem is both an object, a thing well made, and a man speaking, finding the meaning in his experience. Academic attitudes that enable the reader to regard the poem as something other than a meeting place, where two minds come together to grasp a meaning which is important to both, and which may question both, and change them, have to look for playgrounds elsewhere. "The world as a life" also complements with personal terms the relationship between self and world which Jacques Maritain expressed philosophically: "we awake in the same moment to ourselves and to things". Together they indicate the process of thought in George Oppen's poems: the seeing of things which is simultaneously a self-enlightenment.

George Oppen has an acute sense of all that is not himself, but in relation to which he finds himself. For him, love does not merge selves but recognises and companions the other, sharing meaning and the search for meaning. His answer to Whitman's incorporate ego containing multitudes, and infinitely permeable, in 'Myself I sing', is that a man "finds himself by two. /Or more." He is a poet capable of great tenderness, who like Williams has a special appreciation of the warmth and courage of women.

'Sara in her Father's Arms' is perhaps George Oppen's finest short poem:

> Cell by cell the baby made herself, the cells
> Made cells. That is to say
> The baby is made largely of milk. Lying in her father's arms,
>   the little seed eyes
> Moving, trying to see, smiling for us
> To see, she will make a household
> To her need of these rooms — Sara, little seed,
> Little violent, diligent seed. Come let us look at the world
> Glittering: this seed will speak,
> Max, words! There will be no other words in the world
> But those our children speak. What will she make of a world
> Do you suppose, Max, of which she is made.

Love and wonder are the emotions of this metaphysical poem. In George Oppen, as with all major philosophical poets, the primary emotions are not disconnected from the intellect but issue in thought. So, here, seeing the baby with love and wonder stimulates perception of the nature of creation, first biological, in the process of growth, then human in the making of a household, and a world. The baby, the 'seed', has the violence and diligence with which things are made to serve human needs. (A conjunction of qualities which speaks eloquently of the experience of pioneer settlement still haunting George Oppen's culture.) The need, however, is to make a household, and here, as in other poems, George Oppen sees the woman as the source of human sustenance and the creator of order. 'Household' receives from the poem its full meaning: of the house and its inmates, the home that contains and sustains them. The act of making such order depends upon seeing and speech. Sara is already "trying to see, smiling for us/To see", and to see, as the repetition shows, is to form a relationship between the seer and that which is seen, and at the same time to become a conscious self. The natural, instinctive being achieves human creativity with faculties of vision and speech that are as innate in the baby as the creative properties of cells. Words do not create nature, but they are "in the world"; active in the formation of human order, they enable the woman to seek the meaning "of a world... of which she is made".

'Sara in her Father's Arms' combines intimacy with clarity, and a concentrated strength of thought and expression. These qualities, which make George Oppen so stimulating for the reader who is prepared to meet his mind in the poems and see with him, make him difficult for the critic who believes — as I do — that the most useful thing he could do, at the risk of being clumsy, would be to give some idea of how George Oppen actually uses a poem to see.

'Return' is a fine example of his extension of "the imagist intensity of vision" to a process of thought. It accordingly shows how George Oppen, though, as he has acknowledged, indebted to Ezra Pound, is one of the very few modern poets to show, in his poetic practice, an intelligence equal to Pound's. George Oppen's poems demonstrate, in Pound's words, that "all poetic language is the language of exploration". And because "the image is the word beyond formulated language",[14] we can be made to see what we can indicate only with difficulty.

'Return' begins by invoking the medieval sense of the world:

> *This Earth* the king said
> Looking at the ground;
> *This England.*

The allusion to Shakespeare's *Richard II* seems to compound John of Gaunt's famous speech of prophecy in Act 2, Scene 1 with Richard's salute to his native ground on returning from Ireland. In any case, the important conjunctions are between 'Earth' and 'ground' and 'England', which together form an image of the world as the king's absolute possession, the reality he names and on which his order is founded, and whose eternal immutability he takes for granted. The poem then returns immediately to the present:

> But we drive
> A Sunday paradise
> Of parkway, trees flow into trees and the grass
> Like water by the very asphalt crown
> And summit of things
> In the flow of traffic
> The family cars, in the dim
> Sound of the living
> The noise of increase to which we owe
> What we possess. We cannot reconcile ourselves.
> No one is reconciled, tho we spring
> From the ground together —

"Crown/And summit of things" continues the regal imagery but applies it not to the king, at the apex of an hierarchical order, but to the asphalt of the parkway, the public world where all merges, (as the lines flow together). The Oppens share this with others, "in the flow of traffic/The family cars". The people are at once part of this world, flowing with it anonymously as "trees flow into trees and the grass", and shut off, in their cars. "Family", as is often the case in George Oppen, is a source of order in an alien or unreal world. It has this meaning here, in contrast to "the dim/Sound of the living/The noise of increase", but the confined family is part of the flow, too, and owes "what we possess" to "the noise of increase". True to a common sense in Oppen, of *his* place both inside and outside American society, the images depict a world which is at once shared and isolating, and in which between people, and between people and their 'ground', there is no reconciliation.

In the second movement time and place change easily again — for the space of the poem is the poet's mind — but with another organic image following the image of people springing "from the ground", and the poem opens further into a meditation upon time and creation, natural process and man's relationship with the earth. Here George Oppen sets the force contained in "the miniscule Sequoia seed", seen in the museum, and the time of the full-grown and disintegrated redwood tree, against "the streets of the living". With an echo, as on several occasions in his poetry, he recalls T.S. Eliot, another poet with a feeling for the ocean, and the oceanic reaches of evolutionary time; a poet with whom he has something imaginative in common, but against whom he defines an opposing sense of the ground of human existence:

> This is not our time, not what we mean, it is a time
> Passing, the curl at the cutwater,
> The enormous prow
> Outside in the weather.

Contemplation of this leads George Oppen not to prayer, as "time not our time" led Eliot in 'The Dry Salvages', but to a sense of "desertion,/ Betrayal, that we are not innocent/ Of loneliness", and to turn to the living, to those closest to him. The passage that follows is one of the most tender and intimate in all his poetry:

>   Mary,
> Mary, we turn to the children
> As they will turn to the children
> Wanting so much to have created happiness
> As if a stem to the leaves —
>
> — we had camped in scrub,
> A scrub of the past, the fringes of towns
> Neither towns nor forest, nothing ours. And Linda five,
> Maybe six when the mare grazing
> In the meadow came to her.
> 'Horse,' she said, whispering
> By the roadside

With the cars passing. Little girl welcomed,
Learning welcome.

As in 'Sara in Her Father's Arms' the emotion carries George Oppen's thought about the relationship between nature and the human world, which are reconciled here. "This England" was the name given to "this Earth", the king's possession, representing "the medieval sense" that "seems innocent, the very/Ceremony of innocence that was drowned", but was not innocent, as George Oppen says quoting W.B. Yeats near the end of the poem. But here is innocence — the little girl whispering 'Horse' is not possessive, or claiming dominion, but is "welcomed,/Learning welcome". It is a true relationship, and of course, totally vulnerable . "The rest is", George Oppen says,

> Whatever — whatever — remote
> Mechanics, endurance,
> The piers of the city
> In the sea.

The final movement of the poem returns to the city, to "whole buildings/ Razed, whole blocks/Of a city gone/Among old streets/And the old boroughs, ourselves/Among these streets", and to a particular incident from the social and political upheavals of the Thirties. From a world made homely by the mutual welcome of child and horse we move to violent deprivation — and its resistance by Petra, defending her children and her neighbours against eviction. Petra and the incident are actual, not symbolic; but she, true to her name, gives a meaning to 'endurance', and a sense of completeness to the "*whole* buildings". The meanings stand though the buildings have gone. "How imagine it?" George Oppen asks. And finally:

> But how imagine it
> Of streets boarded and vacant where no time will hatch
> Now chairs and walls,
> Floors, roofs, the joists and beams,
> The woodwork, window sills
> In the sun in a great weight of brick.

It is a statement and an exclamation. As for the questions it contains — how imagine the life of that time, now it has gone? How imagine that which is real, beyond imagination? — any answer would be an imposition upon the poem and an insult to its honesty. 'Return' is a profound, subtle, and inevitably inconclusive meditation on man's changing social relationships, and his relationship with the ground of his existence, based on the ancient metaphor of human life as a tree, in the context of time and the forces of nature. It is also, (and this the word 'meditation' may belie), "the world as a life", a poem in which the thought proceeds exploratively, with "imagist intensity of vision", each image having the integrity of lived experience. And when in this poem George Oppen turns to Mary he makes explicit what is usually implicit in his poems, that for him the world is a life shared. The medieval 'Western wind' is one of his motifs, and he admires Wyatt's poetry — not surprisingly, since there is in his own a similar emotional intensity and wholeness. The language of Donne's "each has one world and is one", or of Arnold's sudden intimacy in 'Dover Beach', or of Hardy's evocation of places charged for him with the presence of Emma, is in no case George Oppen's language. He is, however, essentially a love poet, who has in common with these poets an acute sense of love as a stay and a strength in an endangering world. Love is not an escape for him but a sharing, and a shared meaning.

The act of seeing places George Oppen in a world, but seeing also distances him from the world in which the majority live:

> 'Whether, as the intensity of seeing increases, one's distance
>   from Them, the people, does not also increase'
> I know, of course I know, I can enter no other place
>   ('Of Being Numerous' 9)

Yet it is this fact, and George Oppen's honesty in face of it, that enables him, in 'Of Being Numerous', to write the most penetrating poem about the possibility of poetry in our time. And all his poems exist in the awareness of this critical problem; for the possibility of poetry depends upon the possibility of meaning. Questions about the poet's relationship with his people, with those with whom he shares a language, are necessarily the most important questions about what poetry is, and what it means. In George Oppen's circumstances, which are those of most poets in the West, there can be no justification for a Wordsworthian confidence that searchings of the self will penetrate the ground of humanity, and the poet looking into himself speak to and for others. Nor is it in uncritical populism that the poet will find the people, but only, perhaps, in exploring his complex and troubled relationship with them, which includes his distance from them. It is relatively easy, of course, to evade the problem of meaning altogether, by catching a poetic style from the time or writing according to the expectations of a past poetic convention. George Oppen is one of the most important modern poets because he has done neither but has tested every word for its meaning, in full awareness of the subtlety as well as the power of meaninglessness in the modern world. The truth of George Oppen's poetry is the truth of his poem 'The Gesture'. Whether writing of things shared or of things seen in the light of "the shipwreck/Of the singular", he has never had a bauble to sell but has always held "something/In the mind which he intends/To grasp".

Notes

1. Recollected by Zukofsky in an interview with L.S. Dembo, *Contemporary Literature*, Spring 1969, p. 203.
2. Interview with L.S. Dembo, *Contemporary Literature*, Spring 1969, p. 160.
3. *Ibid.*, p. 161.
4. L.S. Dembo, 'Oppen on his Poems: a Discussion', *George Oppen Man and Poet* (ed. Burton Hatlen), 1981, p. 204.
5. All quotations from the poems in this essay are from *The Collected Poems of George Oppen* (New Directions, 1976).
6. George Oppen, 'The Mind's Own Place', *Montemora* 1 (Fall, 1975), p. 133.
7. Simone Weil, *Gravity and Grace* (1952), p. 37.
8. Charles Tomlinson, *Some Americans: A Personal Record* (1981), p. 63.
9. William Carlos Williams, *Autobiography* (1948, New Directions, 1967) p. 362.
10. See, for example, Burton Hatlen and Tom Mandel, 'Poetry and Politics: A Conversation with George and Mary Oppen', *George Oppen Man and Poet*, p. 29. The line occurs in Charles Reznikoff's *Jerusalem the Golden* (1934).
11. *Ibid.*, p. 29.
12. Louis Zukofsky, 'An Objective', *Prepositions* (1981), p. 12.
13. Burton Hatlen and Tom Mandel, 'Poetry and Politics: A Conversation with George and Mary Oppen', *George Oppen Man and Poet*, p. 25.
14. Ezra Pound, *Gaudier-Brzeska* (1916, 1960), p. 88.

"The boundaries or our distances":
George Oppen's 'Of Being Numerous'

I

Whenever we consider the complexity of 'Of Being Numerous', or George Oppen's scepticism, or ontology, or dialectical method, the force of his moral witness in the poem should be borne steadily in mind. 'Of Being Numerous' is a fundamental exposure of the bankrupt ethic of modern capitalist society, which produces insanity and despair. The poem, written at the height of the Vietnam war, is also an indictment of America's involvement. It is more than this alone, for Oppen's outrage is at once present in the poem, and a disturbance intensifying the guilt, disillusioned idealism, and fears for the future which are other shaping emotions.

He can make the indictment with Imagist dispassion:

> It is the air of atrocity,
> An event as ordinary
> As a President.
>
> A plume of smoke, visible at a distance
> In which people burn.[1]
> ('Of Being Numerous', 18)

"The air" is the appearance; it is also the air on which we and all living things depend for our existence, and the air carrying presidential words and images. "The air of atrocity" is "A plume of smoke, visible at a distance": the image of the war, seen on TV screens by millions of Americans and people throughout the world, and even by combatants, looking down from plane or helicopter at distant signs of their action. The appearance is "a plume of smoke"; the reality is people burning. Thus, Oppen reveals the ordinary event that is an atrocity, by disclosing the meaning of words that ordinarily obscure it, as smoke hides burning people from their killers. What the eye sees is "a distance/In which people burn" — it is that "distance" which makes possible both the atrocity and the evasion of meaning and responsibility.

George Oppen locates the atrocity and the evasion in the same place: "An event as ordinary/As a President". The poem is the work of a poet who has mastered imagism as a method of moral perception; it also shows what he has learned as a political poet from Blake - ways of exposing ideological systems which conceal the sources of their power and mythologize the relations of cause and effect, and ways of revealing the actual relations, even in the very "air".

Or in the city, as Blake's "hapless Soldier's sigh/Runs in blood down Palace Walls":

> A city of the corporations
>
> Glassed
> In dreams
>
> And images —
>   ('Of Being Numerous', 2)

"Corporations" should be a word of embodied meaning, uniting people in a body; instead, it is a mere ghost of its former self, an abstract denomination of capitalist institutions, hidden powers which make life unreal. "Glassed", like Blake's "charter'd", concentrates the thing and its social effects: a city of windows, not windows through which one might see other people, but the facade of big business mirrored in dreams and images; a glassy place, a place of glazed eyes, a place which exists vicariously for the sake of hidden powers. Terms like alienation and reification are not abstractions in Oppen's city; rather, they *are* that city, a world of "irrelevant objects", where "life loses/ solidity, loses extent".

The imagist technique, as exemplified in the passages considered above, serves Oppen well in his remorseless exposure of corruption and meaninglessness. But of course, 'Of Being Numerous' is not exclusively imagist in technique, and its passages or parts are used not only to develop meaning, but to qualify or question or change it. Thus, in section 18, at least three words — "visible", "distance", and "people" — are key words in the poem as a whole, so that their meaning in the section is not self-contained, but subject to further illumination, and testing, from their use in other parts. The poem has the complexity of experience. Oppen writes from his life, subjecting the ideals and images which he values to the same testing that he applies to the public world; indeed, the pressure of the poem arises in part from his denial of the ordinary 'common sense' distinction between his life and the public world. Section 19 resumes the concentrated perception of the preceding part and both shifts and extends it:

> Now in the helicopters the casual will
> Is atrocious
>
> Insanity in high places,

> If it is true we must do these things
> We must cut our throats
>
> The fly in the bottle
>
> Insane, the insane fly
>
> Which, over the city
> Is the bright light of shipwreck

The statement with which this begins has been won from the images in Section 18: we know now what an atrocious event is, and that it is the act of "casual will". Further, we know that it is a function of "Insanity in high places", which are neither the helicopters nor the President alone but the "air", the "distance" between appearance and reality. Now, what was implicit in section 18 is explicit: "If it is true *we* must do these things...". The insanity can be seen, but not escaped from. This is not, at this point, an admission of complicity on the poet's part, but the image of "the bright light of shipwreck" implies it, confirming that the poet above all is one who sees at a distance. There is no escape from "insanity in high places", except in the insanity of total isolation.

2

> 'Whether, as the intensity of seeing increases, one's distance
>   from Them, the people, does not also increase'
> I know, of course I know, I can enter no other place
>
> Yet I am one of those who from nothing but man's way of
>   thought and one of his dialects and what has happened
>   to me
> Have made poetry
>
> To dream of that beach...
>   ('Of Being Numerous', 9)

In an interview with L.S. Dembo, George Oppen said of the quotation in this passage, from a letter which he had received from a student, Rachel Blau (later, as Rachel Blau Du Plessis, an acute interpreter of his work), that "It was a profound and painful question that I had asked myself in her words". "I've written", he continued, "a whole poem to establish, if I could, the concept of humanity, a concept without which we can't live. And yet I don't know that poetry is not actually destructive for people... It does lead to the growing isolation of the poet."[2] The question is particularly "profound and painful" for Oppen, because it strikes at the roots of his way of seeing, the method of thought which he has constructed from "the imagist intensity of vision".³ The question itself defines his area of concern as a poet; it is his 'place'.

The affirmation of 'Of Being Numerous', 9 is strong. It is of himself as a poet rooted in humanity, one who has "made poetry" from his experience and "man's way of thought and one of his dialects". But at the word "poetry", as the sentence crosses the line break, the confidence breaks down:

> Have made poetry
>
> To dream of that beach
> For the sake of an instant in the eyes,
>
> The absolute singular
>
> The unearthly bonds
> Of the singular
>
> Which is the bright light of shipwreck.

The transition is a leap — *from* faith, the faith that, in the terms of a favourite quotation from Jacques Maritain, he has suffered the things of the world and spoken them and himself out, to the vertiginous doubt that his poetry has done other than isolate him, in a dream of "the absolute singular". Indeed, "Have made poetry//To dream" may be read as implying deliberate choice. Certainly, 'Of Being Numerous' would be a much less complex poem if Oppen's attitude to isolation were not ambivalent. But while he sees it as "shipwreck" he sees it as "bright light", too. "To dream of that beach/For the sake of an instant in the eyes" suggests an annihilating ecstasy. There is a strong mystical impulse in George Oppen's poetry, and his sense of belonging with humanity, to "man's way of thought and one of his dialects", though equally strong, cannot always contain it.

Metaphorically speaking, fear of sharing Crusoe's fate influenced Oppen's abandonment of poetry for twenty-five years. 'Party on Shipboard', in *Discrete Series*, was the last poem he wrote before the long silence. He has said that it contained the whole of 'Of Being Numerous', and while this is an amusing exaggeration, it is true that the question, metaphysical and political, which 'Party on Shipboard' fails to answer is the same question that the long poem asks. "The sea incapable of contact/Save in incidents", in 'Party on Shipboard', is a metaphor for humanity, which exists as a whole but cannot be known except in contact with individuals. As Oppen has said, the poem "doesn't manage to see the whole" — a failure which he then related directly to his reasons for giving up poetry, which he had earlier described to Dembo as "pressures of conscience". "There were some things I had to live through", he said, "some things I had to think my way through, some things I had to try out — and it was more than politics, really; it was the whole experience of working in factories, of having a child, and so on".[4] In another interview, he ended a similar statement with a memorable phrase: "I thought most of the poets didn't know about the world as a life".[5] The implications are clear: the failure of 'Party on Shipboard' "to see the whole" threatened to isolate him as a man and condemn his poetry to an arid particularism. He knew that he had not found himself or humanity, and could only find them together, through experience in the world.

Twenty-five years later, however, when he returned to the same question in 'Blood from the Stone', his first poem after the silence, he brought to it a scepticism sharpened by political disillusionment:

> What do we believe
> To live with? Answer.
> Not invent — just answer — all
> That verse attempts.
> That we can somehow add each to each other?

The question is political, but not only political, for Oppen now or at any time. "What do we believe/To live with?" is a metaphysical question, which scorns the isolation of politics and metaphysics from each other.

The story of George Oppen's poetry is of a steady commitment to the construction of meaning, in the knowledge that meaning is public and the individual belongs to humanity. It is a story of almost intolerable tension, arising from a struggle with despair and the failure of an ideal. 'Pro Nobis' records Oppen's failure "to arrive/At an actuality/In the mere number of us". In political terms, he lived the tragic failure of left-wing politics to carry the activism of the 1930's into a reshaping of American society. Much cynicism has fed, often vicariously, on the general failure, in Europe and America, of inter-war socialist and communist ideals, and neo-conservatism has been a common response of intellectuals to their disillusionment. An important reason why this was not the case with Oppen was that his political thinking was more deep-rooted than most, and that while he felt the failure bitterly, he was able to distinguish what was illusory about the ideal from the reality of the need which it had promised to fulfil. 'The People, The People' is his most bitter poem:

> For love we all go
> To that mountain
> Of human flesh
> Which exists
> And is incapable
> Of love and which we saw
> In the image
> Of a woman — We said once

>   She was beautiful for she was
>   Suffering
>   And beautiful. She was more ambitious
>   Than we knew
>   Of wealth
>   And more ruthless — speaking
>   Still in that image — we will never be free
>   Again from the knowledge
>   Of that hatred
>   And that huge contempt. Will she not rot
>   Without us and die
>   In childbed leaving
>   Monstrous issue —

In this instance, the refusal of closure admits the possibility of despair. The poem's anger at American materialism is in proportion to the beauty of the ideal which it has destroyed, and despair feeds on the prospect that the present evil will produce a worse future. But the poem is not a rejection of 'the people'. On the contrary, it is a fairly comprehensive self-criticism, which condemns a false image. Oppen begins by recognising the need for love which drove him and other idealists to see "that mountain/Of human flesh" "In the image/Of a woman", and the suffering which gave the image beauty. He speaks throughout the poem "in that image", and the effect is to release the bitterness and to judge the ambition of wealth and the ruthlessness of American society, yet also to show the inadequacy of the ethic on which the image of 'The People' was based. Nothing in the confession of failure in 'The People, The People' or its recording in 'Pro Nobis' diminishes the seriousness of "What do we believe/To live with?". This remained, for Oppen, a question of fundamental ontology, at once uniting the political and the metaphysical, and implying the problem of the one and the many. Martin Heidegger's thought pervades Oppen's, and is changed by it, for Oppen lived the same questions of meaning, but through a radically different experience and politics. The title of 'Of Being Numerous' has the stress of two of Heidegger's key terms, *Dasein* and *Mitsein*, and concerns the "being-in-the-world" that is necessarily "being-with-others". This is a measure of the poem's ambition, which, in terms of modern philosophy, challenges Milton's in *Paradise Lost*. The substance of the poem is Oppen's experiences, his dialect, the pressure of a failed idealism upon a continuing fundamental need, the people and the streets and subways of New York; and in and through all Oppen's thought seeks "a justification of human life".[6]

3

"Rescue" is an important term of George Oppen's poetry. A straightforward example of the charged meaning that the word has for him occurs in 'Return', where Petra beating a washpan out of her window gathers "a crowd like a rescue". In this instance, in a specific political act, it is the very virtue of communal solidarity, which makes human survival possible. 'Population' deals with the concept metaphorically:

> Like a flat sea,
> Here is where we are, the empty reaches
> Empty of ourselves
>
> Where dark, light, sound
> Shatter the mind born
> Alone to ocean
>
> Save we are
> A crowd, a population....

Here, in another fine instance of Oppen's exceptional verbal care and deliberation, "save", which obviously means except, also has the meaning of the verb 'to save', and therefore says that our being "a crowd, a population" saves "the mind born/Alone to ocean" from shattering in its isolation in a world empty of human meaning.

"Save" in 'Population' looks forward to the concept of "rescue" in 'Of Being Numerous', but is under less pressure from Oppen's dialectical method:

> We are pressed, pressed on each other,
> We will be told at once
> Of anything that happens
>
> And the discovery of fact bursts
> In a paroxysm of emotion
> Now as always. Crusoe
>
> We say was
> 'Rescued'.
> So we have chosen.
>   ('Of Being Numerous', 6)

We speak of Crusoe being "rescued" when he was taken off the island, implying that society saves the individual from isolation. In the context of this section, however, scepticism points the irony of the 'choice'. Oppen's gift of concentration is strongly present in the opening line: "We are pressed, pressed on each other". We are crowded together, pressured, made to serve or to crush each other; we are passive, and manipulated by the press, ("We will be told at once/Of anything that happens"). In these circumstances, can we really say that "we have chosen" the meaning of "rescued"?

The following section approaches the question from another direction:

> Obsessed, bewildered
>
> By the shipwreck
> Of the singular
>
> We have chosen the meaning
> Of being numerous.

In section 6, the choice arose from pressures of the crowd. In this section, it arises in response to the insanity of isolation. What, then, *is* "the meaning of 'Of being numerous' "? Of course, there is no easy answer. Even the whole poem is not the answer, rather, existing in the dialectical tension between the "pressed" crowd and the "obsessed, bewildered" individual, it attempts to think through the question; the question which Oppen has lived, and is living as he writes.

4

"Truth also is the pursuit of it", George Oppen wrote in 'Leviathan': "Like happiness, and it will not stand." But if truth "will not stand", a whole society, which stops pursuing it, may live the lie of believing that it has attained it. This, I think, is the significance of images of stasis and of freezing which recur in Oppen's poetry. In 'Of Being Numerous', 5, for example:

> The great stone
> Above the river
> In the pylon of the bridge
>
> '1875'
>
> Frozen in the moonlight
> In the frozen air over the footpath, consciousness
>
> Which has nothing to gain, which awaits nothing,
> Which loves itself.

The self-adoration of an age which believes that it has achieved everything is projected in an image of temporal finality: '1875'. As if a bridge, built for the passage of people were ever "finished", perfected, complete. Only a mind may think so whose complacency leaves it no energy to pursue the truth, and no sense of the future. Bridge and footpath are ways over and on; only a "frozen" consciousness, which may be the mind of a society, congealing its very "air", "awaits nothing".

The end of the great sustained lyrical passage which concludes 'A Narrative' contains a similar image:

> I thought I had encountered
>
> Permanence; thought leaped on us in that sea
> For in that sea we breathe the open
> Miracle
>
> Of place, and speak
> If we would rescue
> Love to the ice-lit
>
> Upper World a substantial language
> Of clarity, and of respect.

"The ice-lit/Upper World", like "the great stone... Frozen in the moonlight/ In the frozen air" over river and footpath, is the mere 'worldly' consciousness imposed on "the open/Miracle/Of place", which is an image of what may be experienced but not, ultimately, defined, though we may understand it as akin to Heidegger's 'Being', that which the attentive poet 'speaks'. Oppen's "substantial language/of clarity, and of respect" is the language that "rescue(s)/Love". It is a language of substantives, as Oppen's language insistently is: "the little words", which are most nearly transparent to what he called, in discussing "the circle of the visible, the primitive", the "great, tremendous astronomic relations". These relations are "not only not nothing, because they're so tremendous but they're not nothing within a little place where we sit".[7] The significance of this for the city in 'Of Being Numerous' is that it is both "frozen" ("A city of the corporations//Glassed/ In dreams//and images") and a place of "the great, tremendous astronomic relations". In respect of the latter, Oppen's kinship is with Melville, Whitman, Emerson and Thoreau. He is not subject to agrarian nostalgia, but he has inherited the pioneer's sense of America. While living in and writing from New York, in 'Of Being Numerous', he is, in the largest sense of the word, a 'nature' poet, who looks down through the glass and stone and steel to the earth under the pavements, the sea under the piers, the original wilderness.

5

'A Language of New York' differs too much from 'Of Being Numerous' to be thought of as merely its earlier version, but is sufficiently similar to bring out the great superiority of the later poem. By virtue of Oppen's uncharacteristic discursiveness in 'A Language of New York', 4, he gives a simplified, explicit statement of a method and prime concern of 'Of Being Numerous':

> Possible
> To use
> Words provided one treat them
> As enemies.
> Not enemies — Ghosts
> Which have run mad
> In the subways
> And of course the institutions
> And the banks. If one captures them
> One by one proceeding
>
> Carefully they will restore
> I hope to meaning
> And to sense.

Sections 13 and 17 of 'Of Being Numerous' develop the same thought, but more subtly, with the test of images. In the former, Oppen writes of people who have no regard for the substantive, but who "develop/Argument in order to speak". "They become/unreal, unreal, life loses/solidity, loses extent, baseball's their game..." His distance from populism, immediately evident here, is then strongly affirmed:

> They are ghosts that endanger
>
> One's soul. There is change
> In an air
> That smells stale, they will come to the end
> Of an era
> First of all peoples
> And one may honorably keep
>
> His distance
> If he can.

"Soul" may give one pause, if only to confirm the significant religious and even theological presence in Oppen's diction. In adapting a favourite passage from Søren Kierkegaard's *Fear and Trembling* in section 16, he omits all references to "the world of spirit"[8] which Kierkegaard was writing about. But the omission makes little difference, for the positive side of "the singular", developing from the position of "sincerity" from which Oppen as a poet began, reflects not only Heideggerian personal authenticity but also Kierkegaard's *hiin Enkelte* ('the Single One'). True, it is "the world" that Oppen believes in, ("I believe//in the world//because it is/impossible," he writes in 'Myth of the Blaze', wittily adapting a famous saying attributed to

Tertullian), but the world as Oppen apprehends it, like Heidegger's 'Being', has the numinous character of a theist's God. There is a "distance" that makes possible acts of atrocity and evasion of responsibility for them. There is also a "distance" without which personal responsibility is impossible, the distance from those without substantial being, which "one may honorably keep//...if he can". This distance also depends upon language; it can only be kept by one who uses words with care, restoring them "to meaning/And to sense".

'A Language of New York', 4 calls words "Ghosts/Which have run mad/ In the subways". 'Of Being Numerous', 17 begins: "The roots of words/Dim in the subways". In Oppen's poetry, 'subway' is sounded as a devaluation of one of his key words, so that it is virtually the equivalent of 'subhuman'. For Oppen, 'way' has a value close to Heidegger's *Weg*, and both resonate with the meaning of *Tao*. It is "man's way of thought", "Truth" which "also is the pursuit of it". True to Oppen's grounding of thought in experience, "way" is related to "road", and "root"/"route", too.

The following passage from Mary Oppen's *Meaning A Life*, describing her travels with George in America in 1927, is, in retrospect, a poignant illustration of this point:

> We were in search of an esthetic within which to live, and we were looking for it in our own American roots, in our own country. We had learned at college that poetry was being written in our own times, and that in order for us to write it was not necessary for us to ground ourselves in the academic; the ground we needed was the roads we were travelling. As we were new, so we had new roots, and we knew little of our own country. Hitch-hiking became more than flight from a powerful family — our discoveries themselves became an esthetic and a disclosure. The people we met, as various and as accidentally met as thumbing a ride could make them, became the clue to our finding roots; we gained confidence that this country was ours in a sense which we hadn't known under our parents' roofs. The sense was not only a patriotic but also a personal one, for as people generally accepted us, we felt comfortable and at home in our country. I have never felt so at home in any other land.[9]

In view of the subsequent history, which included a long period of exile from American injustice, this is, to say the least, poignant. It should be borne in mind as a kind of preface to George Oppen's poetry, in case its origin in patriotic feeling should be overlooked. I quote it here, however, because it is the clearest possible illustration of the connection between American "roots", or "ground", and the actual roads of America, which is crucial to an understanding of *Of Being Numerous*, the whole book, but especially the title poem and the closely related 'Route'. The passage shows that the Oppens' personal experience embodied their country's two most powerful ideals, whose tension has defined a good deal of the American experience and

American literature: settlement and exploration, a dualism whose dialectical relationship involves complex tensions between individual enterprise and communal solidarity. Theirs was an individual venture, but they travelled the roads with other people, who were "the clue to our finding roots". The movement was at once extensive and in depth: "the ground we needed was the roads we were travelling". The preoccupation with "new roots", as distinct from 'tradition', had a profound effect upon George Oppen's metaphysics.

Of course, he never wrote naively about a common world to be located in the "ground" or on the roads of America. Estrangement within the city, or, rather, from the mental structures of capitalist society, already defines the method of *Discrete Series*. Yet the tragedy of failure "to arrive/At an actuality/In the mere number of us," which is both Oppen's and his country's, may be felt acutely in the juxtaposition of Mary Oppen's words with 'Route', 8, which, because Oppen believes in poetry as communication, with its basis in the speech of a people, is one of the most extreme statements of the difficulties facing the modern poet:

> Cars on the highway filled with speech,
> People talk, they talk to each other;
>
> Imagine a man in the ditch,
> The wheels of the overturned wreck
> Still spinning –
>
> I don't mean he despairs, I mean if he does not
> He sees in the manner of poetry

The wreck is not Crusoe's, on an island, but a car wreck beside the highway. The man is still in a world in which cars are "filled with speech" and "people talk, they talk to each other"; he is in this world, yet he is thrown out of it, too, in a sudden sickening impact with the ground on which the road has been built. He is still in the world of human communication — there is nowhere else for a man to be, unless he is dead or mad — but he "sees" it — both the "roots" of speech and the "route" which his society has constructed to travel on — with the clarity of violent estrangement. And with that vision, that seeing "in the manner of poetry", he has to speak. The view from the ditch is much the same as the view from the skyscraper, in 'The Building of the Skyscraper'. There "on the verge/Of vertigo," we look down through empty space, through the meaninglessness of certain words. "But there is something to mean".

6

In the city, the way that is the pursuit of truth ends in the closed system, what

Oppen calls in 'Vulcan', "the subway's iron circuits". There,

> It is not easy to speak
>
> A ferocious mumbling, in public
> Of rootless speech
>
> ('Of Being Numerous', 17)

The greatness of 'Of Being Numerous' is that it wins "a thing/Which is" from the struggle with meaninglessness, and speech from the extreme difficulty of speaking. The discontinuous, elliptical, fragmentary style is at once a response to the difficulty, and a result of Oppen's insistence on the primary value of the substantive,[10] which he refuses to skate over on the heels of argument, and which he encloses in completed sentences only at decisive moments.

'Of Being Numerous', 11 is a particularly fine example of the style's virtues in its response to extreme pressure and its affirmations:

> it is *that* light
> Seeps anywhere, a light for the times
>
> In which the buildings
> Stand on low ground, their pediments
> Just above the harbor
>
> Absolutely immobile,
>
> Hollow, available, you could enter any building,
> You could look from any window
> One might wave to himself
> From the top of the Empire State Building —
>
> Speak
>
> If you can
>
> Speak
>
> Phyllis — not neo-classic,
> The girl's name is Phyllis —
>
> Coming home from her first job
> On the bus in the bare civic interior

> Among those people, the small doors
> Opening on the night at the curb
> Her heart, she told me, suddenly tight with happiness —
>
> So small a picture,
> A spot of light on the curb, it cannot demean us
>
> I too am in love down there with the streets
> And the square slabs of pavement —
>
> To talk of the house and the neighborhood and the docks
>
> And it is not 'art'.

"*That* light/Seeps anywhere, a light for the times": this is the light of the isolated individual, but of isolation that has become a common condition, the "consciousness/Which has nothing to gain, which awaits nothing,/Which loves itself". Like the date set in "The great stone/Above the river," the buildings of the city are "frozen". They "stand", they are "absolutely immobile//Hollow, available". But their availability is not openness; this is not a public space in which people can speak with each other; availability means that anything can be bought. In this "hollow" place, where the isolated are "dead", in an "exhausted" world, there is nothing to mean and no one to encounter except oneself; even the highest window has the function of a mirror, from which "One might wave to himself". From the annulled distance between people, in their common condition as ghosts, the absolute distance of meaninglessness, nothing, complete emptiness threatens. Having brought the image to this point, Oppen staggers,[11] almost despairs, and in great stress, which the lines and silences brokenly enact, at the seeming impossibility of communication, come words of absolute need: "Speak//If you can///Speak".

What he speaks is a name: 'Phyllis'. At once, the almost intolerable tension relaxes and an affectionate human contact leads to the further relaxation of humour: "– not neo-classic,/The girl's name is Phyllis". The picture that follows presents the girl's experience. Here, Oppen's capacity for affirmation of values which are mundane (in the true sense of the word) is beautifully expressed: "Coming home", "her first job", "the bus", "in the bare civic interior", "Among those people", "the small doors/Opening..." In fact, every word, the substantives and the relations among them, all present the experience, its meaning and its happiness. "So small a picture,/A spot of light on the curb." But "small" as "the small nouns" in 'Psalm' are, "The small nouns/Crying faith/In this in which the wild deer/Startle, and stare out"; small as "the smalle raine" of the medieval lyric 'Western Wind', whose meaning for Oppen helped to make the word one of his most affirmative. Unlike the light that "seeps anywhere", "a spot of light on the curb" is clearly defined; it has substantial reality. So does the space of "the bare civic interior", in contrast to the space of the buildings which "stand on low ground". The former is real, a place to be among people, the latter unreal, a place "Glassed/In dreams//And images". "From the top of the Empire State Building", Oppen has literally come down to earth. "To talk of the house and the neighborhood and the docks" — as Charles Reznikoff ends his first *Testimony*, a work which Oppen loved and admired, with "ships, harbors, rivers". As Oppen said: "Just things, just things there, and it's amazing what they do".[12] And if it is not "art", then "art" means nothing.

7

"I too am in love down there with the streets." Oppen is, primarily, a love poet, in the common sense that he writes both of and from his love for his wife and daughter, and in Wordsworth's definition of the poet, "carrying every where with him relationship and love". 'Of Being Numerous' contains an absolute personal affirmation:

> Not truth but each other
>
> The bright, bright skin, her hands wavering
> In her incredible need
>
>
> 33
>
> Which is ours, which is ourselves,
> This is our jubilation
> Exalted and as old as that truthfulness
> Which illumines speech.

The four lines of section 33 may be compared to the four lines of 'Western Wind': they too form a perfect love poem. It is a poem which concentrates Oppen's most precious values, the values he has lived by, in the relationship in which he has lived. Here is complete integration of body and mind, self and ourselves, truth and speech. In this light, the big words are embodied and united in the flesh: 'jubilation', 'exaltation', 'truthfulness', 'illumination'. Yet this can hardly be compared to "I too am in love down there with the streets", not only because a primary human relationship cannot be compared to anything else, but also because "down there" locates a distance which makes integration impossible. The words are carefully placed in the sentence. Oppen does not say the streets "down there", as though he were looking down on them from a high building. He is "in love down there with the streets," which implies when he is there, and also a particular neighbourhood, not the city as a whole.

Distance determines what is seen. Thus, in 'Of Being Numerous', 13 Oppen is seeing the "shoppers,/Choosers, judges" from a high critical overview; in fact, he is categorising them, in a Kierkegaardian perspective, from the extreme distance which is honourable because "They are ghosts that endanger//One's soul". Then, in the next section, he is engaged with, or not "altogether disengage[d]" from, "those men//With whom I stood in emplacements, in mess tents,/In hospitals and sheds and hid in the gullies/Of blasted roads in a ruined country". He names two of his companions in the war, Muykut and Healy, and the naming, as always with Oppen, is the moment of greatest transparency and clarity, when he speaks "a substantial language/Of clarity, and of respect". This, in turn, provokes a question and a self-reproach:

> How forget that? How talk
> Distantly of 'The People'.

But the distance, momentarily closed in memory, is not in fact reduced, and Oppen continues to see, not "Muykut and a sergeant/Named Healy,/That lieutenant also", but "'The People'//Who are that force/Within the walls/Of cities//Wherein their cars//Echo like history/Down walled avenues/In which one cannot speak". In terms of his metaphors, he is back in the ditch looking up at the highway, or on the skyscraper vertiginously looking down.

Oppen does not idealise the companionship he remembers. He "stood" with "those men" "in emplacements, in mess tents,/In hospitals and sheds and hid in the gullies/Of blasted roads in a ruined country". The context does not demean them, but it does define the brutality and destructiveness of their shared circumstances. Oppen is careful to give the meaning of the location: "blasted roads in a ruined country". The picture is a small, telling instance of the tragic irony common in modern literature, whose writers have found a sense of community in the experience of war, but rarely in the city.

Distance from others, in the loss or attenuation of common bonds, can make the critical or sceptical mind savage, and embitter the poet who is unable to find a way of carrying relationship and love into the world. While this was not the case with Oppen, the clarity with which he sees the city and its inhabitants can be a very cold light. In view of this fact, I want to risk a brief and highly contentious digression. My justification for doing so is that the question it raises has come to haunt me during an intensive period of reading Oppen and thinking about the principles of Imagism and Objectivism, and while I am prepared to admit that it may be mere confusion or a shadow, I believe that the work asks for it to be raised, and that it is relevant there, not merely a private obsession.

8

George Steiner, in a penetrating discussion of the elements in Heidegger's thought which fitted in with the ideology of Nazism, quotes Heidegger, in 1933, on the "hard clarity" with which the philosophers, reunited to the *Volk* through the National Socialist revolution, will return to their work of questioning the meaning of existence. Steiner calls "hard clarity" "a characteristic bit of ontological-Nazi idiom", and comments: "Heideggerian 'resoluteness' (*Entschlossenheit*) has more than a hint of the mystique of commitment, of self-sacrificial and self-projective élan preached by the Führer and his 'hard clear' acolytes".[13]

The phrase has disturbing echoes. Ezra Pound's aim "to produce poetry that is hard and clear"[14] defined the methods of Imagism and Vorticism, which were decisively influenced by the thought of T.E. Hulme and the ideas and example of Gaudier-Brzeska, too. A way of making is a way of seeing, of apprehending the relationship — the distance — between subject and object. Pound, Hulme and Gaudier all manifested a strong masculine will. It is evident in Hulme's conviction that "it is only by tradition and organization that anything decent can be got out of man",[15] in Gaudier's desire to master his materials and express the artistic emotion in terms of formal arrangement, and in Pound's "ego-system", his "organization of the world around a character, a kind of masculine energy",[16] which Oppen is not alone in finding in the *Cantos*. The problem with these ideas is that they are both a taproot of much that is valuable in Modernism, and capable of a terrifying misapplication in the social and political sphere. Thus, Gaudier's perception of "mass" in sculpture seems to have influenced his perception of human "masses" in the war, which he saw as "a great remedy", the mechanism of a necessary reduction: war "takes away from the masses numbers upon numbers of unimportant units".[17] The tragic irony of his words scarcely needs comment; he has forced the artist's disinterest to an intolerable extreme, and his great work, to say nothing of his fate, lends nothing but the horror of a grotesque parody to the image of the war as a sculptor, working on the material of humanity. It is more disturbing to find Pound, as he remembers Gaudier, writing in cold anger, in 1934: "What we call social necessity is nothing but the temporary inconvenience caused us by the heaped up imbecilities of other men, by the habits of a dull and lazy agglomerate of our fellows, which sodden mass it is up to the artist to alter, to carve into a fitting shape, as he hacks off unwanted corners of marble".[18]

"The language of poetry naturally falls in with the language of power".[19] Thus Hazlitt, on *Coriolanus*, responding to the repressive politics of the English governing class after the final defeat of Napoleon. Hazlitt was talking about a poetry with its roots in the hierarchical order of church and kingship, and was not thinking about Shakespeare the poet of unaccommodated man. But the question is relevant to the poetry of this century, too, and haunts it as the figure of Coriolanus haunts the poetry of T.S. Eliot, a broken figure of lonely pride, separated from others by his way of seeing them. Is it possible that Objectivism, or any poetry with its roots in Imagism, necessarily isolates the poet from the world he 'sees', thus making him singular, one against the many, the people that he organizes with his perceptions, so that, irrespective of his personal attitudes and beliefs, his art is inherently incapable of expressing the experience of community?

It might be thought that Pound's concern that poetry should use the language of "common speech" would moderate the more severe implications of his view of society as a "sodden mass". But there are no democratic sympathies inherent in the Modernists' preoccupation with common speech. Pound and Hulme both demanded an exactness in the use of language which is not common, but expresses the artist's individual way of seeing and produces what Hulme called "the exact curve of what he sees whether it be an object or an idea in the mind", or, more succinctly, "the exact curve of the thing".[20] Clearly, this differs from the aim of a populist or a democratic poet, and is far removed from both the inclusiveness of Whitman's ego, and an 'open field' poetry in which many other 'voices' besides the poet's may be heard.

As far as its possible application to Oppen's poetry is concerned, the argument so far has glossed over two important facts. Seeing with the eye is an act that always implies distance between seer and thing seen, and the more detached the subject is, the more will the world appear to be a world of objects. Seeing in this way makes possible the separation of self from world which, in turn, enables the self to manipulate or prey upon the world. But Oppen's seeing is not primarily visual; rather, it is a seeing of relationships, in nature and society, among words. Moreover his thought, like Heidegger's and Maritain's, is anti-Cartesian: it denies the primacy of self as a knowing subject, and replaces it among the things of the world. Furthermore, he is not directed by masculine will, but highly receptive to the feminine, and open to mystery. All the same, the 'I' and mind of his poetry are always his, the quotations always adapted to what *he* is saying; which has to be the case when sincerity or personal authenticity is the aim, and indeed these are among the virtues of his poetry. Yet it is hard to be certain that the great strain between the one and the many in 'Of Being Numerous' is not built into the very method which seeks to define "the boundaries/Of our distances". Oppen courageously asks "Whether, as the intensity of seeing increases, one's distance from Them, the people, does not also increase". But this is not the same as to ask whether it is the intensity of *his* way of seeing, rather than of all seeing, that isolates the one from the many.

9

The light in which the city is seen in 'Of Being Numerous' is harsher and bleaker even than the light in *The Waste Land*. For example, there is nothing in Eliot's poem as cold as this:

> In two dozen rooms,
> Two dozen apartments
> After the party
> The girls
> Stare at the ceiling
> Blindly as they are filled
> And then they sleep.
>
> ('Of Being Numerous', 23)

The stark ugliness of the picture — the girls staring "blindly as they are filled," an act as functional as filling a car with petrol — is more horrible for its lack of the prurience and voyeurism of the episode with the typist in 'The Fire Sermon'. The clincial eye sees a general condition whereas the emotional atmosphere of the scene in *The Waste Land* reflects the sickness of the one who sees it. A distinction must be made, though, between the emotional coldness of diagnostic vision, and the realism of a poet who is capable of looking steadily at brute fact. Oppen is the latter. He is fully engaged emotionally in presenting women as the source of warmth as well as life in the city, and his sense of absolute lovelessness is correspondingly all the greater. There is no *frisson* of sexual feeling in the picture, only the ugliness of a meaningless act.

The fundamental difference between Oppen and Eliot manifests itself in their attitudes towards myth. Thus Eliot, partly through the influence of Dante, assimilates his "unreal city" to the state of Limbo. The same identification of fellow citizens with unformed souls is shown in his symbolic use of the London Underground in *Four Quartets*. Certainly, the "ferocious mumbling" of Oppen's New York subways resembles the "twittering world" of Eliot's Underground/Limbo, and Oppen's city in parts of 'Of Being Numerous' is at least as "unreal" as Eliot's. The great difference, however, is that Eliot assimilates his city and citizens to a mythic pattern, which prejudges their 'fate' in terms of a closed system, but Oppen tries strenuously to cleanse words of mythic associations, revealing the difficult necessity of choice and personal responsibility. His New York is the city of the historical present, its unreality a consequence of myths and dreams and false images. He knows that he shares in the unreality, and struggles against it to speak "a substantial language". However great his isolation from the people, he knows that he is not in fact 'outside' them, for there is nowhere outside to be. His is "a language of New York", because he is of the populace flowing through the city.

"*A* language", not "*the* language", of New York. 'Of Being Numerous' explores the distances *within* a shared language, between poet and people, and the gap which meaning has to leap could hardly be shown more pointedly than in the juxtaposition, in section 17, of subway graffito and the poet's response:

> There is nobody here but us chickens
>
> Anti-ontology —

But the poem continues:

> He wants to say
> His life is real,
> No one can say why
>
> It is not easy to speak
>
> A ferocious mumbling, in public
> Of rootless speech.

Who is "he" — the graffito writer, or the poet, who knows what 'ontology' means? The distinction between them, marked as an abysmal gap in the preceding lines, is lost. It is lost, not from failure of clarity, but because Oppen, struggling to "speak" "in public" is subject to the common unreality of "rootless speech". His refusal to assume special privileges as a poet, and his struggle to construct meaning in full awareness of his implication in the destructive unreality which he sees, make 'Of Being Numerous' a poem that goes to the roots of the crisis of meaning and communication in modern poetry.

There is a major, instructive difference between 'A Language of New York', 5 and 'Of Being Numerous', 20. The sections have the same subject — War, and the people's response to news of war — and, in part, the same words. But in the earlier poem the question "Who escapes/Death?" is followed by:

> Whether or not there is war, whether he has
> Or has not opinions, and not only warriors,
> Not only heroes
>
> And not only victims, and they may have come to the end
> Of all that, and if they have
> They may have come to the end of it.

The parallel passage in 'Of Being Numerous' is very different:

> But who escapes
> Death
>
> Among these riders
> Of the subway,
>
> They know
> By now as I know
>
> Failure and the guilt
> Of failure.
> As in Hardy's poem of Christmas
>
> We might half-hope to find the animals
> In the sheds of a nation
> Kneeling at midnight,
>
> Farm animals,
> Draft animals, beasts for slaughter
> Because it would mean they have forgiven us,
> Or which is the same thing,
> That we do not altogether matter.

The main difference between the two 'answers' is that Oppen does not include himself in the first, which is concerned with what "they may have come to the end of" (like the baseball crowd in section 13, who "will come to the end/Of an era"), whereas in the second he shares "failure and the guilt/ Of failure" with "these riders/Of the subway". He too stands condemned for the failure of an ethic, the failure evident in the Vietnam war, in the "rootless speech" of the city, and in loss of hope for the future. It is much for which to accept the guilt, but it is implicit in the passage, in meanings which the poem constructs, and in the reference to Hardy's poem.

'The Oxen' at once expresses Hardy's nostalgia for faith and projects a wistful image of the unity of creation, with the neighbours gathered "in a flock" picturing "the meek mild creatures" kneeling in reverence at the birth of Jesus. It is not a soft-centred poem but combines tender feeling with clear-eyed scepticism. Its presence at this point in Oppen's poem is in harmony with his similar qualities, but also, in the implicit parallel between the oxen and the young Americans drafted for the war, introduces a terrible irony, which leads to the blankness — which is not resignation but may be despair — of the last line. It is significant that he chooses the moment of that birth, seen through the eyes of Hardy's poem, to express his guilt at the ethic which has failed the young. Despite the sharp irony of "the sheds of a nation", the image, reinforced by the feeling of Hardy's poem, carries Oppen's belief in the clearly defined, the rooted and in-gathered, as the ground of community. It is a belief — perhaps it would be better to describe it as a sentiment —

which coexists with the value he places on the pursuit of truth, and on newness and an exploratory poetics. Hence the crucial importance in the poem of the young poets' tragic loss of "the metaphysical sense/of the future", as he calls it in section 26.

But it is not the young poets alone, it is "we" who "cannot defend/The metaphysic/On which rest//The boundaries/Of our distances". The words are a node from which all his concerns spring. The distances are at once between the one and the many, the relationships between people, and temporal, defining the relationship between past, present and future. The bounded distance is also the "limited, limiting clarity", which Oppen describes in 'Route', 1 as "the most beautiful thing in the world", and his only "motive of poetry". It shone in the 'things' of a primitive people who "were patient/With the world", in section 12. It is in the "spot of light on the curb", and is lost in "*that* light seeping anywhere", and in "the air of atrocity".

Oppen's fear for the young caught in the snare of the past calls to mind a passage from Kierkegaard's *Fear and Trembling*:

> Whatever the one generation may learn from the other, that which is genuinely human no generation learns from the foregoing. In this respect every generation begins primitively, has no different task from that of every previous generation, nor does it get further except in so far as the preceding generation shirked its task and deluded itself. This authentically human factor is passion... Thus no generation has learned from another to love, no generation begins at any other point than at the beginning....[21]

In Oppen, a similar existential urgency reinforces his conviction of each generation's need to construct new roots from the elemental foundations, and Kierkegaard's terms translate easily into his:

> How shall one know a generation, a new generation?
> Not by the dew on them! Where the earth is most torn
> And the wounds untended and the voices confused,
> There is the head of the moving column
>
> Who if they cannot find
> Their generation
> Wither in the infirmaries
>
> And the supply depots, supplying
> Irrelevant objects.

For Oppen, the meaning of life is constructed in the pursuit of truth, in struggle and exploration, and he comes close to despair in his fear that in a society going round and round in a closed system established in the past, with its "infirmaries" and "depots, supplying/Irrelevant objects", the young can make no way through.

Yet, however much it bears the weight of "irrelevant objects" a genuinely exploratory poetry like Oppen's is continually alive to the unknown, which means that it does not accept the closure of despair. It may be a name that "cries faith":

> There can be a brick
> In a brick wall
> The eye picks
>
> So quiet of a Sunday
> Here is the brick, it was waiting
> Here when you were born
>
> Mary-Anne
>   ('Of Being Numerous', 21)

How may we understand this, a bare minimum of words yet with complex relations of time and choice and possibility among them? Perhaps by recalling 'Blood from the Stone', 111: "To a body anything can happen,/Like a brick. Too obvious to say./But all horror came from it". Or perhaps in the light of Oppen's patience with the world, and his refusal "to reduce the thing to nothing". 'A Language of New York', 7 begins: "Strange that the youngest people I know/Like Mary-Anne live in the most ancient buildings". The girl is enclosed in the sentence, trapped in Oppen's emotion and his way of seeing, her freedom encumbered by his opposition between youth and the old city. In the later poem he comes much closer to "Clarity// In the sense of *transparence*", "Clarity in the sense of silence". It is as though he were standing at a window looking out. There is the brick. There is Mary-Anne. What will she make of the world she was born into? The question is addressed to her — they are face to face, with no mirror between them. He does not know the answer; it is not predetermined. His act of naming is a profession of faith in the person or thing named.

Notes

1. All quotations from the poems are from *The Collected Poems of George Oppen*, New Directions, 1975.
2. *Contemporary Literature*, X, 2 (1969), p.173.
3. *Ibid.*, p. 161.
4. See *Ibid.*, p.174 and L.S. Dembo, 'Oppen on his Poems: A Discussion', *George Oppen Man and Poet*, ed. Burton Hatlen, The National Poetry Foundation, (1981), pp. 201-202.
5. Burton Hatlen and Tom Mandel, 'Poetry and Politics: A Conversation with

George and Mary Oppen', *George Oppen Man and Poet*, p. 25.
6. George Oppen to L.S. Dembo, *Contemporary Literature*, X, 2 p. 164.
7. George Oppen is discussing his poem 'Philai Te Kou Philai' with L.S. Dembo, *George Oppen Man and Poet*, p. 211.
8. Søren Kierkegaard, *Fear and Trembling* and *The Sickness Unto Death*, translated by Walter Lowrie, Doubleday Anchor Books, (1954), p. 38.
9. Mary Oppen, *Meaning A Life*, Black Sparrow Press, (1978), p. 68.
10. "I'm really concerned with the substantive, with the subject of the sentence, with what we are talking about, and not rushing over the subject-matter in order to make a comment about it. It is still a principle with me of more than poetry, to notice, to state, to lay down the substantive for its own sake." George Oppen to L.S. Dembo, *Contemporary Literature*, X, 2, p. 161.
11. 'And that's when the poems sort of stagger now and then, when I talk about despair." *Ibid.*, p. 173.
12. Burton Hatlen and Tom Mandel, 'Poetry and Politics: A Conversation with George and Mary Oppen', *George Oppen Man and Poet*, p. 44.
13. George Steiner, *Heidegger*, Fontana, (1978), p. 114 and p. 117.
14. Ezra Pound, 'Preface to *Some Imagist Poets* 1915', in *Imagist Poetry*, ed. Peter Jones, Penguin Books, (1972), p. 135.
15. T.E. Hulme, *Speculations*, ed. Herbert Read, (1924), p. 116.
16. George Oppen to L.S. Dembo, *Contemporary Literature*, X, 2, p. 170.
17. 'Vortex Gaudier-Brzeska (Written from the Trenches)', in Ezra Pound, *Gaudier-Brzeska*, The Marvell Press, (1960), p. 27.
18. *Gaudier-Brzeska*, p. 144.
19. William Hazlitt, *Selected.Writings*, ed. Ronald Blythe, Penguin Books, (1970), p. 284.
20. *Speculations*, p. 132 and p. 137.
21. *Op. Cit.*, p. 130.

Crossings and Turns: the Poetry of John Matthias

John Matthias, who was born in Ohio in 1941, and is a professor of English at an American university, has written a number of poems set in East Anglia, where, at intervals over a period of several years, he was able to make his home. *Northern Summer*, his new and selected poems, published by Anvil Press in 1984, also contains poems set in Europe, poems which make extensive use of Polish and Russian materials, and a long poem set in his new home outside America, in Scotland. America appears rarely in his poems, and then usually in retrospective scenes, but the fact of his being American strongly affects his experience of other places. John Matthias's poetry is intrinsically interesting, but, for a British reader in particular, it gains an added interest from his use of the 'matter' of England and Scotland. In this, he contributes to a fascinating and very diverse body of poetry about Britain by contemporary fellow Americans, including Ronald Johnson and Ed Dorn, who belong within a larger, and equally diverse, tradition, which is not confined to poetry but embraces Emerson and Henry James, as well as Ezra Pound and T.S. Eliot. The visits of an American to Britain, with a perspective on the island that no British poet could have, draw out the most obvious meanings of the words of my title, (which I take from the titles of two of John Matthias's books but use neither to exhaust his meanings nor always to adhere to them). The 'crossings' are between Britain and America, the 'turns' are in the poet's mind as he looks from continent to island, island to continent. The concern of this essay, however, is not exclusively insular, since John Matthias's work raises issues of general relevance to the situation of poetry in Britain and America today.

'The Situation of Poetry' is the title of a book by Robert Pinsky, another outstanding poet of Matthias's generation. There, Pinsky states as his thesis: "that we learn many of our attitudes towards language and reality from the past, and that it takes considerable effort by a poet either to understand and apply those attitudes, for his own purposes, or to abandon them. The alternative to such effort may be to lapse into mere mannerism or received ideas. Significantly, the argument at this point is similar to part of what Eliot in 'Tradition and the Individual Talent' said about the historical sense: the poet who wants to avoid being a mere imitator must work at understanding poetry written in the past, in order to find his way in the present.

The great first generation of Modernists — Pound's 'Renaissance' of the early twentieth century — learned to make things new by applying traditions which they partly recovered and partly created. Admittedly, the recovery *and* creation greatly complicates the idea of tradition, which in this context is not the inherited gift of a stable society. Nevertheless, for contemporary poets the traditions of their Modernist predecessors provide a large part of the "attitude toward language and reality" in terms of which they define themselves. To be innocent of the knowledge of modern poetry is almost certainly to condemn oneself to imitation of pre-modern conventions; the adoption of modern styles without understanding their necessity leads equally to shadow poetry; but a sense of the presence of the literary past, including Modernism and its traditions, which can free the poet from "mannerism or received ideas", may also impose on him a great burden of self-consciousness, so that he feels bewildered by the possible choices before him, and crushed by the anxiety that everything worth doing has already been done.

While being seldom bewildered and never crushed in his poems, John Matthias is often anxious. For example, in 'The Stefan Batory Poems', reflecting on an older poet's comments on his poems, he writes:

> My attraction to quotation, commentary, pastiche: exhaustion? or the very method of abstention that he recommends? Many days I'd be a scribe, a monk — and I, like monk and scribe, am permitted to append the meanings that my authors may have missed. "He abandoned himself to the absolute sincerity of pastiche".... Otherwise? Poets know too much.

What is the "too much" that John Matthias sometimes feels he knows? That is, what is the poetry which, on the evidence of his poems, comprises the traditions of which he thinks of himself as a scribe?

To begin with, he knows the works of Ezra Pound, founder and chief impressario of Anglo-American Modernist poetry, and David Jones, the writer who (with Charles Olson in America) did most to extend the range of Modernism after the Second World War. Setting aside their great differences, what these two poets have in common is comparatively 'objective' methods of isolating and patterning the truths embodied in historical, mythical and literary materials. Both are makers of shapes, but both also perceive the poetry inherent in 'things' (in this sense, words, names, facts, and signs, as well as objects), and therefore renew the idea of the poet as a kind of scribe who 'reads' the order of the world, and records it truly. Good poems written by their methods greatly transcend the experience available to any individual ego. (It should also be said in passing that Pound's greatest follower in America, William Carlos Williams, developed Poundian methods and applied them to the things of his native locality. It would require another essay to discuss why Matthias has moved in the geographical direction not of Williams and Olson but of Eliot and Pound).

The oppositions within modern poetry can be exaggerated, especially when there are poets like John Matthias who cross what hard-liners regard as a border and exclusion zone. All the same, for the sake of definition, I will risk a generalisation, and say that the main division is between those who, like Jones and Pound, find the self in the order of the world, and poets with a strong autobiographical impulse, who draw the world into themselves. Robert Lowell is notable among the latter, a poet who, with John Berryman and Sylvia Plath, extended the scope of the personal 'I' over inner experience, in poems which reflected the terrors of modern history in the self. But it is Auden who stands behind the so-called 'confessional' writers, while keeping a sense of the world's objectivity: Auden, poet of the age of anxiety, whose self of the later poems — quirky, opinionated, wise, gross, devoted — moves in a world whose bones are beloved geological facts, and which is ineluctably historical, and redeemed. He too is a crucial figure for John Matthias, whose knowledge is not confined to these poets, but who defines himself, in part, through highly individual 'crossings' of the different methods which they represent.

The poet as scribe is a lover of names. "To begin with a name", says John Matthias at the start of one poem, and he does, often. He sometimes virtually makes poems out of them, too. There is the second part of 'A Wind in Roussillon', for example:

> The train departs from Austerlitz on time.
> After Carcassonne, Tuchan,
> wheat and barley dry up in the sun
> & trees appear hung heavily
> with cherries, lemons, oranges.
>
> Red tiled roofs are angled oddly
> on the little houses in the hills below Cerdagne.
> Gray slate's left behind.
>
> By the tracks
> a villager has nailed up a goat's foot
> and a sunflower to the door
> that opens on his vineyard
> circled by a wall of heavy stones.

Place-names, proper nouns, clear-cut images and lines, surprising detail, all combine to create a strong sense of the external world, in which the poet's presence is implicit as the man who sees. Some of the pleasure of reading *Northern Summer* comes from writing like this, and three of the finest poems, 'From a Visit to Dalmatia', 'Poem for Cynouai' and 'A Wind in Roussillon' itself, owe much of their success to this method. The scribal love of names manifests a respect for things existing in themselves, and for the experience of other people embodied in their actual words or artefacts. John Matthias's historical poems are accordingly made largely by his deployment of names, facts, and quotations. In 'Poem for Cynouai' he speaks of a world "where names are properties of things/they name", and his art of naming often suggests the identity of name and thing, especially in his poems set in East Anglia, where long human occupation has woven together language and landscape. Occasionally, as in 'East Anglian Poem' itself, his respect for the materials leads him to lean too heavily on them, and results in lists and incantations of names. He knows, however, that long-occupied places have undergone most historical change, and that it is reflected in language. Consequently his awareness of processes of change is often expressed through the 'crossings' and 'turns' which words themselves undergo. John Matthias also has a great liking, reminiscent of Wallace Stevens's, for exotic names. But this belongs as much to his autobiographical impulse as to his delight in flamboyance and oddity or his scribal fidelity. Running through names in his moods of uncertainty or dislike of his own American identity, he is part shape-shifting magician, part clown enjoying a comic turn. In 'The Stefan Batory Poems', he has Prospero whispering in one ear and Lenin in the other — tempters that nicely represent the dualism of a disciple of facts and a verbal wizard.

The historical sense, as Eliot said, "involves a perception, not only of the pastness of the past, but of its presence". For a number of contemporary poets, however, it also involves, often in social and political terms that Eliot would not have accepted, a perception of the processes and connections that make a society. The result is that, for them, the past is present as a moral pressure, raising radical questions about cause and effect, justice, motivation, meaning. This may be seen, for example, in John Matthias's finest historical poem, '26 June 1381/1977'. Briefly, this concerns connections among the following: the Peasants' Revolt in Norfolk, Henry Despenser, Bishop of Norwich, who put it down, but attempted to keep the leader's head from banging on the cobbles as he was dragged behind a cart to his execution, the dyer Geoffrey Lidster, who led the revolt, the reredos given to Despenser by the Norfolk nobles for putting down the revolt, the restoration of the reredos in 1977, and the reaction to it of various sightseers. But while any sketch of the main connections is bound to sound clumsy, the poem lives in its imaginative recreation of key events and its meditation upon them. It is both vivid and properly tentative, respecting what cannot be known about the dead yet searching for meaning, and responding to the past in the knowledge that it is the present, above all, that is under question:

> And us with our heads still on our necks?
> With books in our laps,
>
> Stupid or giddy, gawking —
> Us with the eyes still in their sockets

And tongues still in our mouths —
Where do we travel, where

Do we think we can go —
All of us, now, staff, of one, life?

The modern consciousness is historical even when it is also religious, as the most notable British and American poetry of recent years amply bears witness. Together with such poets as David Jones, Geoffrey Hill and his near namesake Roland Mathias, John Matthias has a religious attitude towards the past. He is aware of what in 'Epilogue from a New Home' he calls the "ancient charge: to/read whatever evidence in lives or lies appears,/In stones or bells – transform, transfigure then whatever/comedy, catastrophe or crime, and thus/Return the earth, thus redeem the time". To read the evidence, transform, transfigure, return, redeem, and (in '26 June 1381/ 1977') restore: these key words describe the aims of the commemorative poet, who works for memory against oblivion, but knows that justice cannot be done to a past that is regarded as static and dead, but only in its living connections with the present, which require of the artist imaginative recreation as well as fidelity to facts. John Matthias's readings and transformations of East Anglia have something important in common with *The Anathemata* and Geoffrey Hill's poems concerning English history and Roland Mathias's involvement with the Welsh past. But there are also good reasons why his historical poems have a different psychological emphasis from the British poets'.

This may be seen, for example, in his 'Double Derivation, Association, and Cliché: from *The Great Tournament Roll of Westminster*'. For a start, the poem's title amply confesses its self-consciousness. Then, although there is some overlap of subject-matter with Hill's 'Funeral Music', Matthias even in his more sombre passages creates, not "a florid grim music", but theatrical rhetoric and even something like a carnival atmosphere:

> Or Richard Gibson
>   busy
> with artificers and labour, portages and ships:
> busy with his sums and his accounts:
> for what is wrought by carpenters & joyners,
> karrovers & smiths...
> (Who breaks a spear is worth the prize)
> Who breaks a schylld on shields
> a saylle on sails
> a sclev upon his lady's sleeves;
> who can do skilfully the spleter werke,
> whose spyndylles turn

> Power out of parsimony, feasting
> Out of famine, revels out of revelation:
> Out of slaughter, ceremony.
> When the mist lifts over Bosworth.
> When the mist settles on Flodden.
>
> Who breaks a spear is worth the prize.

The atmosphere owes much to the poet's delight in historical words and names, but it is more important to note that the theatricality befits his subject, which is man the actor or player.

As I have shown, John Matthias's poems are dense with historical detail. He is acutely aware of time, in landscapes where different historical strata lie side by side, in which he looks for pattern and order:

> There's a plague pit
>   just to the edge of the village.
> Above it, now mostly covered with grass,
>   a runway for B-17s: (American
> Pilots back from industrial targets). Tribes
>   gathered under my window;
> They'd sack an imperial town: I'll wave
>   to my wife at the end of the Roman road.
>
>   ('Epilogue from a New Home')

For him, to make a home in Britain means to 'dig down', to know the place in historical depth, but his home-making also honestly reflects his self-consciousness as an outsider. The result of this is that his poetic motives differ from the purely celebratory impulse of Ronald Johnson in his *The Book of the Green Man*, (with whom he otherwise, in his more scribal poems, has something in common), and also from the British poets' explorations of their problematic, mixed heritage (though, again, he shares more than their unease). John Matthias's 'crossings' are also of angles of vision, from self-conscious outsider at one extreme to settled occupant at the other. He does not fake his relationship with place, claiming to belong where he does not, or to know more than he does, but writes from the effort to make contact, uneasy at his endeavour. His poems consequently have a nervous intensity, and a restless, quick perception of what he is attempting. And he writes in full awareness of his psychological need to imagine other people, other places, other times. It is this awareness, above all, that accounts for the large element of play in his poems, which at times gives the earlier ones in particular an extreme, and, to me, strained ingenuity, but also stimulates the wit and exuberance that make him at best an exceptionally entertaining poet.

In 'Clarifications for Robert Jacoby', John Matthias reminds his cousin of

> all those games
> we used to play: the costumes,
> All the sticks & staves, the whole complicated
> paraphernalia accumulated to suggest
> Authentic weaponry and precise historical dates,
> not to mention exact geographical places.

The clarifications are of parts of 'Double Derivation...', in which he speaks of himself as reaching "for words as in a photograph/I reach for costumes in a trunk". Thus, he locates the source of his historical imagination in his boyhood passion for historical games, rituals, dressing up. While this certainly helps to account for what I have described as the carnival atmosphere of some passages of his historical poems, it also belongs with a characteristically modern sense of an intimate relationship between childhood and the historical past, which we also find, with different emphases, in Geoffrey Hill, David Jones and Seamus Heaney. As with these poets, John Matthias in his way is serious about the relationship, for as he says in 'Double Derivation...':

> In proper costume, Homo Ludens wears
> Imagination on his sleeve.

In other words, Matthias the poet knows himself to belong to the species Homo Ludens. Not surprisingly, therefore, there is more of Johan Huizinga's philosophy of play, which distinguishes man from the animals and inspires the creativity which shapes the human world, in John Matthias's poetry than there is Marxism.

But if he writes more in the spirit of Huizinga than Marx (or of Prospero than Lenin), he is far from forgetting the claims of a reality that refuses imaginative transformation. In fact, there is often a duality in his poems which prevents the play from becoming merely indulgent, when, in terms of 'Clarifications for Robert Jacoby', "reality itself" disturbs the "elaborate rituals". A fair summary of this important dimension of his work might be that the poet at his creative play makes poems that are themselves worlds, but makes them out of the stuff of reality, which exists independently of him, makes its own claims, questions the poet, and calls him to witness all that is not himself.

John Matthias's position of outsider in Britain and Europe has evidently heightened his feeling for language and for languages to an acute sensitivity. His use of verbal records is an art in itself, and he combines scribal precision with the play of one kind of language and point of view against another. Indeed, his Scottish poem, 'Northern Summer', is effectively a test of languages against reality and against each other, and therefore fittingly concludes the book with his furthest development of a characteristic method.

Here, for example, the void of absolute subjectivity contrasts with a space occupied by human experience, a space which is seen differently through different languages — guidebook, Romantic, the styles of different generations, and so on — which the poet who wants to be more than a tourist must be able to interpret. Understanding languages as the medium and depository of other people's experience also enables him to see things from unusual angles, in 'crossings' and 'turns' of words, as when in 'A Wind in Roussillon' he throws a sharp ironic light on Mrs Thatcher and the Falklands war:

> In French, the words of Mme T. about les îles Malouines sound nearly as bizarre as ads for the religious kitsch at Lourdes translated into English in the same edition of *Le Monde*.... "A see-through plastic model of the Virgin with unscrewable gold crown enables you to fill the image up with holy water from a tap." And Mme T., *qui a félicitée les forces armées*, swells in French to the dimensions of a Bonaparte: *les plus merveilleuses du monde... le courage et l'habileté ont donné une nouvelle fierté à ce pays et nous ont fait comprendre que nous étions vraiment une seule famille.*
>
> Et nous, les os: vraiment une seule famille.

The same historical sense is at work here as in the poems set in the past, revealing the connection, or more often, the disconnection, between what is said and the way of saying it. This is shown by the way the turns of language, French into English and English into French, and their juxtaposition, disclose the extraordinary nature of what the familiar words would conceal.

Other qualities and methods of John Matthias's poetry may be seen in this passage. As well as those already mentioned, there is his combination or alternation of poetry and prose. This allows him both a considerable range of reference and discourse, and a lyrical development of image, phrase, or motif, like "les os" and "une seule famille'. The passage also illustrates how he finds in rich and diverse materials from various sources the motifs which guide and extend his perceptions. Here, for example, "une seule famille" represents the concern he feels most strongly; expressed in poems which seek connections between people divided by time or space, and in poems of personal relationships, it looks back to "staff, of one, life" in '26 June 1381/1977' and to 'Poem for Cynouai', in which he explores, with intense feeling, wit, and tenderness, the relationships of "father, father-son, and daughter" (his father, himself as son and father, and his daughter) who, with time, are "changing places painfully". For, of course, it is not only words that make patterns or tangles when they cross each other, or that turn meanings inside out — it is human beings that play many roles in their lifetime, influence each other variously in life and death, and are generally held for good or ill in a web of changing relationships.

In his combination of lyrical and discursive voices, as in subject and concern, John Matthias has an exciting range. As I have attempted to show, he writes in some poems from tension between a scribe's respect for the integrity of his materials and a magician's freedom to transform them, and in many poems he brings together the contrasting gifts and is fully present as himself, both scribe and magician. In fact, he is a very engaging presence — funny, honest, intelligent, generous — and this in turn greatly increases the scope of his language. The imagist and objectivist side of Modernism tends towards the puritan virtues — a poetry working by omission, which, in Robert Pinsky's terms, abandons many of the attitudes toward language and reality that the poet has learned from the past, and produces, at best, work of great purity and concentration. The sacramentalism of David Jones, on the other hand, though it creates an immensely richer universe, tends equally to exclude the personal self as either poetic agent or poetic subject. But the poet's use of his self with all its strengths and weaknesses need not close him to the external world, or lead to disintegration — it can lead as well to the inclusive embrace and serious playfulness of a great comic actor. In his refusal to see these possibilities as mutually exclusive choices, John Matthias's achievement is already impressive, and, with the resources and talent at his command, the prospect of his future work is as exciting as it is unpredictable.

John Ormond: The Accessible Song

Definition of a Waterfall (1973) includes eleven poems from John Ormond's previous substantial collection, *Requiem and Celebration* (1969), which gathered together work written over a period of about twenty-five years. In many ways this was a remarkable book, powerful but also frustrating, in which a strong individual talent could be seen in the process of working through influences that were at once stimulating and inhibiting. Some of the eleven poems carried over into the new collection show minor revisions, but all have the stylistic maturity of Ormond's latest work; with the benefit of hindsight it is easy to see that they were the inevitable choice for a book that contains the best of his poetry to date. It seems to me that their selection is a clear illustration of how a major phase of creative development can produce in an artist a matching critical self-awareness. I believe that in *Definition of a Waterfall*, John Ormond emerges as an important poet.

His poetry is both entertaining, with no superficial difficulties to hinder understanding, and profoundly appealing. This is a broad introductory statement, but one carefully chosen to indicate a rare combination of qualities. With John Ormond's work, the poem that comes alive at first reading and offers no superficial difficulties, remains to tease the imagination with meanings that are untranslatable into prose. He has a narrative and dramatic gift; he has wit and humour and he is a brilliant descriptive writer. 'My Grandfather and his Apple-Tree', 'Organist', 'Johnny Randall' and 'Full-length Portrait of a Short Man' embody memorable characterizations.

The characterizations are built up, in part, by some striking descriptions which risk, but do not succumb to, caricature and sentimentality. But even in these poems, where Ormond's gifts as an entertaining storyteller are most in evidence, it is plain that the effects of his poetry cannot be explained merely by reference to these gifts. Just as his vivid descriptions of appearances almost invariably become metaphors which disclose the nature of a person or a thing, so the narrative-dramatic-descriptive mode, with its seductive but not shallow attractions, serves the aims of one who is primarily a symbolist. Although this may be obvious in the early poems collected in *Requiem and Celebration*, it is far more effective here, largely because the poems work symbolically through credible realistic narratives and sensuously particularized descriptions. If symbolism is a universal language, in poetry it is spoken only by those who have made it their own through personal experience. Despite the talent and dedication that John Ormond showed in his early work, I feel that he was trying to use a language of symbols created by others, principally Dylan Thomas. In the poems of his maturity (mostly written since 1965) he has achieved a true symbolism because he has found a distinctive voice; speaking as himself he has found his own proper materials, eloquent of a reality beyond appearances.

The presence of a central symbol is obvious in 'My Grandfather and his Apple-Tree'. The poem tells a credible story (no doubt it is a true one, but not all true stories are credible), where the apple-tree to which the Nonconformist miner grafted "a branch of cooker" because its sweet fruit "budded temptation in his mouth", was a real tree rooted in a real garden in a South Wales community. But it also has the symbolic force of 'the tree of the knowledge of good and evil'. It is a forceful because an unforced symbol, natural in the Nonconformist community to which the poet's grandfather, a deacon at Ebenezer, belonged, and inevitable for one with memories of such a background. Yet the symbol in the poem cannot be interpreted as the man himself would have interpreted it, in orthodox Christian terms. For him, since guilt was engendered by the sweetness of life, sweetness contained evil, and had to be tempered by the sour fruit of rigid moral discipline. But I do not think the poet is calculating his effects merely to invert this morality, so that sweetness becomes symbolic of natural good, sourness of doctrinaire evil. The poem's complexity subverts rather than confirms any view of life in which such pairs of naked opposites explain its meaning. The man grafted "the sour to sweetness" because he wanted "the best of both his worlds". But he was a man of two worlds in more than one sense. "A wild and drinking farmboy" he left the land "for dark under the field six days a week", but

> All light was beckoning. Soon his hands
> Untangled a brown garden into neat greens.

Thus "both his worlds" comprised life above ground, where his instinct for creating order in the natural world prevailed, and work underground, submitted to in order to marry and pay the rent: light and dark. But they also comprised the sweetness of life itself and the sourness of a sense of sin. Inevitably the symbolism of good and evil seen in a Christian context is juxtaposed ironically with these other pairs of opposites, light and dark, sweetness and sourness, an instinct for creating natural order and discipline, adding to the complexity of a poem that is largely concerned with one man's attempt to integrate the warring extremes of human nature. It is a fine poem, which can be seen as relevant to a society and an age. It is also a memorable character study. And in relation to John Ormond's underlying themes, it reveals his use of a traditional religious symbolism in an unorthodox way. It seems to me that he is not primarily concerned with good and evil in moral terms, but rather with using the conjunction of light and dark, sweetness and sourness, good and evil, as a symbol for the relationship of life and death. The old man has his own terms of reference, which are perhaps as valid as any, for what perplexes all men, but I think the poet, the grandson, sees them in another context; that he is seeking to understand life, and how it is to be lived, when seen as inseparable from death. This is, of course, an ancient quest for understanding which predates Christianity, and whose symbolism is manifest in cromlech and stone circle, labyrinth and cauldron of rebirth. This, too, is the direction in which the poems in *Definition of a Waterfall* move, from personal and ancestral history in a place dominated by the religion of the chapel to an apprehension of the religious symbolism of myth.

In his excellent introductory essay, 'The Poetry of John Ormond' (*Poetry Wales*, Summer, 1972), Randal Jenkins has spoken of Ormond's "anxiety to involve us in his painful awareness of mortality, and in his perplexed search for the wisdom to understand it." The painful awareness and the search for understanding are at once apparent in the poems about people and place with which the collection opens. In "My Dusty Kinsfolk', for instance, awareness of the dead's presence manifests itself as a sense of their livingness and his mortality:

> Continue
> To tenant the air where I walk in the sun
> Beyond the shadow of yew.
> I speak these words to you, my kin
> And friends, in requiem and celebration.

When the living and the dead are seen as fellows, requiem demands celebration, celebration requiem. Similarly, his imagination is much preoccupied with the juxtaposition of geological and human time scales:

> We placed you where a vein of coal
> Can still be seen when graves are open.
> The Dunvant seam spreads fingers in
> The churchyard under Penybryn.

The phrase "spreads fingers in" suggests an intimacy that many would find chillingly sinister; but this is not how the poet apprehends it. Here, he is expressing his sense of a kinship that is almost kindly between the stuff of the material world and the substance of flesh. (The kinship is, of course, a commonplace of metaphor, as in 'vein of coal'). Whether it is felt to be kindly or not, the properly human response is requiem and celebration for living and dead alike.

'My Dusty Kinsfolk' is a good poem, but it is not fully mature Ormond; it still has a hint of the more abstract death acceptance embodied in the stone/bone imagery of the early poems. In the later 'Letter to a Geologist', for example, he is able to use a more flexible tone in expressing a far more personal response to a similar theme. There, he shows his fascination with geological time in images that convey real excitement:

> The shifting land you've shown me: off-shore
> Islands in green counties; tide-ways
> 500 million years of age under the plough;
>
> And desert sands stranded in river-cliffs
> On Deeside, come from the Sahara.

From Thomas Hardy to David Jones this is a vision the modern imagination has thrilled to. Then, very movingly, John Ormond sets against geology, as Hardy invariably does, another scale of time:

>   Let us tell
> Some part of earth's true time together soon
>
> With a drink, a song — the lullabies you sang
> My children, come sing them again before sleep;
> Let us say to each other words of a common world.

The play of a quick intelligence, the ability to express a wide range of feeling, from awe of "the shifting land" to poignant awareness of "earth's true time" and celebration of "words of a common world", characterize most of the poems in *Definition of a Waterfall*. Ecstatic appreciation of beauty informs his most beautiful poem, 'Certain Questions for Monsieur Renoir'. For the most part, as I have said, he is a symbolist; but although he knows and uses the terms of philosophical and metaphysical approaches to the perplexities of existence, he places an absolute trust in none of them; if his symbolism has affinities with Vernon Watkins's, his sense of the irrevocable moment has something in common with Hardy's, who found no consolation in philosophy.

In 'After a Death' the poet finds a slug's trail on the kitchen floor, among the possessions he has inherited. In one sense the slug, "him who wasn't mentioned in the will", is a symbol of mortality; indeed, a slug "who entered from the garden once" (after feeding on fallen apples, no doubt), which provokes the wry comment: "I have inherited him with all the rest". Yet the effect of the poem, as of others concerning death, is neither sombrely elegiac nor portentously allegorical; it is rather that death induces a sense of perplexing mystery, of 'other presences' in life, presences that falsify expectation, subvert philosophies of order and leave a man knowing only that he does not know. Naturally, symbolism can be used, as in Vernon Watkins, to convey a radiant certitude; but Ormond uses it to intimate mysteries that do not appear to derive from belief in an orthodox creed.

Sometimes, if the effect cannot be properly described as sombrely elegiac, he faces up to a desolating blankness. This is so in 'The Key', one of the half dozen best poems in the book. The first five stanzas describe the key of the poet's old home, a key rarely used because "our door/Was nearly always on the latch", and create an impression of the warm life of the place:

> This room
> Saw paths of generations cross;
> This was the place to which we all came
> Back to talk by the oven, on the white
> Bench. This was the home patch.

But, at the end of the poem,

> The key
> Engages and the bolt gives to me
> Some walls enclosing furniture.

The last line has a staring blankness that derives from the contrast with all that has preceded it. In John Ormond's characterizations, too, the people are brought to life so vividly it is a shock to realize that the originals are dead. This is the inevitable effect of celebrations that are also requiems. *Definition of a Waterfall* is a collection that earns the right to include a version of 'The Hall of Cynddylan', probably the greatest of all requiem-and-celebrations.

Creating a lively impression of chapel in 'Organist', he writes of the moment of communal vision

> When, pentecostal, guilts were flung away
> Fortissimo from pinnacles of fervour,
> When all were cleansed of sin in wild
> Inaccurate crescendoes of Calvary,
> Uncaring, born again, dazzled by diadems
> In words of a Jerusalem beyond their lives....

This passage exemplifies one of the strongest thematic links between the poems in the book concerned with personal and ancestral history and those concerned with prehistory and myth, at the same time as it discloses one of John Ormond's primary themes in the imagery and symbolism in which it is most frequently embodied. The theme is revealed by the phrase "a Jerusalem beyond"; its symbols and images are drawn from music.

It is clear that he is intimate with traditional Christian symbolism, but that for him the symbols carry an archetypal significance instead of a dogmatic truth. Indeed, I think it has to be seen that his primary themes derive from a traditional Christian background, so that the quest for understanding which leads him to prehistory and myth has its origin in the belief which filled the chapelgoers with a joyous sense of being 'born again', and the chapel with "words of a Jerusalem beyond their lives". Similarly, there is in his work a powerful impulse to celebrate the sweetness of life, and to graft the sweet apple to the sour one of death without "the sour half" taking over, that is reminiscent of the vigorous individuals he commemorates. In short, both the themes and the qualities of the poems in *Definition of a Waterfall* are shaped by the people and places which some of those poems celebrate.

A recurrent theme of John Ormond's poetry, expressed in the symbolism of ancient myths and in symbols derived from the 'language' of music, is a yearning for what to the chapelgoers was (and is) "a Jerusalem beyond their lives". Isolated and described as a theme it sounds portentous, but it is present in the poems as a structure of feeling which can take many forms, including a desire to return to the beginnings and to be 'born again', and which can be called archetypal only if it is understood to be a felt reality, part of the texture of living experience. Thus in 'Salmon' the fish

> ache towards the one world
> From which their secret
> Sprang,

and

> They unravel the thread to source
> To die at their ancestry's
> Last knot, knowing no question.

'Saying' envisages a language other than any known to man, which the poet rejects as absurd though it may disclose an ultimate paradisal reality which he must remain outside, a prisoner in his own human languages. In 'The Birth of Venus at Aberystwyth',

> The sea still tells the story in its own
>
> Proud language, but few understand it;
> And, as you may imagine, the beauty of it is lost
> In the best translations available....
> Her different world was added to the world....

I do not think it is a great distance from "a Jerusalem beyond their lives" to "her different world"; it is the distance, some would say the regressive distance, from Christian to mythic awareness, and from dogma to archetype. In 'Tricephalos' the third face of the god also has a vision, embodied in a characteristically fine musical metaphor:

> I await wisdom wise enough to know

> It will not come. The inaccessible song
> Upon whose resolution we, awake, expectant,
> Yearning for order, lie, is the one tune
> That we were born for. Its cadence
> Shapes our vision and our blindness.
> The unaccountable is my stone smile.

It is a religious theme and John Ormond, like most symbolists, is a religious poet who works in a ground where creed and the certainty that there is one truth have broken back into the myths, archetypes and perplexities to which these assurances gave a temporary, limiting shape. He is a religious poet, too, insofar as the keynote of his response to the world is awe, which he is capable of making others feel. This is particularly true of 'Ancient Monuments':

> Turn and look back. You'll see horizons
> Much like the ones that they saw,
> The tomb-builders, milleniums ago;
> The channel scutched by rain, the same old
> Sediment of dusk, winter returning.

"What they awaited we, too, still await".

Clearly related to the theme I have illustrated above is a preoccupation with rebirth. In 'Full-length Portrait of a Short Man' Will Bando died "where an unended/Dream of shelter brought him". Twice, in 'Salmon' and 'Ancient Monuments', John Ormond uses the image of a cauldron with unambiguous but unobtrusive reference to the Celtic Cauldron of Rebirth, probably the original of the Holy Grail. In each instance, as is fitting, the image is not to be interpreted in terms of a fixed belief. It is, perhaps, a word of the language we do not know, of "the inaccessible song".

But the song is inaccessible; John Ormond evidently experiences its haunting silence, and the experience makes him a true symbolist, with something to add to the tradition which can be modified only by those who discover its language from within. The inaccessibility is also symbolised by the telling juxtaposition of 'Winter Rite' and 'Tricephalos'. In 'Winter Rite' neophytes approach the god with three faces, invisible under the water of the lake:

> We do not expect to see him,
> He allows us to approach and accepts our gifts
> With the silence of all gods.

In 'Tricephalos' each face of the god speaks in turn. The third face, in the lines I have already quoted, affirms the existence of "the inaccessible song". It seems that even for a god ultimate 'resolution' and 'order' belong to a world outside his world; the men can only listen to the silence of the listening god. But the final paradox I would like to draw attention to in a poet who has such a keen sense of the paradoxical nature of existence is that his preoccupation with a secret language should be expressed with such lucid eloquence, and in rhythms that approach the condition of the art which is his symbol for the inaccessible reality.

The Poetry of Anthony Conran

Whether he is conscious of it or not, for whom the individual poet writes is a principal factor sustaining his imagination and shaping his poetry. To claim to write for oneself alone is to posit or reveal a self closed on the outside but split within, since language is a medium of communication: one cannot talk at all without talking to someone, even if it is only oneself. The nature of the other, whether it be social group or individual or part of the divided self or God, will be implicit in both the language and the form of the address; for the object of words informs their means. Alienation, however, by which the self assumes or is forced into isolation and defines its identity in opposition to all others or to all common worlds, is now the state of some important Western writers and of most trivial ones. This state is often romanticized, and the alienated poet is in fact heir to Romanticism, to the last phase of a movement which began — with Wordsworth, for example — as a deepening of individual consciousness to the point where it discovered its continuous existence with humanity, and ends with desperate solipsism, the self communing with the self in a limbo walled with mirrors, cut off from the meeting place of common experience. The anguish of this state is still producing some notable death songs; but in Britain and America the poets who, in David Jones's words, "intend life" are seeking ways out. Though there could hardly be one way alone, all ways must find or re-create relationship between the poet and others and embody it in the form and language of the poem. The societies of England and America are, of course, especially fragmented and alienating; but there are other areas in which the traditional role of the poet makes his present choice of ways critical for the survival or renewal of civilized human contact. The Anglo-Welsh situation, for example, is one in which the poet can choose between the way of alienation, which must ultimately lead to the far reaches of the absurd where all ideas of poetry become meaningless, and alternative ways of sustaining relationship.

Anglo-Welsh poets are in general highly conscious of the responsibilities of their position between the Welsh language and culture and the Anglicising influences of their medium. Several of them are realizing the potentialities of this unique position to create a poetry that is — at least to an English reader — more Welsh than English. By embodying Welshness, English in Wales acquires some of the value of the primary tongue: it becomes more native, more the speech of relationship, and enriches the English language at large by extending its capacity for expressing the life of a distinct culture. The gain is twofold; but since the position is a critical one, sheer unconsciousness of its dangers can produce a twofold loss. There is, above all, the danger of the Anglo-Welsh poet becoming an agent of alienation, less by willing it than by blindly adopting the manners and assumptions of his alienating medium. Not necessarily, but aided by the poet's default, English can trivialize, divide and isolate. This will happen even if the poet talks sincerely about his love of Wales, but without Welsh culture informing his work; for it is in the culture and its forms that relationship inheres. To my mind, of all Anglo-Welsh poets Anthony Conran has the clearest awareness of this situation, and the intelligence, imagination and skill to meet its challenge. It is, therefore, a matter for grave concern that his achievement has been too little regarded in Wales, though that is exactly what one would expect to happen elsewhere.

A superficial reading of his *Poems 1951-67* could leave one with the impression that Anthony Conran is a late Romantic, primarily a love poet who explores his universal themes through use of ancient mythology, and a private mythology created from a landscape of slate, water and fern, and in language strained by its combination of archaic and modern elements. (He is capable of using "compound gravitation field", "your sweet tyranny", and "doublethink" in a single poem.) An equally superficial reading of *Spirit Level* (1974) might suggest that at a certain point he became self-consciously modern, though one could hardly fail to attend to the 'Gifts' with which the selection ends. These misreadings are, in fact, a simplification and overstatement of my own. Subsequently, I came to see that his achievement as a poet writing in English can be fully appreciated only within the Welsh context. He is, in short, an essentially Anglo-Welsh poet who indelibly marks the language not only with his use of Welsh material, but with the alien purposes and forms which he makes it serve. The measure of his success is, then, the degree to which he makes those purposes and forms native to the language.

I have recorded my initial response in order to indicate how misleading it can be to approach Anthony Conran's work with expectations fostered by reading contemporary English poetry. It is relevant, on the other hand, to consider him in relation to T.S. Eliot and Robert Graves, whom he has acknowledged as influences on his early work, but with the proviso that the Welsh context remains fundamental. There are a few echoes, especially of T.S. Eliot, audible in *Poems 1951-67*. Influence on the verbal level is, however, of little importance. Far more important, I believe, are T.S. Eliot's idea and practice of 'impersonality', and Robert Graves's *The White Goddess*. These are important for having indicated ways in which the poet could escape from the single point of view of the self, and therefore from poetry limited by the perspective and emotions of the dominant, confined ego, and both release the unconscious springs of imagination and create a poetry of relationship. What is apparently archaic, then, and may at first embarrass — Anthony Conran's disclosure of his source of inspiration in the 'darkness' of certain girls he has loved, in his Introduction to *Poems 1951-67*, and his comment on 'Three Swans on the River of Death' in his contribution to *Artists in Wales: 2* (1973) "With this poem I was formally bound apprentice to the muses" — can be seen to be the mark of a mind deeply concerned with the sources of imagination in the unconscious and in extra-personal experience. It is a mark of barbarism, on the other hand, when a poet ceases to think of himself as a medium or servant of poetry, and regards poetry as a medium for expressing himself.

Anthony Conran is an uncompromising critic of what he calls "the poetry of personal definition" and "the anglicising school of self-expression". Nowhere even in his earliest published work do we find him completely seduced by either. In 'Three Swans on the River of Death', for example, the earliest poem to be included in *Poems 1951-67*, the muse commands the poet:

> Give me green words and blood
> And a strange locality to dye
> My froward unborn whiteness with the leaf
> And pastoral homesteads of a name –

It is not the self that asks to be born in order to impose its image on the world, but the mysterious union of forces which "the woman" embodies and which it is the poet's task to give "a local habitation and a name". There is, however, in his considerable body of work, evidence of conflict within the poet between this calling and the temptations of isolating self-expression, and a corresponding search, attended by many and various discoveries, for the ideal form relating self and others in a sustaining pattern. Ritual as the ceremonial binding of relationships is one of Anthony Conran's primary concerns — as a theme requiring urgent attention, but also as a form within which relationships can be enacted naturally and tenderly, in the freedom of the order which the ritual celebrates. Indeed, in his brilliant Introduction to *The Penguin Book of Welsh Verse* (1967), he calls ritual "the art of community living" and stresses its opposition to the bourgeoisie's "cult of individual fulfilment and sincerity". This recognition — deriving from the roots of Welsh culture — determines the direction of his thought and the significance of his formal preoccupations. It shows, also, how poetic form is intimately related to the form of the society to which the poet belongs.

'Solstice', another early poem, concerns the poet's failure to participate in a binding rite:

> And for us, mankind, though we pretend dislike
> For this chill season, surely some gruesome love,
> Some rite, is re-enacted. Even I,

> Mufflered to twice my size, suddenly blaze,
> Pilfer from flame a dance-step. Then, as my legs
> Die down in shame, with anxious glances I walk
> Deliberately cold, being
> Human in both modes of defeat.

The poet is both "I" and "us, mankind". He almost participates in the fire-dance of spring, putting off his individual personality and uniting himself as man with mankind, and man with nature. But he both fails in this, fearing the "gruesome love" of the fertility rite, and is anxious lest others should have witnessed his eccentricity. In this instance, "being human in both modes of defeat" was surely inevitable, since the rite is no longer a socially-given form but a re-creation of the solitary imagination. Nevertheless, here and throughout his work he is searching for ways of overcoming all that defeats the union of "I" and "mankind", and man and creation.

The superb 'Rain', a later poem which the poet himself describes as "almost a fertility rite, set in a London park", shows the union enacted on a cosmic scale where imagery of art and music, religion and sex, embodies the human world. In 'Elegiac Ode for R. Williams Parry', on the other hand, which is surely Anthony Conran's finest early poem and among the most significant Anglo-Welsh poems ever written, the Welsh poet with "his shepherd voice" is commemorated as being at one with his community and with the creation to which its pattern belongs. Significantly, speech is imaged as an organic part of the fundamental structure of the social body:

> Wherever, in the yellow bones
> Of speaking, phrase turns its fingers
>   To touch our bodies,
>   Your immanent ghost
>   Walks proudly in bright eyes.
>
> Whether a gypsy begs water;
> Whether old quarrymen debate
>   By ramshackle bus
>   Football or bible,
>   Or grumble about cold;
>
> Whether the new teacher forgets
> His children no longer listen;
>   Whether ovation
>   Ends the charm, or no,
>   Or the bard goes hungry;
>
> In all gay words, in all complaints,
> Blasphemies or valedictions,
>   The eyes tell their tale,

> Poet, whose homeland
> Harks to the summer stars!

Since speech is part of the structure of the body to which gypsy and quarrymen, teacher and children belong, words are as much a part of them as touch and can be used for all human purposes, not just the creditable or happy ones. The common culture embodied in a common language is an organism in which men and women know themselves and know each other as parts, and with a knowledge that releases human potentiality, not a form of self-consciousness or sentimentality. This is partly what a "homeland" is, but not all; for it "harks to the summer stars" and is part of the universal ordering. The idea of home occurs again and again in Anglo-Welsh poetry, and is often the occasion of nostalgic longing; it is one of Anthony Conran's strengths, however, that the idea — if that is not too abstract a term — embraces relationships that are at once specifically social and profoundly metaphysical.

The act of naming is important to most poets. Once again, however, in his perception of the named and the nameless we can see the comprehensive pattern of Anthony Conran's thought. In 'The Swan', one of his *Mythological Poems* 1959-61, the poet says:

> There is only one gift a man finds good:
> The gift of the original speech
> There was in Eden, the naming craft,
> Acceptance of a man as a man,
> A woman as a woman to this man,
> And God as God.

The emphasis is placed not on personalities but on the primal pattern of relationships in a religious vision of the creation, on "a man as a man", "a woman as a woman to this man", and "God as God". What "the region of the summer stars" means in a Celtic context, Eden means in a universal one: the 'original country'. It is important, therefore, to realize that the Wales to which Anthony Conran has committed himself with a fine sense of its history, literature and society, is for him primarily the 'original country'. I say 'is' instead of 'is a symbol of' because it seems to me that he understands the relationship between the human and the sacred to be actually realized in ceremonies that bind the community to forms instituted out of time. But, of course, no less is true of any Christian.

This is made clear in another fine poem, 'The Harbour'. The poet and his friends have come to a small seaside town that seems familiar, though on an "unexpected seacoast". Here, "all premonitions find their landscape" and "all origins release". The "strangeness" of the town is really familiar, because it belongs to the place of origins that is also man's ultimate and only home. In the church, where they attend a wedding of their friends, for the poet

> Bride and groom are almost any bride and groom,
> Their histories forgotten, condensed by the two candles
> And folded into the paired image I now see.

This 'anonymity' of the bridal pair extends to all who enter the town and participate in the ceremony:

> Anonymous, all enter the whitewalled town,
> And with a sweet lack of the heart's concern
> Meditate here on what has been, what is,
> What shall be: for till you leave this seaport
> All's timely true, nothing is unforeseen.
> A legend has it that this town, called Cana,
> Was where Adam first saw Eve; and therefore
> The anonymous is sweet here, and no trouble
> Of being alone vexes the heart's unnaming
> Of what was known, and now is strange as childhood
> For ever transfixed in the harsh yelp of gulls.

The identification of this place with Cana is literal not symbolic, in the same way that the communicant partakes of Christ's body and blood not of bread and wine symbolising it. Cana, the place of miraculous transubstantiation, is Eden too: so the sacrament of marriage also celebrates the primal union of man and woman. This, then, is the "original country" where "all's timely true" because the ceremony in time re-enacts the timeless pattern. "Unnaming" does not lead to the desolation of a lost identity, but to the roots of being, far below divisive personality, where a man is revealed as a man, "a woman as a woman to this man", and "God as God". But it is a wedding, a specific ceremony in a place that is precisely yet mysteriously rendered, not a vaguely romanticized vision, in which the miracle recurs.

It can be seen, then, how the relationship between the named and the anonymous, and the timely and timeless, is more than just a theme for Anthony Conran, and why it is ritual itself, not the idea of ritual or the expression of ritualistic feeling, that concerns him. But since he has a profound sense of order, of cosmos, it is not surprising that he should have a correspondingly acute awareness of chaos. This is apparent in 'The Marsh', which *Poems 1951-67* prints as a poem in four parts, but *Spirit Level* as four individual poems. Either way, the connections among them are evident, and I shall speak of it as a single poem. It could be seen as the objectification of a state of profound anguish, but the objectification leaves no trace of the excessively personal. "I am marsh", the poet writes, and, like Proteus, proceeds in the poem to become that particular chaos into which a long process of evolving civilization and biology has relapsed. The poem might be read on one level as a metaphor for the chaos from which the poet is saved by a woman, but it subsumes this personal meaning under a form embodying the redemption from unbeing of man and nature:

> Isis of compassion, radius,
> Road of my healing,
> Against whom the lustful wind
> Now mutters, and is calm –
>
> Gather the speckled courage from my silt,
> Make cosmos pivot on deed
> And my opened eyes know East from North,
> Flicker tall shadows; be man.

A later poem, 'Prospero's Dream', is even more disturbing than 'The Marsh' in the intensity of its anguish. For Anthony Conran in this poem, Prospero is surely the individual at his greatest possible distance from mankind and God, quintessential embodiment of the secular mind's urge to know everything — in fact, to become a self-creating god. Thus the monologue begins with a statement of total opposition between self and world ("Look what the world does. I am marooned") and recalls the birth into isolation of the completely sceptical yet 'omnipotent' intelligence ("I was a god") who cannot accept his place in nature as man, child of God:

> I remember my tugging lips at the breast which flowered me like a bee.
> I remember the recalcitrant dribbling of water onto the rocks.
> Even the red ants on the floor took care to involve me.
> Even dog dirt was a splendid intellectual conundrum.
>
> Then, cold salted my cheeks. Grey sky blinked as I looked up into emptiness.
> My loneliness ached in the hungry bowels of the sea.
> Hands had taken my struggling feet, comforters were bound round me like chains.
> I was adrift in the wicker cradle of myself.
> The yelp of gulls instructed me with a friendship I could neither trust nor disbelieve.
> I learnt the specious navigation of the tides.
> I mastered the way of the moon and half-suspected her of fraud.

D.H. Lawrence, a poet formally very different from Anthony Conran, wrote some of his most haunting poems about the perils of falling into knowledge of the self, out of "the hands of the living God". I believe that Anthony Conran, too, would probably describe this as the kind of hell to which we are most prone, whether as rationalists or poets, and that his contempt of "the poetry of self definition" reflects a true awareness of where it leads. And, of course, even the poet who 'intends life' may know in himself the desolation of all self-consuming illusionists, as this hard-edged, raw-nerved poem shows.

Naturally, in an essay it is impossible for the critic even to point to everything he has noticed and valued in the poet's work, and he is in danger of obscuring its variousness with his selectivity. Since this is so, it must just be said that the three fine longer poems in *Poems 1951-67*, 'The Mountain', 'Guernica' and 'Day Movements', are an index to the variety that characterizes the whole. Nor can the recent *Gifts* be considered adequately here, because they represent an achievement to which a whole essay of this length could scarcely do justice. It will have to be enough in this place if my sparse comments can indicate why I believe them to be easily among the most important poems by any poet of Anthony Conran's generation, and among the most hopeful for the future.

It should be clear from his own writings (for Anthony Conran is, alas, the best interpreter of his own work; indeed, lack of proper critical response to it in Wales has made him one of the few), and from this interpretation of them, why he maintains that

> A third person poetry can no longer enact a civilization. The
>   poet cannot stabilize his art
>   in the tarnishing medium of I and IT.

He believes, however, that Welsh poetry offers an alternative. "Welsh poetry is second-person poetry. A poem praises, satirizes or laments within the magnetic field of I and Thou. The giving and receiving of gifts, like the giving and receiving of poetry itself, formed the central arch of Welsh civilization; and the celebration of gift and giver an important sub-division of the Welsh poetic art". His *Gifts* are, in fact, the consummate expression of a complete system of belief about the nature and purpose of poetry towards which Anthony Conran has been working for at least fifteen years, in relating his own practice to what he has learnt from the study and translation of Welsh poetry. Like other poems written at least as early as 1956, these are designed as part of the rituals, whether birthdays, weddings, christenings or the ceremonies proper to all relationship, that express and confirm an ordered world; and they prove the truth of his contention (in the Introduction to *The Penguin Book of Welsh Verse*) that "Formal praise, if it is well executed and right for the occasion, can be a most deeply satisfying thing". The poems are skilfully disciplined in form, and allow considerable freedom to the speaking voice and to the development of thought that is often metaphysical in subtlety and subject. The poems are therefore instances of the freedom within order which the rituals celebrate. When he chooses to do so, Anthony Conran is second to none in his rendering of objects; but there is all the difference in the world between the objects in these poems – the conker, the silver spoon and the spirit level are just three examples — and things described by an observer with the aim of capturing their thisness, or by one who wishes to define himself in relation to them. The objects are, in fact, not rendered as things at all, but as gifts and therefore as emblems or symbols of relationship within the ordered world. In giving the spirit level, for example, he writes:

> I pray for you through this emblem
> That each of you in each,
> The straight wood, the bubble of oil,
> True centre reach,
>
> And right-angled with the world,
> Hold its full sphere
> With the delicate poise
> Of the hoof of a deer.

Often, as in 'Heron', there is extreme metaphysical concentration in his philosophical and imaginative definition of the proper relationship of man to woman, and the human order to the divine; yet the poems are rarely difficult and never obscure. It should be said, also, that most of the *Gifts* (and to my mind 'Spirit Level', 'Three Lily Seeds', 'Silver Spoon', 'Heron' and 'Jasper' in particular) are beautiful, wise and serene, an extremely rare and unfashionable combination of virtues in modern verse. Indeed, the remarkable thing about them is their ability to "enact a civilization". In his essay in *Artists in Wales: 2* (1973), Anthony Conran asks: "How can such a poem, starting life as a present to one person not as an intimate token of affection but as a public gesture to honour him at some important point in his or her life — how can such a piece be a serious work of art, able to communicate outside the immediate circle for whom it was written?" Certainly, the ordered world celebrated by ritual and embodied in particular communities, has to be acknowledged as the meeting place of a minority within contemporary Western society — though a far larger minority than the bulk of modern art would lead one to infer. Nevertheless, accepting that world and offering themselves as part of it, these poems also enact a community where I and Thou and the emblems belong to an order defining and sustaining them, and where language used wisely and with cultured naturalness is real speech. It is necessary to add, too, that as 'Christmas Song' and 'Six Poems about God' show, poets with a strong awareness of the sacred are usually far more aware than others of the limitations of words. And of the importance of words; for if words can only unname the Word, all human order and relationship is to some extent dependent on the state of our common language and the poet's use of it. He can either accept the breakdown of significant human contact in the uses to which he puts his art, or, like Anthony Conran, work for contact against the trend.

John Tripp: *Collected Poems* 1958-78

Of bards, John Tripp writes:

> In places where the language is spoken
>   they dissolve into the people....
>   ('Bards')

This is something neither he nor any of his fellow Anglo-Welsh poets could be said to do. (Today, it is probably equally inapplicable to most well-known Welsh poets.) However, because the idea of the poet as a man of his people is still potent in Wales, and because there are areas of rural and industrial Wales where community exists, the poet who is an outsider in Wales is likely to feel isolation far more acutely than most poets do in societies where their alienation from the people is taken for granted, and even romanticized, often by the poets themselves. These feelings may be exacerbated for the Anglo-Welsh poet by his guilt at not speaking "the language", and his guilt at having a softer life than his hard-worked ancestors but with what he feels to be less human worth to show for it. He may then feel almost equally ill at ease in Welsh-speaking rural Wales and the Anglicized industrial South — but with that special kind of unease that can occur only at home. This, generally, is John Tripp's situation. It makes him familiar with what he calls, in a poem on Dylan Thomas in New York, "the old black factor, chill of aloneness", and places him on the border between belonging and not belonging. From there he looks one way towards dissolution into the people, and the other towards loss of identity. He is where the sense of individuality — of being singular, and a singular being — is most intense and most discontenting. As far as most readers and writers of poetry nowadays are concerned, he is, in the words of one of his admired Conrad's characters, "one of us".

Language offers John Tripp less comfort than it offered Dylan Thomas. For Tripp is without a religion or a myth, and has no use for the symbols or metaphors by which harsh realities may be transcended and discords made harmonious in another dimension. In the final poem of his *Collected Poems*, 'Praise at Llanstephan', he sets his feelings beside the faith of a religious artist:

> The artist was gentle and kind, secure
> in his praising skills. I only felt
> things were what they appeared to be
> and behind them was nothing.

It is a bleak note on which to end a book that, on the whole, neither makes nor induces negation, but it records a feeling and not a dogma. An important feeling, however: one denoting the blackness against which his compassion is exercised and his comedy enacted. We should also see against this his healthy fear of softening the reality of suffering with words of false hope or imaginary comfort. The poignancy of tone and detail in his poems of personal loss, most notably 'Separation', is one outcome of his determination to see things as they appear to be, rather than as he or anyone else might wish them; another is the compassion which pervades his *Collected Poems*, and is shown for animals as well as people, but especially for those who, like Dewi Emrys, are brought to "the skidding edge". Heir to the spirit of Idris Davies and akin to Glyn Jones, but without his verbal opulence, John Tripp is a poet on the realist side of Romanticism.

John Tripp's poetic character, his language and stance, is as demotic as Dylan Thomas's and Vernon Watkins's are hierophantic. Without either their symbolism or R.S. Thomas's "deciduous language", his word hoard is popular modern prose and speech, though as one would expect of an admirer of Roland Mathias and Geoffrey Hill, his 'historical' poems use words appropriate to their periods. He can write a heavily adjectival verse, coming up pat with words advertising disgust, dereliction and decay. He can be too prosy (but is often very funny in his prosaic verses, as in 'Mission'), and also a self-parodist. 'Weymouth in August' has these weaknesses:

> Pink-and-white candyfloss squashes underfoot
> as I'm swept on a pokerface tide
> of Cockney and Taff, Yorkie and Pak
> towards a Bingo Bonanza. It is useless
> to struggle. In the plastic caff, years of grease
> cake on the fan blades, and whiffs
> of chip-fat float through the Xpelair....

Here he is ostensibly at his most uncompromisingly anti-poetic, but actually relishing the seedy atmosphere (significantly, he has a Graham Greene novel with him). Weymouth, however, is not his country, but somewhere too alien for him to feel uncomfortably at home in — he is much better on Penarth between the wars. Usually, in his poems detailing urban dereliction or the high life of the lowly, he avoids both using his settings as a metaphor for spiritual death-in-life, with which T.S. Eliot's example addicted many would-be poets of the city, and romanticizing squalor. Both ways of seeing are from a height. But John Tripp is a democrat: his run-down or tawdry places are lived in either by himself or by people like himself. He is a kind of Anglo-Welsh Philip Marlowe. He knows what the more desperate existentialists are talking about, but has a sense of humour which keeps him on the unpretentious side of the absurd. He will often turn on himself with biting irony, and then with a jest imply that the fate of such a wretch is a matter of small moment. In such poems he is funny, serious, sad; and sophisticated, not at all unliterary. When in 'On my Fortieth Birthday' he writes:

> I am piling my rubbish against oblivion,
> stacking it against the dark.
> If you go up to Aberystwyth
> you'll find my name mis-spelt in the dust.

the full significance of the lines depends on our recognising the allusion to *The Waste Land* and the Biblical meaning of 'dust', and also, perhaps, that in Aberystywyth in summer, TRIP may be written in the sand.

One of John Tripp's principal gifts is his ability to capture the look and feel of a place or a period, and often both, in a few lines. Here, for example, is a deserted airfield:

> Flung down between useless scrub and good farm marl,
> it sits there like some patrician folly
> nobody wants, unmarked on maps,
> with one riddled windsock, dented oil-drums and a few
> rotted chocks, old sand seeping from bags
> on the gun emplacements.
> ('Airfield')

The place is depicted, characteristically, not for its atmosphere alone, but to present the world of those who are to be celebrated and commemorated. In 'Airfield', these are the men who flew on missions from this place during the Second World War. John Tripp sees them with a quizzical affection, implying the distance between his world and theirs with a beautifully right, but slightly critical and even mocking use of their language:

> Seeing it, I think of the brash squadrons
> bundled off to their dates
> in that jubilee of turbulence,
> the posthumous gongs and citations
> for an élite of valorous wings.

But he sees them above all with a gratitude and respect which the honesty of his ambivalent reaction underlines:

> Would I be here but for that kind
> of fealty to a striped flag....

Significantly, it is their fealty to a national cause as well as his personal debt to them that he acknowledges.

Despite his self-presentation as an outsider, and his anti-bardic poetic character, John Tripp in some of his best poems is fulfilling an important traditional role of the Welsh poet. Writing of the *Cynfeirdd* in his review of Gwyn Williams's *The Burning Tree*, David Jones quoted the line in *Y Gododdin* which may be translated "The bards of the world appraise the men of valour". "One could hardly put it more clearly than that," he wrote. "The poetry of the 'first-bards' was concerned with a recalling and appraisement of the heroes in lyric form" ('Welsh Poetry', *Epoch and Artist*).

John Tripp in some of his most powerful poems appraises "the men of valour". One could hardly put it more clearly than that. Nor is it only men he appraises, but also creatures such as a tomcat and a Welsh terrier which are heroically true to their natures. His tomcat is naturally a killer, but not, like Ted Hughes's (in 'Esther's Tomcat') "unkillable". It is a resilient, enduring, but finally vulnerable mortal outcast that earns Tripp's respect, not a savage, elemental principle. Violence holds no excitement for him, but he honours the spirit that comes up against a hard world, and instead of giving way, has to be beaten. Animal or human, most of his heroes are battered within or without, but not self-defeated, and most endure under stress. There is his old family doctor, for instance;

> He was the Doctor, serving six forgotten
> poor square miles, carrying his leather bag
> wherever it was needed by his people,
> sitting tight within the dignity of an oath
> between the bad hours of his own sickness.
>
> ('The Doctor')

But endurance alone does not win his admiration. Time and again, as in this poem, goodness and loyalty are the heroic virtues he celebrates. These he recognises in David Jones and Idris Davies, too, and honours them in two of his finest poems. David Jones is "one soldier of goodness and truth", and of Idris Davies he writes:

> His goodness seeps down the years to remind us
> of faith to be kept in the ruins.

'A David Jones Mural at Llanthony' and 'In memory of Idris Davies', together with 'Turner in Old Age' and, to a lesser degree, 'Purgatory Revisited', 'Dewi Emrys' and 'A Quest for Light', concentrate his gift for using biographical details and the vivid phrase to evoke the quality of a life. When his admiration is less warm, however, as in 'Caradoc Evans Revisited', his sketch of the man does almost nothing that a brief prose biography could not do, while in the third section of 'Purgatory Revisted', his poem in memory of Gwenallt, admiration for the poet's words (or rather Anthony Conran's translation of 'Rhydcymerau') leads him to quote them excessively. Here, self-criticism has been sacrificed to generosity, a quality amply manifested in John Tripp's *Collected Poems*. It is this, together with its ally compassion, that must be added to the strength perceived in his old headmaster, before the following lines can be applied to the poet himself:

> Sometimes I think
> his kind of iced wisdom is best –
> the goodness of sad reason.
>   ('Headmaster')

Nine years ago, reviewing *The Lilting House* for *The Anglo-Welsh Review*, I found the poems representing John Tripp discursive. They seemed to me to waste their strength of feeling in telling us about his disenchantment, instead of showing it, as in my view much of the writing by the younger Anglo-Welsh poets of that time was doing. As a criticism of those poems (only the best of which, 'Diesel to Yesterday', is included in his *Collected Poems*), I still think it fair. It would not be, however, if applied to this book, the greater part of which consists of poems written in the last decade. Having once written of John Tripp that he "often neglects the means by which poetry shows us reasons for listening", I want now to record that, for me, he is one of the most arresting and moving of contemporary Anglo-Welsh poets.

R.S. Thomas: Prytherch and After

"Iago Prytherch": to an English ear, the name has an exotic, foreign sound, but Prytherch is, 'A Peasant'[1] tells us, "just an ordinary man of the bald Welsh hills". The images in the first ten lines of the poem relate the man and his activities to the land. R.S. Thomas portrays him as an earthy man, solitary, (in a Wordsworthian fashion), hard-working, austere in his way of life, (and in harmony as such with "bald" hills, "crude earth", and "gaunt sky"), apparently without culture or spiritual qualities; indeed, the images stress animality and more than hint at savagery and stupidity:

> Docking mangels, chipping the green skin
> From the yellow bones with a half-witted grin
> Of satisfaction,...

But the portrait already implies some complexity and even conflict in the attitude of the poet producing it. It contains a Romantic, especially Wordsworthian, celebration of the solitary labourer, who is a child of earth, a primitive, and virtually identified with the powers of nature. Yet Prytherch, also, is almost less than human, and in his savagery and vacancy of mind, reminiscent of the "peasantry" as seen by Caradoc Evans, or by outsiders who caricature people they do not understand and are afraid of, because of their difference from the "civilized" norm.

The next lines form a transition between the portrait and its message:

> And then at night see him fixed in his chair
> Motionless, except when he leans to gob in the fire.
> There is something frightening in the vacancy of his mind.
> His clothes, sour with years of sweat
> And animal contact, shock the refined,
> But affected, sense with their stark naturalness.

The vacancy of mind and the fear it engenders, suggested by the portrait, are summed up. But then the attitude of the outside observer is criticised. He is shocked because his sense is "refined, but affected"; while what Prytherch has is "stark naturalness". Finally, Prytherch is celebrated as "your prototype", who "preserves his stock" against the warring elements and even death. "Stock" is rich in meaning, implying inheritance or line of descent as well as animals and material possessions, and preparing, with a backward look at his half-witted, less than human character, for the triumphant statement at the end, where Prytherch, "a winner of wars", is seen "enduring like a tree". With the imagery of warfare, we are reminded that 'A Peasant' was written during the Second World War: a fact which strengthens the celebration by emphasising his strong life-serving qualities, as distinct from his merely stockish animality.

Clearly, like other Romantic artists, like Wilfred Owen, for example, in his position between his men and those guilty of their slaughter, R.S. Thomas stands uneasily, but in a position of creative tension, between his subject and a foreign or unenlightened readership. He himself has "the refined, but affected, sense" shocked by Prytherch, but he sees and values the "stark naturalness". He writes, in 'A Peasant' and in other poems, both as a penitent who humbles his own pride, and as a spokesman for Prytherch who humbles his readers'.

In speaking of his experience as a young curate in English Maelor and later at Manafon, in Montgomeryshire, R.S. Thomas helps us to understand his position in relation to Wales and the Welsh people which strongly influenced his earlier poems. From Maelor,

> I could see the Welsh hills some fifteen miles away in the evening, magical and mysterious as ever. I realised what I had done. My place was not here on this plain amongst these Welsh with English accents and attitudes. I set about learning Welsh, so as to get back to the real Wales of my imagination....
> Manafon was an eye-opener to me. Here I became aware of the clash between dream and reality. I was a proper little bourgeois, brought up delicately, with the mark of the church and the library on me. I had seen this part of the country from the train in the evening through a romantic haze. I now found myself among hard, materialistic, industrious people, who measured each other in acres and pounds; Welshmen who turned their backs on their inheritance... I can remember the lonely figures in the fields, hoeing or docking mangels, hour after hour. What was going on in their heads, I wonder? The question remains unanswered to this day.[2]

The predicament of the romantic, the "proper little bourgeois", of delicate upbringing, bearing "the mark of the church and the library" on him, is not uncommon, especially among English poets since the late eighteenth century. Indeed, in a class society in which poets born into the bourgeoisie desire to get close to "the people", it is a standard predicament, and underlies many a "clash between dream and reality". In the case of R.S. Thomas, of course, the predicament was intensified by his being a priest, with a special mission and service to perform for actual people, and by his beginnings as an Anglicized Welshman, with an outsider's romanticism, and a passionate dedication to repossessing and confirming his Welshness.

Affectation, bourgeois romanticism, Anglicization: these are what R.S. Thomas felt the need to eradicate from himself. At the same time, he was a priest with a duty to bring the gospel's spiritual gift to his parishioners and foster it in them. He was thus in the position of submitting his dream to the judgement of their reality while bringing them to the reality of the spirit. The word *reality*, however, has to be seen in the light of "the real Wales of my imagination", for Thomas is true to his Romantic heritage in both valuing the reality of the imagination and dramatizing the difficult relationship, and at times opposition, between the real and the imagined. For him as priest and poet, the figure of Prytherch or of other labourers — all are essentially one figure: his creation on the basis of real people, encountered, or observed at a distance in the fields — is especially important. The figure is a focus of his conflicts, not a stable 'character' but a symbol through which the poet dramatizes and seeks to resolve his predicament, so that he approaches Prytherch in different ways at different times. We hear in 'The Minister', in respect of some old harvest traditions:

> That was a fad of Prytherch
> Of Nant Carfan; but the bugger was dead.[3]

But this only emphasises Prytherch's malleability as poetic symbol and subject of dialogue — on one occasion his 'death' serves a thematic purpose, but he lives on for R.S. Thomas in all his early books, (with rarer apppearances after *Tares*), because of all he touches in his feelings and questions in his mind.

In 'The Dark Well',[4] Prytherch is "the man/Who more than all directed my slow/Charity where there was need". Again, R.S. Thomas shows his consciousness of his readers, and his relation to them is part of the poem's meaning. He is aware of writing about fundamental realities, but for a sophisticated audience for whom Prytherch is less a man than a "story":

> There are two hungers, hunger for bread
> And hunger of the uncouth soul
> For the light's grace. I have seen both,
> And chosen for an indulgent world's
> Ear the story of one whose hands
> Have bruised themselves on the locked doors
> Of life; whose heart, fuller than mine
> Of gulped tears, is the dark well
> From which to draw, drop after drop,
> The terrible poetry of his kind.

The fact that he is writing a Welsh "story" for English or Anglicized readers increases his self-consciousness. The world listens with an "indulgent" ear, giving him a kind if condescending hearing, but self-indulgently, for compared to Prytherch they are soft and corrupt. The "indulgent world" is the "they" of the opening, who "see you as they see you,/A poor farmer with no name". But to the poet, "you are Prytherch, the man". Here, then, Thomas, who recognises and identifies Prytherch, is mediator between him and the world. He is closer to Prytherch than the world is, closer to Prytherch than to the world, but his distance from Prytherch and relative closeness to the world make the disregarded, suffering man the source of his poetry — as this compassionate poem frankly confesses.

At other times, Prytherch is more part of the poet than outside him. Like 'The Dark Well', 'Temptation of a Poet'[5] presents him as the source of the early poetry. His importance to R.S. Thomas, both as part of him and as teacher, question or questioner, standing outside him, is shown here by the poet's hesitation between describing Prytherch as co-builder of his poetic world, and as one with whom he found it, "lingering on the farm". Now Prytherch tempts him to return to the past, and is virtually identified with nature and the poetry of nature. "With nature's lore green" on his tongue, he tempts Thomas to turn back from his quest for "a spring that my heart fumbles". Thus he figures also both in the poet's skirmishes in the traditional Protestant war between flesh and spirit, and in the Romantic conflict between mind and heart.

Obviously, Prytherch is far too malleable to be consistent, and while he is Thomas's questioner, Thomas himself, as in 'Which?',[6] sometimes asks which of several meanings he represents, and whether he was "a real man". However, he is usually consistent as a survival and defender of an old, pre-industrial way of life in the countryside; one who refuses, in the words of 'Which?', "to change/His lean horse for the quick tractor". But R.S. Thomas can vary even this, as we see in 'Too Late',[7] a poem from the same collection, which describes Prytherch as a servant of the materialism which the poet hates: "a dog/To the pound's whistle", and one who has resigned his "membership of an old nation". He is a victim of "the cold brain of the machine", so that as the machine's destructiveness begins to appear more strongly as a theme in R.S. Thomas's poetry (though present there from the start), Prytherch can serve this too.

Yet, having made due allowance for Prytherch's creative inconsistency as a symbol, we may see that for R.S. Thomas he represents, above all, natural man, in constant touch with the harsh and enduring realities of life. He is in this respect his — and our — prototype. He is Thomas as man the creature, stripped of book learning, artistry, and sophistication; his reality, as opposed to his dream. As man, Prytherch has — unconsciously — man's spiritual need, his hunger "for the light's grace". But he also represents what R.S. Thomas must leave behind him before he can develop further as a religious poet. For Thomas himself is not a man of "uncouth soul", but a pilgrim, called away by intellect and spirit from man's natural condition. It is important to note, however, that he speaks in 'The Dark Well' of "the light's grace", not of grace's light, and while the former may be seen as a metaphor for the latter, the place of supernatural grace in R.S. Thomas's poetry is hard to determine. Indeed, he is among the least devotional of Christian poets, and his mysticism focuses on nature and on God, with little reference to Christ, while Prytherch's "thought's bareness" is identified, in another poem,[8] with absence of "science and art". Nevertheless, in dwelling on Prytherch R.S. Thomas becomes aware of the danger not just of looking back nostalgically, or of repeating himself as a poet, but of celebrating natural man as the ideal.

Not infrequently, we see R.S. Thomas being tempted to celebrate the sufficiency of man's closeness to the earth, as though he were virtually part of it, and to spiritualize the relationship. His development as a religious poet, however, depends upon his recognition of the inadequacy of man rooted in earth. In 'Truth',[9] the man in the fields seems to him always to have been there, while he comes and goes, not just literally, but at "the mind/Calling". He does not deny what the man intimates, that

> the heart's roots
> Are here under this black soil
> I labour at.

He is without question rooted emotionally in the soil. Nor does he deny that nature can survive "the smooth town". In fact, he desires this. However, 'Truth' should not be taken to state his ultimate belief:

> but the truth's here
> Closer than the world will confess,
> In this bare bone of life that I pick.

This is not Thomas's statement, it is what the man in the fields intimates. All the same, for him too, the truth in this essential, hard reality is "closer than the world will confess". But that is to say there is more of the truth here than the world will assent to, not that it is R.S. Thomas's final truth. Stark natural settings, and imagery of bones and bare trees, delineate the austere side of his vision, which in turn expresses his belief that truth is to be found in man's essential condition, stripped of worldly illusions and lies. But that condition includes hunger for "the light's grace" and its absence here makes this an intimation, not of absolute truth, but of truth relative to the world's evasion of reality. The poet has to follow "the mind/Calling", ranging through poetry and other arts, through philosophy and science, if only finally to reject them for a God who is beyond all ideas and images.

In 'Truth', the man in the fields intimates,

> Every right word on your tongue
> Has a green taste.

This recalls "nature's/Lore green on your tongue" in 'Temptation of a Poet', in which Thomas, who has a liking for puns, identifies Prytherch with nature's law as well as nature's lore. Nature's law without "the light's grace" is one thing, however, and R.S. Thomas is not finally its adherent. But nature's lore in the sense of words with "a green taste" is another, and he could not utterly reject it without ceasing to be a poet. That is to say, the words dear to him, which embody or intimate his values, are drawn from nature and the elements. He uses mechanical and commercial terms with distaste and even hatred, and in *H'm* develops his idea of the machine, in evidence as early as 'Cynddylan on a Tractor', into a mythology of evil.

In 'Once',[10] the first poem in *H'm*, man and woman, "confederates of the natural day", go forth "to meet the Machine". In 'Earth'[11] the poet, speaking as man, addresses God:

> Where have your incarnations
> Gone to? The flesh is too heavy
> To wear you, God of light
> And fire. The machine replaces
> The hand that fastened you
> To the cross, but cannot absolve us.

In 'Soliloquy'[12] God addresses man: "Within the churches/You built me you genuflected/To the machine". The most striking single feature of the book as a whole is its development of R.S. Thomas's myth-making faculty. This is a faculty shadowed in earlier work but in *H'm* it is a controlling rather than a subsidiary faculty. The myths are consistent not in telling a single story but in feeling, and in so far as the poems concerned with this theme are metaphorical statements of the cause of man's estrangement from God and from his own nature as his worship of the machine. At first, it may appear that R.S. Thomas's idea of the machine is an abstraction scarcely less injurious to creative thought than the abstracting tendency of the mechanical principle itself; that the dramatic form of the metaphors merely conceals the dogged repetition of a prejudice. On further acquaintance, however, one can see that the machine, if it does reflect an outlook as obdurate as the mechanical principle it stands for, is also being used as a flexible symbol for the processes by which man is divorced from his humanity by the false idols he creates. *H'm* has close affinities, which occasionally extend to phrase and cadence, with Ted Hughes's *Crow* (1970). In each God is a protagonist; in each the influence of *Genesis* is frankly acknowledged, though R.S. Thomas's use of the Judaic Creation-myth is less plastic and truer to the original than Ted Hughes's, and is without the grim and witty irreverence of *Crow*. R.S. Thomas does not rewrite *Genesis* in order to express an anti-Christian vision, but interpolates the worship of the machine as an agent of the Fall, as a prime cause of anguish, estrangement, and evil.

The unity of theme finds expression in the voice's resonant personality, that eloquence over a narrow but intense range of emotion which is characteristic of R.S. Thomas. It is an astringent, deceptively plain voice whose movement and tone embody tension between natural sensuousness and the iron control of conscience: at this stage, images of natural beauty and the feelings they engender enter the poetry only to be checked or contained by the stern perspective of a mind attuned to spiritual discipline. The voice is vibrant with restrained sensuousness, and rarely speaks unless urged to by pain. Like the robin likened to Christ in 'Song',[13] the poet

> Comes to us in his weakness
> But with a sharp song.

At this point in his development, it is plain that R.S. Thomas is not the latter-day Georgian or even the 'nature' poet he has been called, usually by those who are understandably nervous of the religious centre of his work. Nor is it adequate to define him in terms of a tradition containing such poets as George Herbert and Edward Thomas. If he is formally closer to Edward Thomas, his spirit is closer to the Eliot of *Ash Wednesday*; and his anguish is nearer to Kierkegaard's — it is of the *Via Negativa* rather than the dark periods between moments of union with God that Herbert expresses:

> Why no! I never thought other than
> That God is that great absence
> In our lives, the empty silence
> Within, the place where we go
> Seeking, not in hope to
> Arrive or find.[14]

As in the case of George Herbert, however, it is only misleading to call R.S. Thomas a 'nature' poet if the word is meant in its usual narrow sense. 'Postscript'[15] begins: "As life improved, their poems/Grew sadder and sadder". "Improved" refers ironically to the belief in progress which R.S. Thomas does not share. The machine represents materialistic civilization with its commerce and industry, and exclusion of natural and spiritual realities. This is seen dominating the entire physical and mental environment so that, figuratively-speaking, if not quite literally, "the forests/Of metal" cover the world, and

> the one human
> Sound was the lament of
> The poets for deciduous language.

"Deciduous language" signifies more than either words with "a green taste" or nature's lore or law. The phrase unites the language of nature with the language of the Fall, and defines what Thomas means by "human" creation, as opposed to mechanical "production". It is the language of Creation and therefore expresses both spiritual values and man's place in the natural order – for example, all flesh is grass, or light symbolises grace, and the tree the Cross. The union of nature and religion in "deciduous language" is richly imagined in 'The Prayer',[16] in *Laboratories of the Spirit*:

>   Let leaves
> from the deciduous Cross
>   fall on us, washing
> us clean, turning our autumn
>   to gold by the affluence of their fountain.

Indeed, there is a sense in which the language of nature *is* the language of Christianity, for this is not only the language of Christ with his parables of wheat and tares but of the religious spirit at all times and in all places, and we might almost go as far as to say that once the tree as a symbol fails, the meaning of the Cross falls with it.

"Deciduous language" is traditionally the language of poetry, and, incidentally, not infrequently continues to supply the language of value for poets writing of the urban world, with a far more positive attitude to industrial society than R.S. Thomas's. But failure of "deciduous language" in a technological civilization is especially critical for the religious poet. For example, David Jones was acutely aware of the problems arising for the religious poet when words like *tree, water, blood,* and *bread* lose symbolic significance. R.S. Thomas feels the problem of language even more desperately — as a Christian poet, as a 'nature' poet, and as a Welshman using what he regards as a foreign language destructive of the real Wales. The latter respect is a source of tension in some of his later poems in particular, but the problem of language is compounded for him by the inherent inadequacy of words to express religious experience — the inadequacy which mystics have always felt of language to express the reality of God, not only when the language of earth and seasons, of birds, beasts and flowers, loses its potency and even becomes *un*natural for many people. For R.S. Thomas, like David Jones, the Christian order, "deciduous language", and the survival of a Welsh-speaking culture founded on rural Wales are closely interconnected. One consequence of this is that both passionately mythologize history, with the result, in the case of R.S. Thomas, that in some poems he expresses a disdain, even a Swiftian loathing, for urbanized and Anglicized people. This can be repellent, but what usually saves it from being merely a cold, hard arrogance is the suffering in the poems: torment and even self-contempt at the inheritance which originally made him an outsider in "the real Wales of my imagination", and the struggle with himself of a man who knows that charity does not come easily to him.

A positive result of his trinity of concerns is that poems occur throughout his work which celebrate the beauty of nature perceived as the Creation, and experienced in Welsh landscapes. In 'The Moor',[17] for example, traditional natural and religious images — "clean colours", "wind over grass", "the air crumbled/And broke on me generously as bread" — serenely convey his experience of the elements as sacramental: "It was like a church to me". The sense of holiness is experienced without prayer, but with "stillness/Of the heart's passions", and "the mind's cession/Of its kingdom". The point is not of course that R.S. Thomas has achieved the "vacancy" which he ascribes to Prytherch, but that he experiences nature religiously, not as a substitute for supernatural grace, but in his love of the Creation, without desire or mental effort. Natural and religious images are united again in 'The Bright Field',[18] in a field lit by the sun, "that was the pearl/of great price, the one field that had/the treasure in it", and "the miracle/of the lit bush". Again, mental effort ceases with the benediction of a glimpse of eternity, and he realizes:

> Life is not hurrying
>
> on to a receding future, nor hankering after
> an imagined past. It is the turning
> aside like Moses to the miracle
> of the lit bush, to a brightness
> that seemed as transitory as your youth
> once, but is the eternity that awaits you.

It is significant that this is the most radiant poem in the collection, *Laboratories of the Spirit*, in which, with refreshing daring and boldness, he brings the language of science to his attempt to intimate God's unknowable reality. That language has theological point, but it is not the language of love. As David Jones says of "newfangled technicalities", "increasingly exacting mechanical devices", and "creatures of chemicals", in the Preface to *In Parenthesis*:[19] it is difficult to recognise them "as true extensions of ourselves, that we may feel for them a native affection, which alone can make them magical for us". Or it may be that, as R.S. Thomas says in 'Emerging':[20]

> Circular as our way
> is, it leads not back to that snake-haunted
> garden, but onward to the tall city
> of glass that is the laboratory of the spirit.

But it is in "leaves/from the deciduous Cross", in the garden, or in the moor or the bright field, that he is moved to love and praise.

I will conclude with a discussion of *Frequencies* (1978), because it is in my view the culmination of the greatest phase of his writing to date, which occurred during the Seventies, and because I do not think the later books, although containing a number of fine poems, move beyond the position he arrives at there. *Frequencies* continues, with the greater strength and intensity of *Laboratories of the Spirit*, the new movement which begins in the poetry with *H'm*. The movement is not new in the sense of marking a discontinuity between early and later Thomas. But he now asks explicit metaphysical questions, apprehended existentially, in the quick of his being, which he formerly asked in relation to matters like the state of Wales or even his role as priest, from which his techniques made him seem more detached. He sounds vibrancies, and signals given and received, with an unmistakable voice which is now still more urgent, more flexibly expressive, more the voice of a man speaking from the centre of his inner life, and creating powerful dramatic lyrics that seem the effortless outcome of natural speech. He brings new sciences to aid the perennial spiritual pilgrimage, and a more questioning intelligence to the nature of language, the pilgrim-poet's principal obstacle and guide. Comparable to poets such as W.S. Graham, C.H. Sisson and Geoffrey Hill in his concern with the ways in which language mediates or obscures reality, he brings to the problem a tortured awareness, almost unique among living poets, of his equivocal relation to the particular language he uses.

There is one fine poem in *Frequencies*, 'The Small Country',[21] which will be vital to any discussion of R.S. Thomas's Wales:

>   everything
> on this shrinking planet favours the survival
> of the small people, whose horizons
> are large only because they are content to look at them
> from their own hills.

There are several other poems bearing directly on this subject too. But the fact that there are now fewer of these than in his early books does not mean that Wales is no longer a centre of his concern. It means that as his existentialist metaphysics has found ever more direct expression in his later poems, so he has come increasingly to write from inside the experience of being a Welshman who lives the related temporal and eternal questions in his specific part of the world, and therefore to address himself less to a world from which he is in some ways detached. However, this is an increasing tendency, not a position consistently maintained, for in a number of later poems the prophet addressing a people is still a vestigial figure, in process of passing into the man who articulates his essential problematic being, though the language of his poems prevents him confirming that being as wholly, unselfconsciously, Welsh.

If there is a change in *Frequencies* within the movement continued from *Laboratories of the Spirit*, it may be found in R.S. Thomas's position further out on his "peninsula of the spirit".[22] The book contains more poems than ever before in which the sea is setting or metaphor. While the stone church near the sea is still important, it seems that the Church as institution and body of doctrine is now more closely associated with Kierkegaard's Christendom, and the poet looks frequently to the sea as metaphor for that which does not, in the words of 'The White Tiger',[23] confine God within "our definition of him". In these poems the paradox abounds of "this great absence/that is like a presence",[24] but the most palpable images of God are found in depth and height, when the man on the peninsula contemplates the ocean deeps or the night sky, ranging the cosmos for his signs. Although dread and doubt are both either provoked or imaged by these vertiginous spaces, and although the elements as metaphor are not confined to a few fixed meanings, *Frequencies* also contains a number of poems which express the serenity born of awe found in 'The Moor', and elsewhere throughout the poetry, but now more often, and affirming the Christian cosmic order. 'In Great Waters',[25] one of R.S. Thomas's finest lyrics, invokes Christ (the intimate but awesome "you") as having "made an altar/out of the deck of the lost/trawler whose spars/are your cross". In the deeps,

> There is
> a sacrament there more beauty
> than terror whose ministrant
> you are and the aisles are full
> of the sea shapes coming to its celebration.

"Aisles", sounding *isles* — there is certainly a haunting echo of *The Tempest* here — recalls other poems in the collection in which the land, too, is visited by such a ministration, when in Welsh places, whether actual or real in the imagination, signs are perceived of "that which is/beyond time, that is everywhere/and nowhere".[26]

However, poems as real as these do not achieve moments of vision without the poet sometimes knowing his self as "that grey subject/of dread that Søren Kierkegaard/depicted crossing its thousands/of fathoms".[27] In 'Pre-Cambrian'[28], focusing his thought on man's intellectual endeavour down the ages, seen in the context of geological time, he can only say:

> Plato, Aristotle,
> all those who furrowed the calmness
> of their foreheads are responsible
> for the bomb.

Indeed, if his perspective were Olympian, this might be a resounding, memorable piece of arrogance; but it is not — his stance is Kierkegaardian, based on the belief that the leap of faith is the one thing necessary, compared to which all philosophy is itself dangerous arrogance. Looking into the sea, he says:

> What I need
> now is a faith to enable me to out-stare
> the grinning faces of the inmates of its asylum,
> the failed experiments God put away.

As 'The Absence' reveals, the strain is hardly tolerable upon a self which, without faith in the intellect, must retain faith in a sustaining reality which is beyond the power of the intellect to conceive:

> What resource have I
> other than the emptiness without him of my whole
> being, a vacuum he may not abhor?

It may seem that this "vacuum" is a long way from Prytherch's "vacancy", and so in a sense it is. In 'Gone?',[29] R.S. Thomas asks:

> Will they say on some future
> occasion, looking over the flogged acres
> of ploughland: This was Prytherch country?

To which the short answer — given Thomas's achievement — is yes, no doubt some people will. No doubt some may even comment on his guilty feeling of having "flogged" the subject and the land, and his compatriots too. Now, "Prytherch country" is more obviously Thomas country than ever before. In 'Gone?' the suffering man with vacant mind has become one "who has needs in him that only/bare ground, black thorns and the sky's emptiness can fulfil"; needs, that is, which stand for the poet's "emptiness" as he waits on ground bare of everything except the figure crowned with thorns. For the reader, as often in the presence of R.S. Thomas's later poems, there is nothing more to say, nothing to do except turn aside, or share with the poet his self-interrogation, and his questioning attendance on the emptiness.

Notes

1. *Song at the Year's Turning* (1955), p. 21. The poem was first published in *The Stones of the Field* (1946).
2. 'Y Llwybrau Gynt 2' (The Paths Gone By) (1972), *R.S. Thomas: Selected Prose* (1983), ed. Sandra Anstey, pp. 138-139.
3. *Song at the Year's Turning*, p. 87. The poem was first published separately in 1953.
4. *Tares* (1961), p. 9.
5. *Poetry for Supper* (1958), p. 14.

6. *Tares*, p. 42.
7. *Ibid.*, p. 25.
8. 'Iago Prytherch', *Poetry for Supper*, p. 36.
9. *The Bread of Truth* (1963), p. 38.
10. *H'm* (1972), p. 1.
11. *Ibid.*, p. 28.
12. *Ibid.*, p. 30.
13. *Ibid.*, p. 8.
14. *Ibid.*, 'Via Negativa', p. 16.
15. *Ibid.*, p. 22.
16. *Laboratories of the Spirit* (1975), p. 10.
17. *Pietà* (1966), p. 24.
18. *Laboratories of the Spirit*, p. 60.
19. *In Parenthesis* (1937), p. xiv.
20. *Laboratories of the Spirit*, p. 1.
21. *Frequencies*, p. 19.
22. *Ibid.*, 'Emerging', p. 41.
23. *Ibid.*, p. 45.
24. *Ibid.*, 'The Absence', p. 48.
25. *Ibid.*, p. 37.
26. *Ibid.*, 'Abercuawg', p. 27.
27. *Ibid.*, 'Synopsis', p. 44.
28. *Ibid.*, p. 23.
29. *Ibid.*, p. 34.

Roland Mathias: "The Strong Remembered Words"

> Why
> When so much is ended do we still begin?

The question Roland Mathias asks in 'Argyle Street' is that of a poet acutely aware of his place late in time, and burdened by his sense of the contrast between the achievements of the past and his personal inadequacy. *Burning Brambles*, his Selected Poems 1944-1979, reveals an inheritor who is uneasy in his inheritance, which, as a result of his rather complicated family history, (described in his essay in *Artists in Wales*) embraces both Welsh-speaking Wales, in the Rhondda as well as rural Carmarthenshire, and the tensions between languages, cultures, and nationalities of a border people. Yet, taking into account two or more generations, there are few of us who do not have complicated family histories, and Roland Mathias's special unease as an inheritor has an additional cause in his feeling that he is unworthy of the inheritance. This feeling, in turn, reflects the Puritan tradition of which he is, among writers in modern Wales, one of the most faithful sons. The paradox of one who is faithful to his inheritance, especially in his feeling of unworthiness, is central to his poetry.

In a sense, Roland Mathias has remained a borderer, first reclaiming a foothold in Wales through historical research and poems set in Gwent and Powys, then moving deeper into the country, both geographically in his movement west, and in his involvement with Welsh history and culture, but remaining one who, in the words of 'Porth Cwyfan', feels that "I can call nothing my own." Consequently, it is from deep within the tensions and complexities of the Anglo-Welsh situation that he writes, not from some ideal resolution in the achievement of 'real' Welshness. In his autobiographical essay in *Artists in Wales*, he has described himself as standing outside "the house" of Wales, "sorry in my heart to be shut out", and as going on knocking at the door, with "memory and guilt". Certainly, memory and guilt are the main springs of his poetry, but the metaphor is characteristic of his humility towards what he would undoubtedly regard as the primary language and culture of Wales, and it belies his achievement. Here, however, another qualification has to be entered; for achievement is not a word to be used easily of Roland Mathias, not because his poetry does not merit it, but because the Puritan conscience engendering his conviction of personal inadequacy also involves the most radical questioning of all man's actions, works and motives. In consequence, his strong impulse as a praise-poet, born in gratitude to particular people who have given him his inheritance, is partly thwarted by his Puritan consciousness of sin, and wholehearted praise comes through only rarely in his poetry. But when it is released, it flows with singular purity and force:

> It is one engrossing work, this frail
> Commerce of souls in a corner,
> Its coming and going, and the mark
> Of the temporal on it. It is one
> Coherent work, this Wales
> And the seaway of Wales, its Maker
> As careful of strength as
> Of weakness, its quirk and cognomen
> And trumpet allowed for
> The whole peninsula's length.
> It is one affirmative work, this Wales
> And the seaway of Wales.
> ('Laus Deo')

The affirmation of these lines is all the stronger for having been hard won. It is a contention of this essay that Roland Mathias makes of special difficulties his peculiar strength.

Yet it is possible to make too much of the difficulty of the poems themselves, especially in view of the fact that difficulty is a necessary part of much modern poetry. Indeed, a case could be made for Roland Mathias's clarity and directness. There is this, for example:

> Over this valley is a well
> Beating with water and I do not see it,
> The hills are shaped every day afresh with a new hand
> And I do not feel it.
> ('Remember Charlie Stones, Carpenter')

And this:

> I have been here in the fields a year
> And never felt so far, desperately
> Far from the course of Christ
> And of His star.
> ('The Mountain')

There are passages that are equally clear and direct in many of his poems, though in some cases, as with the second of these quotations, they coexist with much more taxing writing, and there are whole poems with these qualities throughout. Among the latter, 'An Age' represents his lyrical gift at its finest:

> The blue singleness of summer was in that air
> And the bushes hazed after the light
> Though it was September gone.
> Is it blackberrying, sun
> And juice in the hand, or a flight
> Of birds shearing over the ferry that holds me there?
>
> The envelope has let an age escape to the sea
> And I am old, but not so
> Old as Mabon taken from between
> His mother and the wall. When
> I was young I saw the sun go
> Purple on my thumb and birds stand shoaling in the estuary.

This is immediately accessible, not because it is simple in means or content, but because of its lyrical movement, emotional impact, and the development of its imagery. The reference to Mabon will tax any reader who is unfamiliar with Welsh mythology, and the concentration of meaning in "the blue singleness of summer" and the child's identification of "blackberrying, sun/ And juice in the hand", together with the man's recapture of the moment within the passage of time, is the result of remarkable poetic organization and imagistic compression. The natural flight of time and the visionary moment that transcends or transfigures it are a recurring theme of Roland Mathias, and 'An Age' embodies it most joyfully, as 'A Last Respect' embodies it most deeply and most movingly, but to claim that he often realises the theme with directness and clarity would be to substitute another half truth for the allegation that he is usually opaque. It is more useful, I feel, to demonstrate the relationship between the strengths of his poetry and the demands it makes upon the reader.

Anne Stevenson, in a perceptive review, has described Roland Mathias's style as "that of a poet bruised by those experiences he most loves, and the density of his syntax mirrors the complexity of his emotion". Syntax and verbal texture are conspicuous features of his style, and both serve meaning. At the outset, in many of his poems published in the 1940's, there is a troubled and partly occluded poetry, in which a strong emotional impulse is impeded by its means of expression, and the very eloquence is inarticulate. This is probably due in some degree to his extreme consciousness of the poem as an artifact, and his preoccupation with the madeness of verbal texture, which owed much to his reading of Hopkins and Browning, and despite the marked independence of his mind, it is probably due in part to the poetic climate of that decade. Later, increasing skill has made verbal texture one of the main sources of pleasure in his poetry, but when combined with his essentially qualifying voice, which is bent on being truthful at all costs, in a largely non-colloquial language, it can also make considerable demands on the reader, as the opening of 'A Stare from the Mountain' amply demonstrates:

> As the sun slants, the best of it over,
> Into the trug of Usk from the summary
> West, masking the struts, the wicker rents
> With plush, with a stuff of shaded
> Greens gentling the upper, thistly fields,
> The thicker bush of forest, ploughland
> Cuts of red already stiff in their winter
> Folds, tricking the human aberration
> Into the same still life, a whole
> Kindred lit with the right intensity,
> Painted safe to a fortunate choice
> Of colours, I stand on Yscir mountain,
> Head above wind level, hearing the north's
> Voice at my nape, putting the frozen
> Questions that the poles demand.

Control of the long sentence, as in Milton or Wordsworth, for example, is a feature of some of the greatest English poetry. It is very difficult, however, for long sentences to succeed when they make several simultaneous demands on the reader. Here, reaching for the meaning of the suspended main clause, it is also necessary to understand and not to forget the subsidiary clauses *en route*. In this and in other instances, Roland Mathias's concern with verbal texture leads him to sculpt each phrase, while his concern with truth nourishes a wealth of implications. In addition, he develops an intricate metaphor, and uses words — "trug". "summary", "gentling" — that are either dialectal, or unusual or ambiguous in context — and phrases, such as "tricking the human aberration" — that require an extra effort of thought. And where is the effort to come from, when the mind is already at full stretch? The question is how to grasp all the meanings of a sentence that is longer than a sonnet and employs the capacity of an imagist poem in every line. Yet in 'A Stare from the Mountain' the effort is rewarded: it is a good poem. It is by no means one of Roland Mathias's most demanding poems, however, and this fact serves to indicate that the line between originality and idiosyncrasy in his poetry is sometimes very fine indeed. At times, he can madden the patient reader (the impatient having turned back at the first subsidiary clause, knotty piece of syntax or dense cluster of words), but there is something heroic about a poet who is so intent on the poem as a made thing, instead of pretending that he is just talking much like anyone else, and on telling his truth, that he makes no concessions to frailty of ear or attentiveness, or to lack of knowledge.

When occlusion occurs in work of his poetic maturity, which he achieved in the 1950's, it results from his struggle to dramatise the difficult relationship between himself and his subject, and is often a necessary part of the poem. But my dwelling on the demands of his poetry must not be allowed to obscure either his splendidly vigorous dramatic monologues, whether in his own person or that of an historical figure, such as Henry Vaughan, Absalom, and Sir Gelli Meyrick, or the emotional directness and force of many poems, such as 'The Flooded Valley', 'A Letter', and 'Departure in Middle Age':

> But I cannot go back, plump up the pillow and shape
> My sickness like courage. I have spent the night in a shiver:
> Usk water passing now was a chatter under the Fan
> When the first cold came on. They are all dead, all,
> Or scattered, father, mother, my pinafore friends,
> And the playground's echoes have not waited for my return.
> Exile is the parcel I carry, and you know this,
> Clouds, when you drop your pretences and the hills clear.

In the first verse of 'Departure in Middle Age', the poet has described himself as "cold/And strange to myself"; this is the "sickness" of the second verse, and it is a characteristic state of the poet. The primary cause of this is stated in 'God Is':

> God is who questions me
> Of my tranquillity

Accordingly, there is little tranquillity in Roland Mathias's poetry, and his Christianity manifests itself principally as a conviction of sin. While R.S. Thomas in his later poems is a mystic concerned with the ways in which God hides or manifests himself, Mathias is a moralist concerned with what God asks of him personally and of man in general. There are more difficult poets who have found a wide readership, and I believe that it is the radically disquieting focus of his attention, together with its mediation by Welsh history and places, that is the main cause of his relative neglect. There has probably never been another time when a preoccupation with sin was less likely to attract readers. The seriousness makes embarrassing demands, even though Roland Mathias, in common with most important modern religious poets, uses the metaphors and images of Christianity — fountain, dust, light, fall, and so on – instead of its dogmatic or technical terms; his use of "covenant" and "justification" does however indicate the specific religious provenance of his concerns.

In 'Channels of Grace: A View of the Earlier Novels of Emyr Humphreys', included in his book of essays on Anglo-Welsh literature, *A Ride Through the Wood* (1985), Roland Mathias has written that Emyr Humphreys's "writing and its preoccupation are the result of Wales's heritage of the last three centuries: they begin in that Puritan seriousness about the purpose of living, about the need for tradition and the understanding of it, about the future of the community as well as the individual, that has almost no place in the writing of contemporary English novelists". These words apply almost equally to his own poetry, and help to explain, incidentally, why neither poet or novelist has had anything like his due outside Wales.

Roland Mathias writes well about people, especially those who could not write or speak for themselves. As he says in 'For Warren Davies, Two Years Dead': "You rarely wrote. I am your remembrancer". And, in 'A Kind of Expiation', a poem addressed to his grandfather, published in *The Anglo-Welsh Review* no. 72: "to deny/The dead a voice is to falter/In justice". The latter quotation indicates that he is not only concerned with memory and loss. His consciousness of time colours much of his poetry with an elegiac mood, and his settings and metaphors taken from an eroding coastline, as in 'For an Unmarked Grave' and 'A Letter from Gwyther Street', produce some of his most evocative and haunting lines. But he is not primarily an elegist in the sense that Thomas Hardy was: for Mathias memory that brings back the pain of loss also demands that justice be done. While visiting historical places invariably provokes a self-questioning which finds him wanting in comparison with the dead, justice requires that he questions the dead, too, even the craftsmen he greatly admires, like Charlie Stones, or John Abel, the King's Carpenter, in 'Sarnesfield'. But the most remorseless questioning is reserved for himself, and his celebrations or commemorations of others are likely to include a self-condemnation, as at the end of 'They Have not Survived':

> For this dark cousinhood only I
> Can speak. Why am I unlike
> Them, alive and jack in office,
> Shrewd among the plunderers?

The Puritan conscience is reinforced by his sense of isolation in a country where he can call nothing his own; indeed, it is relevant to ask whether, in a situation in which tradition has been largely eroded and the future of the community is in doubt, the "puritan seriousness about the purpose of living" does not focus too narrowly on the self, with morbid results for a poet whose strongest words are kept for castigating himself.

This point is worth pursuing if the peculiar demands of Roland Mathias's poetry are to be understood. His conviction of sin is acute, leading to self-dislike: "the smell of a life ill lived" of 'Burning Brambles' is typical, and throughout his poetry the temptations of the flesh are felt and bitterly regretted. He asks in 'The Mountain', "Give me the punishment that saves", and in a much later poem, 'The Green Chapel', he writes that "the fear within/Is the worst, the horror of separation/From meaning", so that physical and spiritual torment, in a condition of penitence, is at the heart of his poetry. For the ill conscience has extreme physical as well as spiritual effects, and the poetry's inwardness with these adds to its demands. Thus, in 'Remember Charlie Stones, Carpenter', Roland Mathias asks, "what in hysteria can I do/But wait, as shell and paper wait, myself/The best time to be thrown away?" and in many poems a state of mind approaching hysteria is held in tension with the life-enhancing qualities of his verbal energy and spirited imagination. At the farthest extreme, verbal pyrotechnics and a sense of complete personal inadequacy cause a particularly uncomfortable tension. This may be seen in 'Not Worth the Record', where the problem with the self — "a failure in such sort/That all despair can use/Is the name" — is compounded by the problem with the intrusive listener or reader. The poem was commissioned for the Dial-a-Poem service, but it is unclear to me whether the poet, for whom the worth of art to artist and audience is evidently closely related to the truth of its questioning, means to reveal or partially mask his disgust at the performance. At any rate, I doubt whether a poem meant to serve such a purpose could ever have communicated a greater unwillingness to be so used!

To expect from Roland Mathias anything other than an art that questions himself and implicitly questions the reader is as impertinent as to expect R.S. Thomas to chat about his poems at the end of a reading: what he has to give, he has given; now, with the poems in our minds, we should go away and submit to their questioning. In both cases, the art is Puritan, but Roland Mathias's is far more grudging with the consolations of nature or affirmative vision, and is morally the more demanding. His is a poetry that is suspicious of everything that is natural and everything that is human, including itself. He shares with Emyr Humphreys what he calls, in his essay on him, "the old Puritan distrust of beauty". As he said in an interview with Cary Archard, printed in *Poetry Wales* vol. 18, no. 4, "Beauty in itself doesn't save". This distrust he has in common with Geoffrey Hill, too, and 'Memling' shows his awareness that art can be a subtle form of moral evasion, safely transposing "the ravisher and the ravished". Nevertheless, he is closest to Emyr Humphreys among his contemporaries, and while the novelist remorselessly exposes the deceptions of the word in his country's most cherished places: bardic chair, pulpit, and political rostrum, Mathias is quick to confess what he calls, in 'The Fool in the Wood', "the cost and bloat/I have of words". His aim, in the words of 'Freshwater West Revisited', is to lay the action bare.

I share the frustration expressed by some reviewers at Roland Mathias's refusal to annotate his historical poems. Yet it also seems to me that this is a positive reflection of his regard for the integrity of the poem, which appears negatively in 'Not Worth the Record', and of one of his most attractive qualities — his stubborn insistence on the importance of people, places, and events outside areas of conventional reference, which in Britain reflects the extreme selectivity of a particular version of English history. Thus, Roland

Mathias, like the Irish poet Patrick Kavanagh, affirms the epic scale of his 'parish', and therefore, by implication, of every other parish in the world, by assuming its human centrality. Many poets of his generation have looked to London; he has remained true to the Romantic rediscovery of an original Christian value: that life here and now, or there and then, in the individual soul and in the particular community, is as important as life anywhere at any time. The only part of his thought that threatens to belie this truth is his tendency to see a more 'real' Wales from which he is excluded, but in practice he has been loyal to the people and places that have made him. He is not a poet to make concessions to those who, whether in Wales or outside, patronise Wales with Anglocentric ideas of 'Welshness'. The consequence of his loyalty is that he has taken his Anglo-Welsh situation far more seriously than all but a few writers with whom he shares it, and he has done so partly out of his humble sense of himself as an outsider who cannot claim to be fully Welsh, and who must earn his place in Wales by the quality of his effort and understanding. This, indeed, accounts for the passion informing the meticulous care of his historical sense, and evident equally in his poems, criticism, and historical writings. Care of this order is both an emotional need and a moral obligation, and justice is its object. As I have already argued, the discomfort at not belonging which reinforces his Puritan conscience thereby helps to ensure that he is much more of an insider than he would ever claim to be, and in his representation and exploration of the Puritan tradition he is one of the small group of modern writers in English who reveal Wales from the inside. Indeed, there comes a point when to speak of a poet's 'situation' is as external as it is to speak of sin or love as a 'theme': Roland Mathias writes from his life in Wales, concerned not with his 'achievement' in the public eye, but with the truth and integrity of the action.

As the conclusion of 'Brechfa Chapel' shows, he has no confidence that the tradition he has inherited will survive into the future:

> Is the old witness done?
> The farmers, separate in their lands, hedge,
> Ditch, no doubt, and keep tight pasture. Uphill
> They trudge on seventh days, singly, putting
> Their heads to the pews as habit bids them to,
> And keep counsel. The books, in pyramid, sit tidy
> On the pulpit. The back gallery looks
> Swept. But the old iron gate to the common,
> Rusted a little, affords not a glimpse
> Of the swan in her dream on the reed-knot
> Nor of the anxious coot enquiring of the grasses.
> The hellish noise it is appals, the intolerable shilly-
> Shally of birds quitting the nearer mud
> For the farther, harrying the conversation
> Of faith. Each on his own must stand and conjure

> The strong remembered words, the unanswerable
> Texts against chaos.

Here, "the strong remembered words" curiously echo, yet contrast with, "the sweet remembered demarcations" and "the remembered things" of David Jones's 'The Tribune's Visitation': "things" which are either in fact or by analogy Celtic. The things of the Catholic poet embody his sacramental religion; they are also the 'matter' of cultural tradition, its substance and spirit. The Puritan tradition, in contrast, is based upon the word: the word of God in the Bible, the word God speaks to the individual heart, and "the conversation of faith" binding people together in small communities centred upon the chapel. It is interesting to note this fundamental difference between the two Anglo-Welsh poets who have entered most deeply into the Welsh past. For David Jones, the things of Wales retained a hope of cultural order against the chaos of modern Britain. They belonged more to his idea of a Catholic, Arthurian Wales than to historical reality, but as a symbol they also belonged to the live current of nationalist thought associated principally with Saunders Lewis, and they invoked something of the incarnational sweetness, the integration of soul and body, and human and divine love, that we find in the world of Dafydd ap Gwilym. But for Roland Mathias, poet of a later tradition, which sets man as a spiritual warrior at enmity with his own nature, it is not things but words that bind people together and unite man with God; it is not things but texts that stand against chaos. But "the strong remembered words" are no longer the conversation of a faithful community. Now, they are the support of "each on his own", as the farmers, "separate in their lands", keep their farms in order, and trudge on Sundays "singly" to chapel. It is the waterbirds that stand for the present state of society, for a people without tradition, and "the hellish noise it is appalls". There is no denying the emotional and rhetorical force of the anger and pessimism here, which are similarly provoked by the tradition-breakers in 'Absalom in the Tree'. Yet it is also possible to think the symbol of the birds too weak, and even too contrived, to carry such a weight of significance. Also, it may recall the fascination with birds of Emyr Humphreys's bard, John Cilydd More, which I take to be, among other things, a prophetic portrayal of the marginalisation of poetry in Wales, as well as in Britain generally, whereby the poet deprived of a centrally human position tends to focus all that he has to say about man, God and society onto a nature that can scarcely bear the pressure of the displacement. In terms of a parallel process, it is also possible to see in the conclusion of 'Brechfa Chapel' a reflection of the alienated individualism that the poem laments, and a tragic involuntary response of a poet who feels a stranger in his own land. But if these suggestions seem to limit the power of the poem, this would be to ignore a conviction implicit throughout this essay, that a good poet is known not by the 'correctness' of his answers according to any dogma, but by the intensity with which he lives the questions, and the integrity of his response to the tensions and complexities to which, as a man living at a certain time, he is subject. In any case, it would also be to ignore the force with which the decay of the Puritan tradition of individual and communal responsibility is dramatised in these lines. And the fact that in his fidelity to that tradition throughout his writing, Roland Mathias has earned the right to his anger and pessimism and embattled resolution. "The strong remembered words" have been the basis of his poetry for some forty years. They are the words he has lived by, words of the tradition from which he derives no false comfort and has none to offer; no comfort at all, in fact, except the comfort of poetry which, in its concern to tell the truth and to embody it, treats the reader as an equally serious person.

"A Big Sea Running in a Shell":
The Poetry of Gillian Clarke

The survival in poetry of a language of primary emotion has in recent years been due mainly to women poets. As the poetry of Gillian Clarke shows, this is not achieved without vulnerability, and the strength of the poetry may be defined in terms of risks successfully taken. Most obviously, her concern with birth and death and love, in emotive metaphorical language, risks inflation, and her directness and simplicity risk sentimentality. What is achieved when she succeeds, as she usually does, is a rare integration of unforced seriousness and strong emotion. Her poetry is also vulnerable in another sense – to an energy that beats against the formal control barely containing it, so that all that is positive and creative and disciplined in her poetry is tense with the pressure of a powerful destructive under-tide. In consequence, a first acquaintance with her work may suggest a pleasurably sensuous, affirmative, fairly predictable poet with whom the reader can feel comfortable: domestic (in the narrow, middle-class sense), natural, essentially female. At a closer reading, however, she emerges as a much more powerful poet, who has no comfort for complacency: domestic, (in the Homeric sense), in her concern for family, home and native land, natural in her deep implication in the rhythms of life and death, female in the interaction of biological and cultural constraints, and satisfactions, from which she writes.

Many of Gillian Clarke's poems have as their occasion an experience of birth or death, and are notable for the intimacy with which she identifies her biological and emotional experience with nature. As she feels the power of fertility and the fragility of each individual life, so her identification with all that gives life produces tenderness and fear. Similarly, the interaction and frequent conflict, of union and separateness characterises her poems of personal relationship, and its most extreme image occurs in a poem about her daughter, Catrin: "the tight/Red rope of love which we both/Fought over". The same duality defines her sense of the larger community, although she finds more interaction than conflict, more union than separateness, in Welsh-speaking rural Wales, which is both her ancestral ground and where she lives part of her life. Nevertheless, she does not escape some consequences of the cultural and social displacement that is almost always at the roots of modern poetry of place, and a shade of idealising nostalgia colours her realistic portrayals of community — with particularly interesting results when she confronts community with her feminism.

The title poem which opens her first book, *The Sundial* (1978), has an image of "the sun/Caged in its white diurnal heat". This reappears as "the sun contained" in 'Harvest at Mynachlog', which ends, after the recollection of a violent death, with the harvesters

> hearing
> The sun roar like a rush of grain
> Engulfing all winged things that live
> One moment in the eclipsing light.

Here, the remarkable concentration of her metaphorical language, which is a major source of her power, may be seen in the half-concealed imagery of lions and waterfalls which Gillian Clarke frequently associates with the "caged" energy of the sun. I should add, though, that I doubt very much whether the concealment here of these images is deliberate. Gillian Clarke is notably a poet with a high degree of poetic instinct and intuition, who thinks and feels and sees within a structure of images and metaphors. She is not a theoretician, and her art seems more touch than cunning. In consequence, she has at best an acutely intelligent, non-rational, unselfconscious power, while her weaker poems are repetitive and more automatic workings of the images and metaphors.

The elemental image of the caged sun, which also recurs in "the savage roar of the trapped sun/Seeding the earth against the stop of winter/When everything that lives will play dead lions," of 'In Pisgah Graveyard', has its counterpart in skull, sea and shell imagery. Thus, the "skull, full up with darkness/As a shell with sea", in 'Lunchtime Lecture', reappears near the beginning of 'Letter from a Far Country' as:

> At first the skull itself makes
> sounds in any fresh silence,
> a big sea running in a shell.

Caged sun, lion and waterfall, skull full of darkness and sea in a shell — all image a trapped energy, a held tension. There are contributory social causes, but this is life in the rhythms of nature, life in the body, as Gillian Clarke apprehends it. The result for her poetry is that it is richly sensuous, full of the life of nature, and at the same time tense with the pressure of the power that gives life, but also, eventually, destroys it. 'Dark' is a word Gillian Clarke overuses; nevertheless, 'darkness' is a presence in her poetry.

Like all poets in the particular Romantic tradition in which she writes, like D.H. Lawrence and Ted Hughes and Seamus Heaney, for example, she is a poet of Keats's autumn. Poets in this tradition, this form of feeling with its corresponding images, may isolate one part of the natural cycle, or emphasise now one part, now another, or image the whole. Gillian Clarke frequently catches nature at the moment of fullness, or the moment after, when the fruit whose seed will continue the cycle is ripe, or beginning to decay. She wins her affirmations from the strong pull of death and from knowledge of the shadow side of the mind. In isolating the beauty that is a work of death, as in her recurrent skull images, she comes close to death-worship, but even when this happens, in 'Lunchtime Lecture' and the recent 'Castell y Bere', for example, the vitality of her rhythms and imagery usually obviates morbid indulgence — yet a taste of mortality remains. But while her fertile images contain death, her images of death hold seeds of life. Thus, in 'Lunchtime Lecture', where the woman's beauty is made transparent to show the bone, the skeleton appears as the tree of life, and again, as in Keats's great ode, the poem intimates the complete natural cycle.

Gillian Clarke's second book, *Letter from a Far Country* (1982), and her later work represented in the *Selected Poems* (1985), make explicit what is implicit in her early poems: that for her the creation is a sisterhood. This is a social vision, which finds her at one with "common supermarket women's talk" and embraces all women, but it includes nature, too, and identification with the mother of nature:

> We share
> premonitions, are governed by moons
> and novenas, sisters cooling our wrists
> in the stump of a Celtic water stoup.
>
> Not lust but long labouring
> absorbs her, mother of the ripening
> barley that swells and frets at its walls.
> Somewhere far away the Severn presses,
> alert at flood-tide. And everywhere rhythms
> are turning their little gold cogs, caught
> in her waterfalling energy.
>   ('Sheila Na Gig at Kilpeck')

The sisterhood is a solace, a shared mystery, a source of creative energy; but again, it is often experienced as a caged energy. And in *Letter from a Far Country*, much more than in *The Sundial*, the negative side of natural process, its enslavement of the woman's body, is compounded by women's social and cultural subjugation by men.

Yet 'Letter from a Far Country' itself, her most consciously feminist poem, speaks of more anger and frustration than it shows. When, near the end of the poem, Gillian Clarke writes of women "mixing rage with the family bread", the word "rage" is surprising, because there is no rage in the poem. This is not because she underestimates the constraints imposed upon her grandmothers in the old patriarchal social order of rural Wales, or diminishes her frustration of an artist bound to family needs. Rather, it is because 'Letter from a Far Country' is a love poem as well as a poem of anger and frustration, and the love prevents rage. Moreover, the love is for features of the very way of life in the Welsh countryside that is shown constraining the grandmothers, so that while they are restive in their world, the poet herself looks back with the restlessness of love towards it. The outcome is, inevitably, a compromise as far as feminist convictions are concerned, but the duality which the poem dramatises greatly enriches it as a work of art and increases its psychological authenticity.

Like many Anglo-Welsh poets, Gillian Clarke identifies a lost integration with the land itself, which evokes feelings compounding nostalgia for childhood with nostalgia for a partly mythologised, historical past, and a sense of the Welsh language as the voice of the land:

> My head is full of sound, remembered speech,
> Syllables, ideas just out of reach;
> The close, looped sound of curlew and the far
> Subsidiary roar, cadences shaped
> By the long coast of the peninsula,
> The continuous pentameter of the sea.
>
> ('Llyr')

In this instance, the difficult feelings arising from the poet's love of English, the imposed language, which Seamus Heaney and R.S. Thomas also struggle with, are resolved by the translation of Shakespeare back into his Celtic sources. If the outcome (though a good poem) seems too comforting to be true, the tendency to see a lost ideal in ancestral Welsh-speaking Wales is balanced in Gillian Clarke's poems by her knowledge of rural work and of rural confinement and deprivation, and her awareness of the separateness of the individual. For the most part, her sisterhood is rooted in a realistic social and natural world, and the people and the Wales of her poems have a substantial reality. In addition, while *Letter from a Far Country* retains the intensity of *The Sundial*, it is much less narrow in its concentration. The later poems call on more of the poet's past and present life, and are open to social change and a threatening external world, with good poems on the destruction of industry and the way of life dependent on it, and terrorist violence. Now, too, she links north and south Wales, and the rural and industrial areas, with more common feeling for both than is usual in Anglo-Welsh writing, and her travels are reflected in poems set in France and the Soviet Union. In her most recent poems, in response to the death of her friend Frances Horovitz, there is an even greater depth and strength of feeling in her treatment of the rhythms binding women to nature, and while her achievement is already considerable, there is the exciting prospect that she may combine a greater openness to the external social world with her primary impulses.

There are outcrops in Gillian Clarke's poetry of an ancient tradition, in which women mediate between man and nature. This may be seen in 'Sheep's Skulls', where she says of the sheep: "They die/On the open hill, and raven and buzzard/Come like women to clean them". This makes the intimacy of women with death, which is also the personal experience in the poems, explicit in terms of a traditional culture. It is not the menial task alone that is at issue here, but, as 'Letter from a Far Country' makes clear, a religious role:

> It is easy to make of love
> these ceremonials. As priests
> we fold cloth, break bread, share wine....

The priestly role of women relates to, but does not wholly account for, the prevalence in her poetry of the images and terminology of sacramental Christianity — transubstantiation, stigmata, cross, wafer, novena, stations, mass — which, displaced from Catholicism, are transferred to nature. Here it serves a dual purpose: as a form of ritual, recalling the sacramentalisation of nature and human love which we find in both D.H. Lawrence and the great medieval poet, Dafydd ap Gwilym, who indeed, does not displace the sacred from the Church, but extends it to nature and human lovers; and as an order imposed upon the fierce destructive energy which I have described as the under-tide of her poetry. It should also be said that the displacement usually occurs in places where religion itself formerly established a whole order binding together the domestic with the natural and the sacred, and thus supports the desire of Gillian Clarke's poetry to recover a lost integration. Furthermore, although she uses a sprinkling of words whose provenance is Welsh Nonconformity, and shows only moderate antagonism, (together with some not unloving awe), towards the patriarchal elders who held her grandmothers in subjection, her religious imagery is predominantly Catholic. The displacement and transference of this imagery may call to mind T.E. Hulme's famous description of Romanticism as "spilled religion" — a generally suggestive formulation which usually proves brutally and stupidly insensitive when applied to any one of the many important writers, since the end of the eighteenth century, who have had a powerful religous sense but no allegiance to any church. I prefer to recall "that tradition, that long, humble, vibrant apology to paganism on which the future energy of Christianity may depend", which Charles Lock names in introducing the poems of Mary Casey. In Mary Casey's poetry the energy contained in her Christianity helped her to recover a language of primary emotion; in Gillian Clarke's poetry, it is the natural energy she rechristens that has a similar effect.

The Poetry of Nearness:
Anglo-Welsh Poetry in the 1960s

I

As an English poet living since 1965 in Wales, who felt certain affinities with the aims and situation of Anglo-Welsh writers, and as a critic, I was involved, if only marginally, in what I am to discuss. Consequently, I shall not give a survey, or attempt, with critical impartiality, to describe all the most important figures and events. My view is, inevitably, personal and selective, leaving out much that is relevant to the theme and only touching on subjects each of which deserves extended consideration. Nor shall I confine myself exclusively to the 1960s, since important work published then was written before, and important work written then was published after the decade. And hindsight changes the look of things, as when the writer neglected or unrecognised at the time is seen to be more significant than some who were lauded then, while other reputations fade. Nor is it possible to draw a firm line between past and present in any literary "period". Edward Thomas's poetry was more widely influential among poets in England and Wales in the 1960s than it had been ever before; toward the end of the decade, some of us were waking up to writings which David Jones had published many years before. While R.S. Thomas was acknowledged, gladly or grudgingly, as leader by many younger Anglo-Welsh poets, others, especially of the older generation, still looked to Dylan Thomas. Vernon Watkins lived until 1967, working on his perennial themes. Other poets, notably Roland Mathias, Anthony Conran and Raymond Garlick, were working in ways that owed little to the dominant influences. Leslie Norris and John Ormond, who had first published poems during the Second World War, achieved a poetic maturity, twenty years later, born of control of an original romantic impulse, but without loss of original imaginative energy. The attitude of compassionate realism associated principally with Idris Davies and Glyn Jones united more Anglo-Welsh poets writing in the 1960s, as it does today, than the "colour of saying" which outsiders generally associate indiscriminately with poets in both languages in Wales. Yet, as the work of Glyn Jones and others shows, realism and verbal opulence are not necessarily incompatible.

Since what I have to offer is largely a personal view, I want first, in order to set out some general points relevant to both the subject and my involvement in it, to quote a passage from my review of *The Lilting House*. This book, edited by John Stuart Williams and Meic Stephens, with an introduction by Raymond Garlick, and published in 1969, is the first major anthology of modern Anglo-Welsh poetry, and a landmark on the terrain which Meic Stephens, with the founding of *Poetry Wales* in 1965, had done much to open up, and which poets were occupying with the new confidence he had helped to give them. The review-article, published in *The Anglo-Welsh Review* in February 1970, was my first critical 'intervention' in Anglo-Welsh poetry. I quote the passage with revisions and omissions for the sake of clarification, not to improve what is callow in the style. Indeed, that is part of its meaning, for in writing as a critic I was at the same time learning from the book in front of me:

> Just as most young English poets would find their initial gratification at appearing in an anthology with T.S. Eliot soon turn to pain in the light of the contrast, so it must be beneficial (as such pain should be) for some of the younger poets in this book to share print with David Jones. *In Parenthesis* is, I think, one of the few great long poems of the century; we shouldn't hesitate now to speak of it in the same breath as *The Waste Land*.... David Jones's learning can be valuable to us now, surely, by showing how the imagination immersed in history can give both depth and perspective to its interpretation of man's life in the present; while it reveals for us the significance of our own Celtic past. I'm not sure what R.S. Thomas means by "the bones of a dead culture".... The culture(s) David Jones draws on crumbles, where it is dead, into the humus we still plant in, or — to drop the metaphor — the Brythonic civilization and the Romans, who found conquest a form of exile, are now part of the land where stone cottages are "the wind's home"; disinheritance, too, is part of the land, its recognition in personal anguish a measure of continuing love. Instead of gnawing the bones we might just think of them as part of our own bodies.... In giving us heroes as diverse as the common soldier of the First World War and Prytherch, both of whom "endure", David Jones and R.S. Thomas do much to justify the claim made by Keidrych Rhys in a poem in this anthology, that "the strength of the common man was always the strength of Wales". One can say of them, as Edmund Blunden has said of Thomas Hardy, that the feeling of their poetry is truly democratic. The ways in which we are made to see Prytherch, and to see and hear Dai and his comrades, distinguish them sharply from other ancestral or contemporary, real or imagined, figures haunting the minds of Anglo-Welsh poets. The effort to feel empathy ... seems to me wholly admirable, an antidote to loneliness, and the best way to take possession of the past; it is also much more common in Anglo-Welsh poetry than in contemporary English poetry, so that one distinguishing feature of the Anglo-Welsh poet is his concern with the past and his sense of tragic discontinuity between past and present.[1]

Looking at this again now, I see the following points which bear on the present subject:

1. A belief in poetry as a struggle to transcend limitations; a struggle involving hard self-criticism and the ability to recognise and admire great poetry. This in turn implies, however vaguely, a sense of poetic community transcending temporal boundaries.

2. The beginnings in my mind of a greater independence from received critical opinions, which was in part a result of alternatives which Wales offered to models and fashions prevailing in England.

3. The conviction that "the imagination immersed in history can give both depth and perspective to its interpretation of man's life in the present".

4. Failure on my part to distinguish between historical and mythological elements in the formation of "culture". The interaction — sometimes the confusion — between myth and history is far more important in modern Anglo-Welsh poetry than I saw at that time.

5. A belief that the past is part of the land; a belief present in various forms in a large number of Anglo-Welsh poems of the period.

6. Recognition of "disinheritance", and that to feel it may be an expression of love for what has been lost. Much Anglo-Welsh poetry of the time exists between the poles of "loss of ancestry" (John Tripp) and "ancestor worship" (Emyr Humphreys), and indeed, shows that, far from being opposites, worship may arise from loss.

7. Realization of "the strength of the common man" and of democratic feeling in Anglo-Welsh poetry; but a misleading attribution of the latter to David Jones and R.S. Thomas.

8. Identification of "concern with the past" and a "sense of tragic discontinuity between past and present" as distinguishing features of modern Anglo-Welsh poetry.

Whether I invoke them all directly again or not, these points provide the bearings of the following discussion.

2

Ronald Johnson, a young American, spent a year in Britain during 1962-63. The result of his travels on foot about the country was a book-length poem, *The Book of the Green Man*, which is one of the most delightful books of poetry published in Britain in the 1960s. In the second movement, 'Spring', he records tracing the course of the Wye from Chepstow to its source on Plynlimmon. Johnson writes with visionary particularity, uniting two traditions: loosely speaking, English Romanticism and American Transcendentalism, or the traditions of William Blake and of William Carlos Williams. Like Ezra Pound and Williams, he quotes and 'reconstructs' other writers' words extensively — his sources in the second movement include

Kilvert, Henry Vaughan, *The Mabinogion*, Giraldus Cambrensis, Blake, Delius, and Tolkien among others — and he remakes a visionary and mythological tradition from the ground he covers. His method works cumulatively and is difficult to illustrate with brief quotations, despite many "luminous details". However, the following is from 'Landscapes and Mandrakes', part nine of the movement:

> Then came, like the Celtic Blodeuwedd
>
> who was made of blossoms of oak
>
> & broom & meadow-sweet,
>
> a green man out of Wales — of more than flowers:
> as if all Hafod
>
> rose up again, & came in strides of vistas into England.
> And Hafod, that most
> sublime of gardens, gone into earth
>
> these hundred years.
>
>
> And with those lost romantic
> promontories, prospects, vapors & auroras,
> rolling
>
> & losing themselves in irregularities,
> was the half-legendary Wales of Giraldus, where a man could command
>
> the birds to sing: '& immediately the birds,
> beating the water with their wings, began to cry aloud
>
> & proclaim him'.
>
> And farther back in time,
> the lineaments clearly discerned of
> *Lothlórien* —
>
> of the *mallorn* trees — & shades
>
> of the Blessèd Isles.[2]

Through his combination of sensuous particulars and literary, mythological and historical references, Johnson partly uncovers and partly creates a tradition from elements present in the literature and the land. It is a remarkable achievement, and one possible only for an outsider. Johnson is more than a tourist; he is, nevertheless, *also* a tourist, one who can cross the border from England into Wales without taking account of the history. In fact, he subsumes history in the legend and myth of his 'Celtic' design, in accordance with a vision that is fundamentally literary. In modern Anglo-Welsh poetry, on the other hand, with the major exceptions of Dylan Thomas and of childhood's imagined world, the landscape is an historical, and therefore political, place. The closest native work to Johnson's of that period is 'The Sleeping Lord', which was first published in 1967, and his Green Man and David Jones's Arthur have something in common as embodiments of earth-rooted, regenerative powers. But David Jones's figure has political significance; as the embodiment of a religious apprehension of reality, Arthur is also a response to the *history* of English dominance in Wales.

Raymond Garlick, in his introduction to *The Lilting House*, noted that, "in the sixties the cohering of the sense of national identity in all sections of Welsh life has kindled a vocation of reconciliation among writers, the most articulate members of the language communities — a concern for unity in bilingualism, an awareness of the one, whole Wales, which also (like Whitman) embraces contradictions and multitudes".[3] Of course, this did not mean that writers were seeking to reconcile the Anglo with the Welsh part of their identity — indeed, almost all thought of themselves, justifiably in my view, as Welsh in all but language, (though that is a large "but"), David Jones being the only Anglo-Welsh poet who attempted to reconcile his dual, English and Welsh, inheritance. As Anglo-Welsh writers drew closer to Welsh writers — for example, David Jones and Emyr Humphreys to Saunders Lewis, R.S. Thomas, John Tripp and Harri Webb to Gwenallt, and Raymond Garlick to Waldo Williams — so, even in the case of David Jones, the differences between England and Wales were emphasised: social, political, and spiritual differences, perceived in the history of a union that was destructive for Wales.

Among the literary events that had a decisive influence on the heightening of Welsh consciousness among Anglo-Welsh poets in the Sixties and early Seventies — the founding of *Poetry Wales*, the publication of Glyn Jones's *The Dragon Has Two Tongues* (1968), of Ned Thomas's *The Welsh Extremist* (1971) and of the anthologies *Welsh Voices* (1967), *This World of Wales* (1968), and *The Lilting House*, and the launching of *Planet* in 1970 — I think the two most decisive were the influence of R.S. Thomas and Anthony Conran's *Penguin Book of Welsh Verse* (1967). And these worked together, since R.S. Thomas was already mediating something of the spirit of the more political Welsh poets, of Gwenallt and Saunders Lewis, for example, who wrote from an historical, political Wales. Of course, there were Anglo-Welsh writers who knew Welsh poetry in the original, and I have foreshortened history by concentrating on the Sixties as a time of connection between Anglo-Welsh and Welsh writers; and of course, much is due to Gwyn Williams as a pioneer translator of Welsh poetry into English; but I think it is true to say that, with

Conran's work, a number of translations from the modern Welsh which are *great poems in English*, and notably 'Rhydcymerau' and 'In Two Fields', entered the consciousness of some Anglo-Welsh poets, and suggested how, in their language, things that were indelibly *not* English might be mediated.

The Sixties in Anglo-Welsh poetry felt to be, in more than one sense, a time of recovery. There was Raymond Garlick's 'Consider Kyffin', for example, in which he invokes Anglo-Welsh poets of past centuries, discussed together for the first time in his pioneering *An Introduction to Anglo-Welsh Literature* (1970): Kyffin, "who wove in both tongues", "John Davies out of Hereford,/ Holland of Denbigh — men who fired/their flintlocks through the border wall/loaded with English words as well", "Lloyds and Llwyds, Vaughans,/ who opened with their quills both veins/of language, giving life to myth — / the forked tongue in the dragon's mouth", and others. Garlick the scholar has brought to light buried treasure, which Garlick the poet celebrates:

> In silted bays of old bookshops –
> shelved and becalmed like ancient ships
> in saffron havens, I have rocked
> their boats, long run aground and wrecked;
> eased dusty covers open, looked,
> clambered inside entranced, unlocked
> each bulkhead page from stern to beak
> and in the cabin of his book
> come on the poet at his ease.
> Some — seamen, scribbling in the haze
> of voyages to where Wales joins
> the world's end: Samwell, Poet Jones.
> Others — upcountry parsons, squires,
> hotblood students in Oxford squares,
> curates penning the Poems of Hughes —
> by candlelight in a creaking house
> under the wheeling universe
> cutting and polishing a verse.[4]

He has recovered an ancestry, a tradition, a living myth — "the forked tongue in the dragon's mouth". These poets are "the root" of the Anglo-Welsh, "but", Raymond Garlick concludes, "you have never heard of them" — where "you" presumably represents all the living Anglo-Welsh, but perhaps especially the poets. Yet, as he knows, Anglo-Welsh poets in the Sixties could hardly be accused of indifference to ancestry — it was rather their sense of a long-standing separate poetic tradition that was, in most cases, weak, and that is the tradition he offers them.

It seemed to me, as an outsider, that the Anglo-Welsh poet, compared with his English counterpart, had certain peculiar advantages, especially in the matter of tradition. Thus, in 'Thanks in Winter', Harri Webb, one of the most passionate, uncompromising poets to take his stand on native ground, records standing by Dafydd ap Gwilym's grave at Ystrad Fflur, on "the day that Eliot died". There,

> The dark memorial stone,
> Chiselled in marble of Latin
> And the soft intricate gold
> Of the old language
> Echoed the weather's colour
> A slate vault over Ffair Rhos
> Pontrhydfendigaid, Pumlumon,
> The sheep runs, the rough pasture
> And the lonely whitewashed houses
> Scattered like frost, the dwellings
> Of country poets, last inheritors
> To the prince of song who lies
> Among princes, among ruins.

After praying for his country, and cursing England, he returns home:

> Caught between two languages,
> Both dying, I thanked the long-dead
> Minstrel of May and the newly silent
> Voice of the bad weather, the precise
> Accent of our time, taught
> To the disinherited, offering
> Iron for gold.[5]

Yet Harri Webb, if "caught between two languages/Both dying", and if one of the "disinherited", is nevertheless, in that place at that time, inheritor of two traditions, English and Welsh, medieval and modern, iron and gold. This is not what the poem says, but it is what it shows. Sharing in "the bad weather" of which Eliot is the "voice", Webb is simultaneously writing a praise poem; partly by participating in it, he reveals the continuing life of Dafydd's tradition, at the same time as he gives thanks for Eliot. To my mind, that is a great thing for a poet to be able to do, as it was for Raymond Garlick to go to the root of "the forked tongue" — even though we know the danger of forked tongues; but where the poet experiences such danger, he may receive a gift that safety never knows. What would David Jones have produced without the tensions of his dual inheritance? But Harri Webb knows the advantages of iron and gold, and implies them. He knows that Ffair Rhos is famous for a family of Welsh poets, so that after many centuries the poetic tradition still holds in the hill community, where houses only look "lonely" and "scattered like frost" to the eye of the disinherited, which he is not, or not entirely. The poem says one thing with a "bad weather" voice; but what it shows is another: a poet "caught between two languages", both alive.

3

Recovery and praise both involve memory and Anglo-Welsh poetry, as has often been noted, is chiefly a poetry of memory. In many instances, it is childhood memory. Leslie Norris has written some of the best poems on this subject since Dylan Thomas's 'Fern Hill'. His 'Water' and 'Early Frost', in particular, are eloquent, controlled poems, which express strong emotion, and avoid sentimentality, by a rhythmic and imagistic presentation of sense impressions:

> Once I awoke in a dark beyond moths
> To a world still with freezing,
> Hearing my father go to the yard for his ponies,
>
> His hands full of frostnails to point their sliding
> To a safe haul. I went to school,
> Socks pulled over shoes for the streets' clear glass,
> The early shops cautious, the tall
> Classroom windows engraved by winter's chisel,
> Fern, feather and flower that would not let the pale
> Day through. We wrote in a cold fever for the morning
>
> Play. Then boys in the exulting yard, ringing
> Boots hard on winter, slapped with their polishing
> Caps the arrows of their gliding, in steaming lines
> Ran till they launched one by one
> On the skills of ice their frail balance,
> Sliding through life with not a fall in mind,
> Their voices crying freely through such shouting
>
> As the cold divided. I slid in the depth
> Of the season till the swung bell sang us in.
> ('Early Frost')[6]

The writing is at once rapt and deliberate, with fine control of the long sentence and verse paragraph, and true to the adult's strong sense of mortality, and the child's sensations and wonder. I think childhood appeals strongly to a poet like Leslie Norris partly on account of its unself-consciousness. This was certainly true of Edward Thomas, with whom Norris feels a strong affinity. As Thomas identified childhood feelings with his idea of Wales, so Norris, a Welshman living in the south of England, returns imaginatively to Wales partly through memories of childhood. But only partly. Norris, like Thomas, has a strong sense of self, and therefore of mortality and of isolation. He has also a strong attraction to community and sense of its responsibilities. The communal sense is expressed in his narrative poems, ballads, and translations from the Welsh, and his collections of poems interestingly contain, and to some extent balance, strong opposing impulses, towards lyrical utterance of the isolated self, and towards the expression of shared humane values and experience. It would be crude, but not without truth, to ascribe these impulses to English and Welsh traditions respectively. From the field of tensions between these traditions some of the best Anglo-Welsh poetry derives its imaginative energy.

In other poets in Wales, including some of the greatest modern poets in Welsh, the light of memory becomes the light of transfiguration. Since it was his perennial theme, almost any poem by Vernon Watkins will provide an example. 'Gravestones', for instance:

> I take a sunflower down,
> With light's first faith persuaded and entwined.
> Break, buried dawn,
> For the dead live, and I am of their kind.[7]

Waldo Williams's 'Mewn Dau Gae' — and 'In Two Fields', Anthony Conran's translation — is one of the modern world's greatest visions of universal reconciliation, through the transfigured experience of shared labour. In this extract, for example:

> And when the big clouds, the fugitive pilgrims,
> Were red with the sunset of stormy November,
> Down where the ashtrees and maples divided the fields,
> The song of the wind was deep like deep silence.
> Who, in the midst of the pomp, the super-abundance,
> Stands there inviting, containing it all?
> Each witness' witness, each memory's memory, life of each life,
> Quiet calmer of the troubled self.
>
> Till at last the whole world came into the stillness
> And on the two fields his people walked,
> And through, and between, and about them, goodwill widened
> And rose out of hiding, to make them all one,
> As when the few of us forayed with pitchforks
> Or from heavy meadows lugged thatching of rush,
> How close we came then, one to another –
> The quiet huntsman so cast his net round us![8]

The communion of "the whole world" in the stillness, in the net of "the quiet huntsman", is given, but it is also worked for, literally, in the common labour. This is what is missing in Ronald Johnson's 'Celtic' design; it is also the vital middle term absent from Vernon Watkins's more intellectual, more 'purely' spiritual vision — the cooperation of people in daily work, in particular, historical places.

"How best remember?" Roland Mathias asks at the beginning of 'For

Warren Davies, Two Years Dead'. "You rarely wrote," he says later in the poem. "I am your remembrancer." Speaking or writing for those who did not or could not speak for themselves is another main function of Anglo-Welsh poetry, revealing its roots in a sense of community — or, more accurately, the desire of some modern Anglo-Welsh poets to share a traditional function of their Welsh counterparts. Roland Mathias remembers people — those who have not survived, those with unmarked graves:

> I will speak to him here, in Cwmcamlais ground,
> The mountains spare and grudging his time
> Against their own. How long is it,
> David, long since your loins were water,
> Since you were carpenter, wed, kept shop,
> Were poor and a theologian, companied
> A nephew wide over Senni and the nearer
> Hill of day? Nothing to tell,
> No fossil couplet, no borrowed stone crying
> The claim of a life against an era?
> You are not worth a second in the slow
> Hardening of Wales, only in the sand
> Of the fallen cliff that was my youth.
> ('For an Unmarked Grave')[9]

The poet speaks for David in speaking to him; he defines his own identity partly through the relationship, and suggests David's identity through his relationships and social functions. David is uncle, married man, carpenter, shopkeeper, poor man, theologian. These define him as one belonging to a particular social world, and the place-names are not romantic counters but locations on communal ground. The effect, however, is the opposite of a sense of security. For Mathias, characteristically, sets the man in his historical time against the measure and erosions of geological time: the mountains' time, "an era", "the slow/Hardening of Wales", (an image with social and geological meanings, indicating a country that is "harder" than when its traditions nurtured such men). Against this temporal and social "hardness", the poet's mind holds David's worth. Again, it is characteristic that Roland Mathias internalises social values, presenting them as precarious survivals in the individual mind. He writes from fidelity to a Puritan tradition of communal memory and individual and social concern, which he sees everywhere eroded. In a number of his poems the tradition appears, usually unobtrusively, in the contrast between two kinds of light: the light of nature, represented by the sun, and the light of judgement. Even in his poems set in the border country between England and Wales, the country in which poets from Thomas Traherne to Anne Stevenson have discovered a visionary light, Mathias is at once resolutely historical and moral. It is by his Puritan seriousness about living, with which he sees himself and his fellows subject to God's questioning, that Roland Mathias restores an equal, deep meaning to places out of the way of most people's regard.

The same is true of Emyr Humphreys, whose *Ancestor Worship* (1970) is a major poetic sequence of the period. For him too, the ancestors still live:

> The air is still committed to their speech
> Their voices live in the air
> Like leaves like clouds like rain
> Their words call out to be spoken
> Until the language dies
> Until the ocean changes
>
> ('Ancestor Worship')[10]

And the ordinary Welshman represents a noble tradition:

> This man is a king except
> He makes his living emptying caravan bins
> And uses English in the shop to avoid giving offence
> To visitors who do not know
> Where they are or who he is
>
> ('Gŵr y Rhos')[11]

These passages are affirmative; but *where*, in the cycle of poems as a whole, are we? In the Wales of the author of *Outside the House of Baal*: a living, complex society, perceived both with love and with an ironical, realistic, sharply critical eye. The results in the poems, as in the novel, are unsettling. There is the frightening 'A Roman Dream', for example, which, as Humphreys's work often does, dramatises the fate of a politically disengaged, idealistic, decent fellow, who becomes a victim of tyranny. And there is 'A Democratic Vista', in which things surely are not what they at first seem:

> Strange sanctuary this, perched on the rising cornstack
> Like a desert saint on a broken pillar
> Staring, eyes unstirring until hill field sea are one
> The procession of thought blurred
> Into the regular rising and falling of a sinewy arm
> And the dry rustle of sheaves.
> Tom Williams, Guto, Dick Williams, Wil Bach, Dafydd Dew and me,
> We are the people; our conversation is smooth and superficial
> Like a veneer of grained wood, curves leading nowhere
> Which was where they started.
> We are the people, for whom politicians shout and soldiers fight
> We sow and reap, eat and sleep, copulate in secret, think
> In circumferences of one dimension.
> We are the sacred people, the secular mystery, the host,

> Whitman's elastic deity, Marx's material, Rousseau's noble savage
> Mayakovsky's beloved —
> Tom, Guto, Dic, Wil, Dafie, and me –
> Reasonably efficient between dawn and sunset,
> God chewing tobacco, God drinking tea, digesting rice.
> We are the people.
> God is not mocked.[12]

Here are the companions at work together in the field: positively, the setting of Waldo Williams's vision; negatively, the scene of a number of trite and sentimental Anglo-Welsh poems. But the oneness of "hill field sea", of thought and labouring arm, is seen by one who is an image of isolation, standing on the cornstack "like a desert saint". Moreover, while speaking *for* his companions, he speaks *about* them as they would not speak about themselves: for example, "our conversation is smooth and superficial/Like a veneer of grained wood, curves leading nowhere". He is an intellectual; he has read Marx, Whitman, Rousseau, Mayakovsky. So, in rural Wales, the others may have done too — if unlikely, it is not impossible: Borrovian idealization of the well-read Welsh "peasant" has more basis in fact than the frightening vacancy of Iago Prytherch's mind. But it is still true that the intellectual speaker, with his ironical tone whose object is exceptionally hard to identify, is not, like Waldo Williams, at one with his companions. He is, rather, 'above' them, literally, and perhaps also metaphorically, in his mind, describing them ambiguously while claiming to be one of them. In this, he is like Michael in *A Toy Epic*, a character representing one of Humphreys's major themes: the ambiguous position of the middle-class Welsh nationalist, who is an idealist calling himself a realist, a leader claiming to be a democrat, an alienated individual who says "we".

In the main, the older generation of Anglo-Welsh writers differ from most of the young poets who have emerged since the mid-Seventies in expressing a strong religious sense, and, in some cases, a specific Christian allegiance — for example, Nonconformist in the case of Emyr Humphreys and Roland Mathias, Catholic in the case of David Jones and Raymond Garlick. This also indicates another marked difference between tendencies in Anglo-Welsh poetry and the general literary climate of England in the Sixties. Without implying a hidden sociological reason for individual choices and acts of faith, I would suggest that there is a relationship between the religious sense of the Anglo-Welsh poets and the cultural inheritance which they seek to possess. Owen Chadwick, in *The Secularization of the European Mind in the Nineteenth Century* (1975), claims that the base of religion lay originally in the family, and in the ritual of the tribe, from which it extended to larger communities. His view, instead of seeing religion as a production of non-religious forces, perceives man's nature as being fundamentally religious, and closely relates man's religion to his need of kinship and continuity. Chadwick quotes a character in Bourget's novel *L'Étape* (1902), who has been converted to

Catholicism: "I've decided to become what all my family was for centuries. I want to get back, down into the depths of France. I can't live without my dead".[13] The words have a special resonance in the context of Wales, where the nationalism shared by many writers in both languages, which was particularly strong in the Sixties and Seventies, is a spiritual as well as political force, and seeks to repossess the past as well as shape the future. Religion as a sense of comprehensive order, identified with the depths of Wales, is what we find, in one form or another, in many modern Anglo-Welsh poets; but rather than being an assured inheritance, it is something they strive to gain. Time and again, in the work of agnostics and Christians, in Edward Thomas and Alun Lewis, as well as in David Jones and Vernon Watkins, and in John Ormond, Ruth Bidgood, Anthony Conran, Gillian Clarke and others, we find intimations of an order encompassing self and community, living and dead, man and nature, man and God. In some it is a glimpse, or a longing, a nostalgia, for a lost 'home'; in others, like David Jones and Vernon Watkins, it is a complete religious philosophy. But in all I feel it is also a belief in what the other language, the first language, holds or has held, so that while intimations of an order which has been lost, but may, perhaps, be regained, is to be found widely elsewhere in modern literature, in Anglo-Welsh poetry the intimations are peculiarly haunting, and often suggest a basis in the people and the land, in the family of the Welsh people and their homeland. The guilt of the Anglo-Welsh, especially in this period, arises largely from their doubt whether their language, originally and to some extent still the oppressor's, can mediate the deep things of Wales.

John Ormond, in some of the most powerful poems of the period, combines awe with scepticism. He also detaches an archetypal symbolism from the evangelical religion of his upbringing and develops it in an original form. This is one way of benefiting from the formative belief while reacting against it, as opposed to full-bloodedly and apparently completely rejecting it, as T. Harri Jones did, in memorably uncomfortable poems. John Ormond displaces awe from the God of the chapel and returns it to the land and its primitive natural and manmade features:

> Turn and look back. You'll see horizons
> Much like the ones that they saw,
> The tomb-builders, milleniums ago;
> The channel scutched by rain, the same old
> Sediment of dusk, winter returning.
>
> Dolerite, porphyry, gabbro fired
> At the earth's young heart: how those men
> Handled them. Set on back-breaking
> Geometry, the symmetries of solstice,
> What they awaited we, too, still await.

> Looking for something else, I came once
> To a cromlech in a field of barley.
> Whoever farmed that field had true
> Priorities. He sowed good grain
> To the tomb's doorstep. No path
>
> Led to the ancient death. The capstone,
> Set like a cauldron on three legs,
> Was marooned by the swimming crop.
> A gust and the cromlech floated,
> Motionless at time's moorings.
>   ('Ancient Monuments')[14]

As the capstone balances, so the poem achieves equilibrium from the conjunction of opposites: movement and stillness, time and timelessness, life and death. The imaginative impulse recalls Dylan Thomas and Vernon Watkins, but the clear, conversational idiom does not. Here and elsewhere, Ormond's unique achievement is to combine the strengths of two important poetic movements: the symbolism of the Forties and Fifties, and the clarity and conversational 'naturalness' associated mainly with R.S. Thomas — though Ormond is more formal than Thomas. Far from detracting from his originality, the combination of strengths reveals the poetic intelligence with which he has responded to the possibilities of different traditions. In his evocation of geological and prehistoric time in these lines, in his feeling for rock and for those who laboriously and skilfully handled it, he shows a land charged with energy and haunted by mystery, and with a continuity of work and religious expectation.

Ruth Bidgood is a quieter poet of haunted landscapes, and her personal, sensitive, colloquial 'voice' sometimes recalls Edward Thomas's. However, she seems less self-divided than Thomas, more settled in her place, and more interested in its permanent features than in using it to reflect inner states:

> Arcadia was never here.
> Ice-needles tortured the thin soil,
> spring snow lay long by the north wall,
> yet the peat-fire had a summer heart.
> Waves of life receding left
> jetsam of stone — grey megaliths
> half-sunk in tussocky grass now
> but still processional on the ridge above,
> leading into a mystery:
>   ('Stone')[15]

In another poem, 'Little of Distinction', she speaks of "the mystery/that complements precision"; which well describes both a main feature of her style and what she achieves in her best poems. Here, in 'Stone', she writes of what has gone — people, a path, "waves of life", but with a quiet, strong faith in the future, which has political implications, but no dogma or programme:

> Only stone lasts here.
> Stone proclaims life, affirms a future
> by virtue of so many pasts,
> yet baffles questioning. As I touch walls
> warm in the sun today, and feel
> so many summers gentle to my hand
> and yet withheld, I would crush stone
> in my fist, if I could, till truth's milk ran.

The last two lines have a contained violence, and reveal the effort and suffering needed for an affirmation which would otherwise seem too easily won.

Like Raymond Garlick in 'Consider Kyffin', Ruth Bidgood sometimes follows R.S. Thomas in admonishing her fellows, and thus admits the distance between herself and her reader into the poem:

> You who love so sadly,
> Weeping at the broken house
> And the fern-choked fields,
> You forget the older time
> Before the walls were built,
> Before the fields were made.
> These tumbled stones are language
> In which a life is written –
> Read, and rejoice that it was lived.
> Drink with joy the silence offered
> In this cup of hills, this Grail.
>   ('Mid-Wales')[16]

Her voice has a certain isolation, her eye a detachment from the conventional view which sees "only dereliction" in the depopulated Welsh hill-country. Yet she offers a quiet answer to those who, like R.S. Thomas, are preoccupied with the death of culture in rural Wales. As she says earlier in this poem: "a story does not stop/At the first chapter,/And a life is not invalidated/By having ended". She has written fine poems of praise and of mourning, poems of great emotional intensity, like 'Burial Path', in which personal emotion, released by the litany of place-names, is finally too much for the religious ritual to contain, and, in her later poems in particular, there is a visionary light:

> I am a latecomer, but offer
> speech to the nameless, those

>   who are hardly a memory, those
>   whose words were always faint
>   against the deafening darkness
>   of remotest hills.
>   For them tonight when I go home
>   I will draw back my curtains, for them
>   my house shall sing with light.
>   ('All Souls")[17]

Like Roland Mathias, whose occasional technique of dramatising 'found' materials she uses at times, and whose historical interests she shares, Ruth Bidgood shows great respect for the integrity of her subject, for the world of past and present time which she feels, but knows to be independent of her existence. The effect of her poems set in the mid-Wales landscape of abandoned settlements is both to reveal the humanity buried in a seemingly elemental waste — as Wordsworth does in 'Michael' — and to affirm the possibility of renewal.

4

In my review of *The Lilting House*, I asserted that "the Anglo-Welsh poet's only *duty* is to the English language". "It is', I claimed, "a truism, and should be a first principle, that a poet's first duty is to the language in which he writes."[18] This enabled Bobi Jones, writing in *Planet* 16, to have some fun at my expense, when, quoting my first statement above, and comparing it with a remark by Meic Stephens, he said: "Jeremy Hooker reaches even greater heights of amoral virginity". He qualified the phrase, however, by adding, "unless I misinterpret him (and I probably do)".[19] Well, yes, I think he probably did, though not without help from my cryptic expression.

I had referred to 'Words', in which Edward Thomas says: "Choose me/ You English words" and describes words as "dear/As the earth which you prove/That we love". I then claimed — and still believe — that "the poet's use of language is the only proof that he loves what he claims to love; it is his only way of doing justice to the world". I should have gone on to explain what, for me, is implicit in this: not that language is the only thing that matters — indeed, if it were possible for a person to care only for words he would not really care about them, for language is a radically social phenomenon — but that a poet's care of words in his poems is inseparable from his care of the world, and therefore, in the deepest sense, his social concern, and for us, his readers, his words *are* the world as he presents it, revealed and transfigured by love, or obscured and disfigured by carelessness. My criticism of some of the poets in the anthology was based on the clichés and slack writing resulting from gestures toward feelings outside the poem, in the poet, as if to feel deeply about something, but to care less about the words, were a sufficient poetic act.

While I recognise that some, and perhaps all, serious modern poets have to face and wrestle with problems arising from alienation, I hold to Wordsworth's definition of the poet as one who carries — or tries to carry — "everywhere with him relationship and love".[20] Through my involvement as a critic in Anglo-Welsh literature, I have come to feel that the most significant thing about the situation of the Anglo-Welsh writer between different traditions is that it offers, as alternatives to forms of writing, thinking and feeling which – often unconsciously — confirm and increase alienation, forms which enact and extend relationship. Anthony Conran in particular has recognised this, as both poet and critic. His critique of "the poetry of self definition" and of "third person poetry" is, to my mind, the most radical and original contribution of Anglo-Welsh criticism. "A third person poetry can no longer enact a civilization", he has written. "The poet cannot stabilize his art/in the tarnishing medium of I and It."[21] "Welsh poetry is second-person poetry", he claims. "A poem praises, satirizes or laments within the magnetic field of I and Thou."[22] The emphasis is on the poet's function and responsibilities, on what he is able to *give*; and this in turn depends upon him being not just a man in society but a member of a community. The community is present, and has a continuous life in time. Thus it is evidently the traditional *Welsh* community which guarantees the function of the Anglo-Welsh poet, as Anthony Conran sees and practises it. Nevertheless, the poems which best express it are alive in *English*, and offer to speak to those whose first, or only, language is English. Significantly, Roland Mathias, the other major critic of Anglo-Welsh poetry — and Mathias and Conran are two of the best critics writing in Britain today — places equal emphasis upon the poet's responsibilities. In his thinking, the principal alternative traditions for the Anglo-Welsh poet — who is more often intricated in them, or drawn instinctively to one or the other, than in a position to choose coolly between them — are romantic separateness and self-expression, with abstract ideals of beauty and art on the one hand, and active, responsible participation in the historical community on the other.

As a newcomer to Wales in 1965, it soon became apparent to me that a strong defensive action was being fought, in Anglo-Welsh as well as in Welsh writing, against the forces eroding communal and national identity. It was during this period that, for some of us, place became the centre of our emotional and intellectual concerns, while others, like David Jones and Roland Mathias, who had possessed a sense of place much earlier, became more conscious of it as a theme. Now, in the Eighties, place has the distinction, and faces the danger, of being increasingly a subject of academic study.

No doubt the sense of place developed in the first instance in response to experience of loss, or "disinheritance", and the general threat of placelessness. Later, I saw more of the depth and complexity of the issues involved, and came to feel that there is practically nothing of importance which the subject of place does not embrace. Of course, the modern sense of place is by no means confined to Wales — the period under discussion produced Basil Bunting's *Briggflatts*, Geoffrey Hill's *Mercian Hymns*, and Roy Fisher's *City*, for example — while, earlier, William Carlos Williams in America, and Patrick Kavanagh in Ireland, had done much to define the poetic value of locality. But the political situation in Wales made the sense particularly acute, and stimulated thought on the subject. Later, I read the philosopher J.R. Jones. In 'Need the Language Divide Us', a lecture given in 1967, he sees the basis of a people's formational structure in "the interpenetrative marriage of language and land". He describes how language, "after being spoken over the generations by the inhabitants of the same region", becomes "a vessel to collect and store their past, and through that a means to form them into a People".[23]

Poetry of place bears J.R. Jones out: it frequently involves inter-relationships of language, land and people. Of course, the interrelationships are not without internal tensions as well as external threats. John Tripp says of "bards", in his poem of that title:

> In places where the language is spoken
>   they dissolve into the people.[24]

But John Tripp makes some of his best poems out of not being at home in the rural Wales of the bards, and out of the differences between that world and his own social reality, to which he brings something of the bardic functions of praise and commemoration. He knows, too, that there are not only positive things to be said about any community, whether Welsh or otherwise. I think it undeniable, however, that a tendency to romanticize and idealize the Welsh-speaking community marked some Anglo-Welsh poetry of the Sixties and Seventies. More recently, especially in the work of younger poets, but with precedents in the writings of Glyn Jones, John Tripp and others, the history and qualities of the English-speaking Welsh of the urban areas have been receiving more of their due. Poetry of place does not speak only with vatic or hieratic accents, as in Vernon Watkins and David Jones. The demotic, sceptical, fraternal voice of John Tripp also speaks *from* place.

In Saunders Lewis's article 'Welsh Literature and Nationalism' (1965), I read:

> There is no longer any faith that makes the deferment of the nuclear war very urgent. So that a particular Welsh experience of this century, the crisis that the Welsh Nationalist Party evokes and was organized to avert, takes on universal reference and significance. Civilization must be more than an abstraction. It must have a local habitation and a name. Here, its name is Wales.[25]

When I first read this, I read *over* the first sentence. Later, I read it again, and was shocked. Here was a seriousness about civilization which regarded human existence without it as not worth preserving. It is a seriousness, focused on the meanings which a people share, with which I have great sympathy. Finally, however, the world of Saunders Lewis, or, for that matter, the world of David Jones, is not my world, and not only because it is Welsh and I am not. Many of us born in the Forties or later know little of what such men mean by 'civilization' except from books — and if *they* got it partly from books, if it *is*, partly, books, that is not what they mean. The things that made us are 'meaner' and more everyday — we may *really* care more for some area which has little or no aesthetic or 'historic' interest, (or it may have, but this is not the primary reason for our care), for a place of family and friends and shared memory, of fields or pavements and privet hedges marked ineradicably by their presence, than we care for a poetic tradition lasting more than a thousand years, or for shining fragments picked up from the European past by an Eliot or a Pound. And we may care more for another history with which the fields and pavements and brickwork are ingrained, for forms of labour and struggle and continuity which do not give rise to luminous details or gem-like flame, or compose "a pattern of timeless moments". In which case, we will probably translate the great words — 'culture', 'civilization', 'tradition' — into things which, in David Jones's terms, we actually love and know. At least, we may value ancient poetic traditions and certain cultural and national continuities, but only if they prove hospitable to the actual things, to the flesh and blood, which have made us what we are — things which, too often, the great Modernists despise.

Now, I associate Saunders Lewis's words with a more general statement, which I can understand in more familiar terms — and interpret only in part as its author intended. This is from Martin Heidegger's essay 'The Thing' and is about the abolition of distance which, nevertheless, produces no nearness:

> Man stares at what the explosion of the atom bomb could bring with it. He does not see that the atom bomb and its explosion are the mere final emission of what has long since taken place, has already happened.... What is this helpless anxiety still waiting for, if the terrible has already happened? The terrifying is unsettling; it places everything outside its own nature. What is it that unsettles and thus terrifies? It shows itself and hides itself in the *way* in which everything presences, namely, in the fact that despite all conquest of distances the nearness of things remains absent.[26]

I see placelessness, which is now widely increasing or in possession, as an effect of imperialism and of technological change. The conquest of distances, shrinking the world, the spaces surrounding us, has, paradoxically, *unsettled* us — that is, removed us from the place, the centre, where we are, and estranged us from things, and from ourselves and from each other. The logical irony is that a people whose forebears conquered and colonised a large part of the globe have been left with little they can call their own, in the sense that it is part of them, and they are part of it, confirming their being in the world. Technology contributes to the process, not by its inherent nature, but by the way in which it is used in the service of a uniform competitiveness or a uniform collectivism. Indeed, while R.S. Thomas seems virtually to blame the Machine for the Fall, for others some actual machines are part of the human lineaments of their place, not to mention instruments for saving life and making it more liveable. Demystification is a process welcomed by most modern thinkers. As an exposure of 'mysteries' concealing exploitative social relations, it is one thing. But it is quite another when in the service of desecration, in the word's literal sense; when it takes away the unique being of person or creature or thing, the essential being originally confirmed by belief in God for whom everything that exists has supreme value and is the subject of care. Desecration, in this sense, has already reduced the world to a chaos of uniformly insignificant atoms; most poets, whether they are religious or not, defend mystery in the sense that they care for the unique and integral being of persons and things.

Poetry of place, whether hieratic or demotic, historical or mythological, is a poetry of nearness, of presence, of the location of meaning in people and things. It resists distances which abolish the meaning of where we are, of life in us, here, in this present place with its historical depth, with forces connecting us to the world at large, with immediacy to the ultimate seriousness of judgement; distances which make us mere echoes or reflections, puppets or caricatures, of centralized powers and the images they generate: in London, New York, or Moscow, but also in Cardiff, Edinburgh, or Dublin. Large claims may be made for poetry of place, especially in its more ideological or mythological forms, as in the work of Charles Olson. I prefer to end more modestly, however, with a homelier parallel. In the last century, numerous naturalists-cum-local historians — usually they were clergymen — made invaluable detailed records of their environments. Ironically, they were influenced, usually unconsciously, by the spirit of imperialism, with its desire to possess the entire world either materially or in the form of knowledge. But they also worked with care and scientific curiosity, like their mentor Gilbert White; and they helped to establish a true relationship of distance and nearness between themselves and the world, by revealing the depth in time, and the extensive, intricate interconnections, within place. Since the 1960s, a number of poets, inspired by a similar reverence, have been exploring their localities, not, usually, to classify the *coleoptera* and *lepidoptera* — though a poetry of fact might require that — but to see the life of place comprehensively and in depth, thus affirming — in Patrick Kavanagh's terms — its epic centrality. Poetry of place is a struggle for the mind with distance, which literally blinds us to where we are and what we have and need. During and since the 1960s, Anglo-Welsh poetry has built on foundations established earlier by poets as diverse as Idris Davies and Glyn Jones, David Jones and R.S. Thomas. It matters less that the poets have, sometimes, substituted new false images of people and place for old, than that they have used and affirmed English as the second language of nearness in Wales.

Notes

1. 'Image and Argument', *The Anglo-Welsh Review* Vol. 18 No. 42, pp. 66-67.
2. *The Book of the Green Man* (1967), p. 45.
3. *The Lilting House*, p. xxi.
4. *A Sense of Europe* (1968), pp. 86-87.
5. *The Green Desert* (1969), p. 45.
6. *Ransoms* (1970), pp. 18-19.
7. *Unity of the Stream* (1978), p. 97. The poem was first published in *The Lady with the Unicorn* (1948).
8. *The Penguin Book of Welsh Verse* (1967), p. 259.
9. *Absalom in the Tree* (1971), p. 18.
10. *Ancestor Worship* (1970), p. 10.
11. *Ibid.*, p. 34.
12. *Ibid.*, p. 36.
13. *The Secularization of the European Mind in the Nineteenth Century*, p. 114.
14. *Definition of a Waterfall* (1973), p. 29.
15. *The Given Time* (1972), p. 40.
16. *Ibid.*, p. 12.
17. *The Print of Miracle* (1978), p. 12.
18. *The Anglo-Welsh Review* Vol. 18 No. 42, p. 71.
19. 'Anglo-Welsh: More Definition', *Planet* 16, p. 16.
20. 1802 Preface to *Lyrical Ballads*.
21. 'Ars Poetica', *Spirit Level* (1974), p. 80.
22. Note on 'Gifts', *Spirit Level*, p. 101.
23. *Planet* 49/50, p. 29.
24. *Collected Poems* (1978), p. 95.
25. *Presenting Saunders Lewis* (1973), p. 144.
26. *Poetry, Language, Thought* (1975), p. 166.

Resistant Voices: Five Young Anglo-Welsh Poets

I

My concern in this essay is with the work of five Anglo-Welsh poets (the oldest born in 1944 and the youngest in 1953) who have come into prominence during the 1980s. They are among the best poets of their generation in Wales, and they are representative of a strong movement among young Anglo-Welsh poets — all worthy of serious individual consideration, which limitation of space prevents me from giving them here — whose work contrasts sharply with a dominant trend of Anglo-Welsh poetry of the Sixties and Seventies, at the same time that it owes much to the confidence won for English-language poetry in Wales by poets such as R.S. Thomas, Roland Mathias, Glyn Jones, Raymond Garlick, Dannie Abse and Harri Webb, and, in some cases, to the practice of the older poets. In other words, while there are important continuities linking older and younger, and living and dead, Anglo-Welsh poets, a change significant enough to be described as a new movement has occurred in Anglo-Welsh poetry since the Seventies. In this essay, I shall try to be just to the work of each poet under consideration, but I shall have to be selective too, and to leave out much of their variety. My aim is to indicate lines of development in each poet's work, to note their affinities and differences, and to relate the poetry to changes occurring in Wales and in Welsh intellectual life during the period. These are historical changes, which, together with the vigorous and exciting historical debate which they have stimulated, I take to be the major influences on poetry in Wales at present.

Of course, it is no new thing for poetry in Wales to be closely involved with history. On the contrary, poetry has been inseparable from history and myth in Wales (or the Old North) for at least fifteen hundred years, in what Emyr Humphreys calls "the Taliesin tradition". The ancient poets praised their princes and their deeds, and remembered royal genealogies and the tribal past. Such acts of praising and remembering combined elements of history and myth and did not distinguish between them. But the poets were more than voices flattering a boastful aristocracy, with little use for fact. Emyr Humphreys writes: "The function of praise poetry in the Celtic world was to celebrate and sustain the social order. In the Welsh context, from the very beginning, this also involved the poet as the voice of resistance, the tireless mouthpiece of the endless process of defending a realm under siege."[1] The myth-making of the poets was a method of affirming tribal identity, which, in Emyr Humphreys's view, is just as necessary with regard to Welsh national identity today. He sees myth-making as "a most potent weapon in the struggle for survival", and says that for "a sensitive young person" it is "the thread which connects him to an honourable past". The inescapable destiny of such a person is to know "both consciously and unconsciously that his own dignity as a human being is linked with the dignity of the national entity to which he belongs".[2] What, though, is the part of the historian in this? In Saunders Lewis's 'Marwnad Syr John Edward Lloyd' (Elegy for Sir John Edward Lloyd), the historian plays for the poet the part which the Sibyl played for Aeneas, leading him to Hades to see the heroes and ancestors. The poet is shown the unity of medieval Europe, the destruction of the unity and of Welsh nationhood, and the survival of both as a potential order contained in the Welsh language. Saunders Lewis found his destiny in this vision, and attempted to make it a modern political reality. It was a way of seeing and feeling which also made him savage in his judgement of Anglicized industrial south Wales — the very society, in fact, in which most Welsh historians and Anglo-Welsh poets writing now were born. Thus when Emyr Humphreys, with a reference to a resonant statement[3] by Saunders Lewis, links modern Anglo-Welsh poetry to the ancient tradition of Taliesin, he quietly signals what would be a revolution in thinking and feeling if the link were to be generally accepted by Welsh-speaking intellectuals: "Even when the poet writes in English, you cannot pluck a flower in Cwmdonkin Park without disturbing a great northern star".[4] The great quality of the tradition is "the secret of creative survival". It is a major concession for a writer identified with language-based Welsh nationalism to say that the Anglo-Welsh poet has access to the secret, and may therefore be its bearer in the English tongue. It is also, to some degree, an implicit qualification of the attitude towards the Anglo-Welsh associated with Saunders Lewis.

Dai Smith describes "the production of Welsh history" today as "a battleground on which rival armies contend". "What we are witnessing is," he says, "the invoking of the Welsh past in the disputed name of the Welsh future.".[5] It is, therefore, a contention between rival ideologies for the identity of Wales. But it is more than this, it is a contention between individual people with vital common feelings and loyalties, as well as strong differences; people subject to the massive pressure of contemporary circumstances, and often self-divided, in a country with powerful communal and cultural traditions, but now ravaged by uncontrolled market forces. In the school of thought associated principally with Gwyn A. Williams, 'traditional' Wales, rural, Nonconformist, Welsh-speaking, is seen as the ideal which has for too long obscured the reality of a large part of the Welsh people, those employed (or formerly employed) in the industrial work which formed the economic base of the whole society, and therefore of the rural world used as a myth to exclude them from consideration, and from Welshness. Understanding of the opposition between this view of Wales, expressed most eloquently by Gwyn A. Williams in *When was Wales?* (1985), and the national idea described by Emyr Humphreys with equal eloquence and passion in *The Taliesin Tradition*, is crucial to an understanding of the new movement in Anglo-Welsh poetry, which was first evident in the late Seventies and has gathered force since the vote rejecting a Welsh Assembly in 1979. It should be said at once, however, that the opposition is not susceptible to treatment in terms of clear-cut polarities, such as nationalism versus socialism. Indeed, the opposition often occurs *within* nationalism, between different ideas of the nation, and *within* socialism, between centralist and decentralist ideas of social organisation, so that in a country in which a significant number of writers are *both* nationalists and socialists, and in which conservative nationalists usually have strong social feeling, it is not surprising to find sensitive and imaginative people self-divided in complicated ways. The poets with whom I am concerned in this essay are all, to some degree, inhabitants of what Raymond Williams calls "that border country so many of us have been living in: between custom and education, between work and ideas, between love of place and an experience of change".[6] As Raymond Williams well knows — and he is, directly or indirectly, a major influence on the "structure of feeling" which most of the young Anglo-Welsh poets share — Welsh "border country" is greatly complicated by being, in addition, a border between two nations and two societies, which may run like a fault line or a marriage bond, or like both, through individual lives.

In Wales, poetry frequently matters as much to historians as history matters to poets. This is true of Gwyn A. Williams, who quotes R.S. Thomas's 'Welsh History' as epigraph to *When was Wales?* and comments: "This fine poem expresses some historical truths. It also sanctifies a monstrous historical lie". Unlike Emyr Humphreys, Gwyn A. Williams understands myth in a sense akin to the historical lie, although he is fully aware of its function of shaping history, as in Geoffrey of Monmouth's *History of the Kings of Britain* or Tudor use of an imaginary British past. Near the end of the book he writes: "The Welsh or their effective movers and shapers have repeatedly employed history to make a usable past, to turn a past into an instrument with which a present can build a future. It was once done in terms of myth, it has been recently and can be again done in terms of history".[7] But perhaps the distinction between myth and history is not quite as clear as it appears in his moving conclusion:

> One thing I am sure of. Some kind of human society, though God knows what kind, will no doubt go on occupying these two western peninsulas of Britain, but that people, who are my people and no mean people, who have for a millennium and a half lived in them as a Welsh people, are now nothing but a naked people under an acid rain.[8]

Here, "naked" has the force of its use in W.B. Yeats's 'A Coat', a poem which, Gwyn A. Williams tells us, "these days, I find I cannot put from my mind". Yeats claimed to be giving away his coat embroidered with "old mythologies", because "there's more enterprise/In walking naked". In the event, however, he changed his poetic coat for one in which the myths were structural, not merely decorative. It seems to me that Gwyn A. Williams doesn't altogether succeed in walking naked, either: he has far too strong a sense of identity derived from belonging to a people for that. Orthodox Marxists tell us that there is no such thing as the people: it is a dream of bourgeois romantics – there are only classes, and the committed individual chooses the cause of the working class. If I understand Gwyn A. Williams correctly at this point, however, he is invoking an entity, the people of Wales, now and with a continuous existence during fifteen hundred years, which has at least as much potency as a national idea as Emyr Humphreys's 'traditional' Wales or Waldo Williams's cloud of witnesses. Indeed, Gwyn A. Williams is the historian as poet of his people, who perceives, as he tells us Iolo Morganwg did, that Welsh poets "had been the rib-cage of the body politic, remembrancers, a collective memory honed for historic action".[9] In this spirit, he honours and does justice to the people excluded from the Wales of romantic nationalism; he restores them to history as a force, and returns them to an enlarged concept of the Wales which is their patrimony. It is a spirit shared by most of the younger Anglo-Welsh poets, who, in contrast to the inclination of Anglo-Welsh poetry of the Sixties and Seventies to focus on 'traditional' Wales, but developing from the example of Glyn Jones and Idris Davies, are extending their concern deep into urban and industrial areas of English-speaking Wales. This usually means, in fact, writing from where they are or where they come from, not only from their social circumstances but from their lives and their parents' lives. The result, according to some critics, is that they lose all specific Welshness. But this is precisely the ground of the larger historical contention, which is about values and about people, and about what constitutes the Welsh people. The contention is the more painful because, as Dai Smith says, "the history of Wales is a tale of divisions in the family".[10] Yet what the poets and historians alike also show, in circumstances of appalling social devastation, is the imaginative and intellectual excitement that may be engendered by a struggle "to turn a past into an instrument with which a present can build a future".

2

In his sense of language and his dexterous use of conventional forms, Robert Minhinnick is one of the most talented poets to have appeared in Wales since the 'Second Flowering' of Anglo-Welsh poetry in the 1960s, and his gift for description and metaphor invites comparison with Glyn Jones's work, which he admires. From the beginning, he has depicted a working world, or, more often, a world strongly marked by the work that was once done there, but has passed into memory with the workforce. He is in this sense a poet of worked historical place: of quarries, for example, or docks, or derelict industrial sites, or a former large estate — all places on his "native ground" in south Wales. He has, too, a gift for describing mechanical skills, and acute sensitivity to what he calls, in 'The Pit',[11] "all the mystery of the mechanic's shed". His feeling for the social and working life of places such as garages and pubs and the kitchen and garden side of country estates suggests a family history underpinning his poetic craft. It is part of his achievement to have built an imaginative world of such real, but seldom regarded, worked or working places and to have depicted the character of the area to which they belong. Moreover, the places are peopled, and not by caricatures. In this respect, his achievement is akin to that of a number of his contemporaries, although perhaps only the people and places of John Davies's suburban coastal north Wales have an equivalent authentic strangeness.

More than anything else, it is his sense of self and of its relation to his native ground that sets Robert Minhinnick apart from his contemporaries. In an early poem, 'Salvage',[12] he writes: "I end exile in a landscape of exhaustion". The self-consciousness is characteristic, and recurs in conjunction with the idea of "salvage" in a number of poems. In 'The Midden',[13] for example: "History's black//Sediment/Lies under my nails. Fine irony./All that survives is what people/Disregard,//The rubbish/Of their lives an eloquent spore". The sentiment is genuine but not original. It is not uncommon now for British and Irish poets to think of their work as a kind of imaginative archaeology, and to feel guilty at the eloquence with which they speak for or of the voiceless dead. Seamus Heaney at once comes to mind in this connection, and Minhinnick's work recalls his in more than one way. But lack of originality here does not matter. Poets who are borderers between a world of mental and verbal skills and a world of manual labour on which they are practically and imaginatively dependent, share a common effort to remember and do justice to the latter. Like Nigel Jenkins in his poems about the remote past, Robert Minhinnick looking at an ancient hoard, finds that: "History is not this gear of bronze,/...Rather, it is how it was used,/The association of metal and mind".[14] Such knowledge is a legacy to their descendants of generations of workers in industry or on the land.

'Burmese Tales'[15] reveals Robert Minhinnick's distinctiveness more effectively:

> Some things there are to salvage from the waste.
> History absorbs this too, and yet
> It is his own perspiration I feel chafe
> As he lifts the webbing on a green
> Insect-thrumming dawn, sucks air. And endures.

> And I could go on and on with him
> Following the mules through the Shan states
> Until the trees become China and the war ends.
> His life my drama in the skull's arena.
> But such imagery the one inheritance.

The empathy with his father's wartime experience is remarkable; so too is the claustrophobic atmosphere, which results in part from the setting, and in part from his internalisation of the experience: "His life my drama in the skull's arena". If imagery is "the one inheritance", then the poem will be a stage for sharing experience which perhaps cannot be shared outside it. It is my impression that something of the kind is true of Robert Minhinnick's poetry generally, which articulates a world that is peopled yet at the same time strangely isolated in the mind. He frequently dramatizes experiences of his grandfather or another family member, which he has internalised, and he frequently reverts to childhood memory. Living the past again in his mind, transforming it imaginatively, he works between history and myth in a peculiarly inward sense, honouring what actually happened but simultaneously turning it into personal mythology.

Robert Minhinnick is a poet of borders or margins: between past and present, self and others, man and nature; and his landscapes are between industrial and rural Wales, or between polluted sea and polluted shore, or on waste ground where strange and exuberant natural forms grow amid relics of derelict industry. In social terms, his world might be described as the underside of late decayed capitalist society. It is a kind of underworld, not of subhumanity, but of people exploited and pushed aside, of the defeated — Minhinnick has a Gissing-like sympathy with them — and of crafty or precarious survivors, poachers, mechanics, the unemployed. As in his poem-sequence on the death of the boxer Johnny Owen, Minhinnick both feels for the victims and shares a sense of complicity with the victimisers. He is capable of political anger, but his conscience is too uneasy to allow him the relentless political passion of Mike Jenkins.

The Ffornwg, a tributary of the River Ogmore, runs darkly through a number of his earlier poems. In 'Eels at Night'[16] it is "the crawling Ffornwg", where he plunges his hand into his own shadow and feels "the slippery texture of congealing eels/Like a wound opened in myself, our common skin". Here he gains "something like knowledge/Of a life joined with mine", and "a joint affirmation of the hollow flesh". The theme recurs in 'Sap',[17] which is perhaps his finest expression of it:

> Yet how often was the only sound
> Not the Ffornwg or our
> White thrash after fish,
> But the thinnest flute of the sap
> Maintaining its single note

A long minute in my head
As I imagined that pressure
Of water rising through the trees,
Streams moving vertically
And spilling in a silent turbulence
Along the boughs, a river

Flowing there beneath the bark,
The sap, singing, even as flesh
Leaned white and stunned
Against the visible current,
And the gwrachen like a small
Green stick swam past the hand.

The river is evidently more to him than a loved place where he played as a boy; it is also where he first sensed a frightening and fascinating oneness with nature, flesh, fish, trees and water joined in "our common skin". To Robert Minhinnick, the Ffornwg and other places of water and dank vegetation are like the wells to Seamus Heaney in 'Personal Helicon': a source of his imagination. Again, it is characteristic that he internalises the oneness, hearing "the flute of the sap" in his head. As in Heaney's *Death of a Naturalist*, imaginative energy springs for Minhinnick from nature's underworld, a dangerous, poisonous, fecund and sexually potent region, where the mind has direct access to the body's knowledge. He is fascinated and horrified by what he knows, and his microscopic eye for insects and plants, as in 'Herbals', is half-admiring, half-afraid. He has a Pre-Raphaelite gift of observation, acute, strange, more than real. He is an observer in a social world, who praises and commemorates in the main tradition of Welsh poetry, but he is also sharply aware of the strangeness and precariousness of the familiar, and of the underworld of man and nature.

In the words of 'The Heart',[18] Robert Minhinnick feels "the utter isolation of us all" in "the predatory world". The personal isolation which he conveys vividly and disturbingly is counteracted, yet also, in a way, intensified, by his internalisation of other people's experience. His recent, long poem 'Breaking Down' appears to be the culmination of a strong tendency of his work. It is a powerful, disturbing poem in which, as in his sharing of his father's Burmese experience, his empathy with the woman suffering a breakdown is remarkable. But the condition of self-entrapment, or of having the world in the head, has recurred from the beginning in his work, and in this poem he shares the experience with more than sympathy inspired by the occasion. Significantly, his description of the barbiturates and capsules in part XI recalls his description of the poisonous plants in 'Herbals'. 'Breaking Down' calls to mind Robert Lowell and, more insistently, Sylvia Plath. Indeed, there is about the tendency I have referred to in his work something of the same chill of detachment with which Sylvia

Plath describes isolation and estrangement. While this may be temperamental, it is also, I think, an expression of a general condition of late capitalist society, in a Wales in which individual minds internalise the inheritance which it is extremely difficult to share in common and to carry through into the future. Robert Minhinnick's strength as a poet derives in large measure from the tension between isolation and his sense of belonging to a larger, working and natural, native ground.

3

Nigel Jenkins's poem 'First calving'[19] begins with the poet driving the cow to the yard, where he stands apart while other men assist in the birth:

> I watched there the obscure passage
> of men's hands and, exiled in crass
> daylight, waited –
>   till a shout
> sent me running big with purpose
> to the stable for a halter.
>
> They flipped to me the rope's end, its
> webbing they noosed around the hoof:
> we leaned there, two of us, lending weight
> to each contraction; the other fumbled
> for the drowning muzzle, the absent leg,
>   said he'd heard that over Betws way
>   some farmer'd done this with a tractor —
>   pulled the calf to bits and killed the cow.

After the successful birth, the calf "like some bones pudding/steaming with life", the poet buries the afterbirth: "to be weighted with a stone,/they said, to keep it from the scavengers". At first, then, he is 'I', with no part in the labour, "exiled". Working with the others, he becomes "we", "two of us". But he does not falsify his relationship with the others by claiming to be at-one with them, or with the work by claiming to be equally expert. The need for his help makes him "big with purpose", eager and active, with a slightly amused consciousness of himself which someone to whom calving is common labour would not have; and at the end he is again detached, respectfully acknowledging the men's special knowledge, and dutifully acting in accordance with it. The poem is about attachment and detachment, about being an individual observer and becoming a participant, learning to work with others at assisting life. It is about a proper way of doing things, in accordance with traditional skills, but in a community where human error occurs, as in the case of the farmer "over Betws way" — (whose clumsiness with a tractor may be Nigel Jenkins's unconscious glance in the direction of

R.S. Thomas and his attitude towards the Machine; although of course it may also be fact). To my mind, it is a good poem, which effectively dramatizes the action and its social and psychological value. It is also interesting in that it is a good representation of attitudes common in Welsh and Anglo-Welsh poetry. These may be defined by reference to its difference from poems on the same subject by Ted Hughes and English poems influenced by him, in which the natural act and the poet's relationship to elemental surroundings are the focus of interest, not participation in a communal labour.

There are other occasions when Nigel Jenkins, speaking for himself, speaks also not only for his generation of Anglo-Welsh poets, but for a tradition uniting poets in both languages in Wales. The most notable instance of this occurs in 'The ridger':[20]

> To describe is to listen, to enter
> into detail with this ground
> and this ground's labour; to take
> and offer outward continuing fruit.

The poet listens and acts; he is recipient of an *organic* inheritance, which he seeks to pass on, but changed, developed, in accordance both with new circumstances and with its principle of growth. The aim appears again in 'Maidenhair',[21] in which Nigel Jenkins says of the fern which he has inherited from his grandparents:

> The maidenhair endures in the Celtic west.
> Theirs they kept whole lifetimes
> in the same narrow pot.
> I'll give it space, learn its ways; help it
> flourish, reproduce, watch me go.

The fern links grandfather and grandmother, values of the farm and domestic interior, and, through association with the coal measures, values of the industrial past and the primeval natural world. The grandfather is remembered realistically, fuming against "progress, the workers and his gout", so that the differences between the man and his grandson are shown. Nevertheless, Nigel Jenkins is not a poet of modern industrial or post-industrial Wales, but of rural Wales, under the shadow of the nuclear threat. Among young Anglo-Welsh poets, he acknowledges the greatest debt to 'traditional' Wales, is, in fact, the most nationalist, and the closest in that respect to poets of the previous generation, although he is close in his radical socialism to Mike Jenkins and Steve Griffiths too. However, while recognising his debt to the tradition, and affirming its continuity by intending to pay it, he is also aware of the narrowness of the way of life which the fern symbolises. The movement of his later poetry is accordingly towards a greater openness, and it includes more of the world, while affirming and extending his loyalty to the Welsh past.

The poems in *Song and Dance* have a verbal care which owes much to Nigel Jenkins's awareness that: "There were words about/that weren't to be trusted".[22] It is significant that the statement concludes a poem about castrating bull-calves, since he is acutely sensitive to the fact that man is a tormenter and murderer of other creatures as well as of his own kind. This links him with the American poet Gary Snyder, to whom he is also connected by his love of shared outdoor work, and generally by the ecological vision, although his social and political concern is more specific, and less 'tribal', than Snyder's. It is not surprising, then, to find that the increasing openness of his poetry is formal, in accordance with post-Poundian poetics, as well as a larger hospitality to content. He has this in common with the English poet Philip Pacey too, and with poets in Wales such as Chris Torrance who form an 'alternative' to the Anglo-Welsh 'establishment'. (I put both words in inverted commas to record my sense of their meanings being relative both to the radical concern and the 'outsider' status of *all* Anglo-Welsh poetry in the context of English centralism, and to the tendency of poetic undergrounds to become alternative establishments.) In my view, the most successful poems in Nigel Jenkins's 'experimental' book, *Practical Dreams* (1983), carry his verbal care into the formal inventiveness, while the less successful develop a new rhetoric and acquire a certain sameness in their collage of diverse contents. In 'Snowdrops', for example, he uses the *form* to think with, but in 'Never forget your Welsh' he accumulates materials to express his angry satire. In several poems, including 'Snowdrops', he struggles *in* the form with the difficulty of writing now — which is a difficulty of both meaning and hoping — and combines crisp imagism with news of a violent world breaking in on the local and the domestic. While he was open to the world outside Wales in poems in *Song and Dance*, he is now more open, breaking conventional poetic constraints with their limitations of subject and response, and attempting to carry his Welsh inheritance outward and onward. It would be a great pity if he were to develop his easier poetic rhetoric, instead of entering into the detail of each poem, with the combination of care and passion of which he is capable at his best.

4

"Only connect", E.M. Forster's famous prescription of liberal concern, hardly envisages the kind of connections that are made, in different forms, in the socio-political imaginations of Mike Jenkins and Steve Griffiths. Mike Jenkins's sense of landscapes of menace, developed in his poems set in West Germany and Northern Ireland, takes on an added historical depth in his poems of Merthyr Tydfil, which he sees both with the eye of personal experience — he lives and teaches there — and with the support of Gwyn A. Williams's historical vision. Like Lewis Lewis, in his poem[23] dedicated to Gwyn A. Williams, he knows "that the rope which held Dic Penderyn/was the same that hauled the cage at a pit". This may also be described as a modern version, without the Christianity, of the political imagination of William Blake, and much that needs to be said about Mike Jenkins's poetry is by way of illustrating the force and ingenuity with which he makes such connections with his metaphorical language. In 'Dic Penderyn on Aberdare Mountain',[24] for example:

> But they did not hear our voices
> built to arch across valley, built to carry
> the locomotive history into the future —
> pulling, not trucks, but the coffins of workmen.

The kind of seeing which this exemplifies connects the physical effort of working people, their actual bodies, or, in this instance, voices, to the history they make, and the places in which they make it. Mike Jenkins's inwardness with the cost of that effort, and the ability of his metaphors to convey it, combine with an acute sense of the movement and opposition of historical forces in his strongest writing, as in 'Chartist Meeting':[25]

> Each wheel was held fast
> as you would grip a coin;
> yet everything went away from them.
> The black kernel of the mountains
> seemed endless, but still in their stomachs
> a furnace-fire roared,
> and their children's eyes hammered
> and turned and hollowed out a cannon.

In general, he makes connections by combining naturalistic description with metaphorical language, and at his best he forges vision, hammering out forms of interaction between people, history and place.

"My body is not my own", Mike Jenkins writes in 'T.V. Afternoon',[26] part 7 of his Merthyr sequence, 'Empire of Smoke', and in 'Memorials',[27] part 5 of the same sequence: "There are men with rising-damp in their bones,/men with germs working double-shifts and overtime/in their veins". His theme here, and a major source of his metaphors generally, is the exploitation of the body, its implication in socio-political action, and the sickness and internal strife that frequently ensue. The bodies of working people are worked on, strengthened, or destroyed or deformed by their work. Working together they shape the physical environment, and form themselves as a united body, gaining political consciousness, and acting on history. Effort, suffering, social injustice and alienation put an intolerable strain on individual minds. It is from the connections among these processes that Mike Jenkins makes his best political poems. Broadly speaking, as I have said, Blake is the master of connections between the ideology and processes of capitalist industrial society. It is the example of Wilfred Owen's war poems, however, that is more often brought to mind by Mike Jenkins's strenuous and sometimes tortured metaphorical language, by his urgent sense of involvement in political warfare, and above all by the connections he makes between physical suffering and mental pain.

Sometimes his strengths coexist with weaknesses in a single passage, as in the first part of 'Empire of Smoke':[28]

> I felt the past like valleys
> mapping out the nerves
> of many of its people
> and saw the paralysed expressions
> of museum exhibits: like Richard Crawshay
> priggish and puffed with fowl and port
> turning you servant with his eyes

Here, the image of nerves connecting people and valleys is subtle, and the line "turning you servant with his eyes" is compact with social history. But the description of Richard Crawshay is overwritten and a caricature; in fact, the poet's "museum exhibit". This exemplifies a satirical facility, itself a product of the facility of retrospective political anger, which in my view marks many of the political poems in Mike Jenkins's most recent book, *Invisible Times* (1986). Overconfidence makes his writing flat and crude, and his caricatures, of opponents or attitudes, are the poetic equivalent of slogans. The real history is always more interesting, and the history which he really cares about, the history of working people, he treats with much more verbal subtlety, richness, and force.

Interestingly, it is the more personal poems in *Invisible Times* which are the most fully imagined. His previous book, *Empire of Smoke*, already hints at this development, with good poems about his grandmother and about birth and, above all, the sequence about his daughter, 'For Bethan'. In 'Birth is a Tidal Wave' his sense of connections culminates when he imagines the foetus participating in cosmic rhythms and the child born into a violent and unjust world. In fact, his vision of nature, of the co-operation of natural forces in creating and sustaining life, and of its social deformations and perversions, is the basis of his political perception and anger. This gives his personal writing a political dimension, and, as in the case of Nigel Jenkins, founds his politics on a vision of man's place in nature, which exploitation and social alienation destroy. 'For Bethan', in my view his best poem to date, connects the personal with the natural and the social, and creates convincing different 'voices'. It is a poem in which Mike Jenkins dramatizes the effort, pain, and release of birth labour, expresses primal emotion, and links an ancient drama of primeval forces with modern hospital methods and conditions. A poet who can write from this imaginative and emotional depth, and with the force of his best historical and political poems in *The Common Land* and *Empire of Smoke*, will surely come to see the difference between these qualities and such poems as 'Military Rule', 'Industrial Museum', 'Police Statement' and 'My Country' in *Invisible Times*, and between these poems and 'I follow her Meandering', 'Tonight the Sun' and 'Stallion' from the same book.

5

The tension and difficulty Steve Griffiths struggles with in his writing may be measured by the distance between the dedication to *Anglesey Material* (1980) — "These poems are for the people of Anglesey, in the hope that they will not be accepted unquestioningly" — and the extreme and, on the whole, necessary difficulty of poems in *Civilised Airs* (1984). Not that *Anglesey Material* is an easy book, but its public and personal dimensions are related in more accessible ways.

Steve Griffiths's "patchworks" of Amlwch are "a pattern of fields and buildings/interlocking with lives". He has "chosen/a folk pattern,/forsaking isolation".[29] He is, however, like many poets of 'place' in recent years, a native returning, with the distance that enables him to see both the pattern and himself in relation to it. In fact, he is intensely self-conscious about the problematic relationship of the personal and the social:

> I come to a poetry of place
>
> having seen the sensitivity of an elite:
> it is in the small comfort of our minds
> that we are important
>
> in a culture of mutual congratulation
> not in the eyes of the excluded
> no matter how humane we think we are.
>
> A small boy in rags who misunderstands
> follows me, pointing derisively, out of my past,
> throwing dried balls of particular poetry.[30]

The last fine complex image implies, among other things, I think, that "poetry of place" is itself excrement when gathered from the lives of those whom it excludes.

Steve Griffiths's self-consciousness as man and poet in *Anglesey Material* is an expression of his good faith: he will not falsify his relationship to the people of the place either by excluding himself from them or by denying his distance from them. He is critical; he sees himself with the same detachment as he sees others, and with the same socio-political imagination; he quotes historical documents and comments on them. This gives his style something of a clear, hard-edged 'objectivist' technique, not unlike George Oppen's at his hardest and clearest. One example must suffice of the many that form one of the book's principal strengths:

> by the old jetty's streaked luxury
> of local stone smeared with seaweed,
> a child's game of construction,
> cost-effective numbered concrete blocks are shifted.
>
> old women with foam-coloured hair work
> through the motions of bright washing on the line
> at their square house, surrounded by the waiting
> blocks, an alien intelligence, administered
> by a Portakabin from Rotterdam.
>
> the track to their house is dangerous to the unauthorised.[31]

The detail and depth of social perception, of seeing and imaging connections, in writing of this quality are much greater than those of a more subjective and romantic kind. Steve Griffiths's Anglesey is a place of "patterns of history, smallest events/in the folding of mountains";[32] it is a place of individual lives and human agency, and of immeasurably ancient elemental powers shaping the land; it is where change "means how one technology/builds up on another, bankrupt of human reference".[33] It is all of these things, and the book's considerable achievement is to show their connections, in and between passages, which move confidently, (and, in the following passage, with some humour) between elemental and social forces, and between cosmic overview and individual experience:

> I have seen the Packet surrounded with green
> menacing light, the clouds heaving like passengers,
>
> running against the Atlantic, its ears flattened.
> The turbines drumming the comfort of power:
>
> the plastic cups in the buffet and the ring of the till
> a statement in the hollow of enormity.
>
> Like lived-in leather, like the skins of seamen,
> struggle ebbs the mailboat to its worn beauty.
>
> Beaten on rainy mountainsides by west winds
> that follow the contours of erosion and recreate them,

> so many people bear this quality: beaten women,
> dark rings under their eyelids,
>
> told they have too many children, balancing
> resignation and fortitude in their eyes.[34]

Compared to *Anglesey Material*, I would not describe *Civilised Airs* as a 'success'; nor, I think, would Steve Griffiths be interested in such a description. It is a book which, in its division into "poems of love" and poems of "social concern" (as the blurb puts it), and in each section, wrestles with the critical difficulty of relating the personal and the social today, and especially in north London, where most of the poems are set, and where Steve Griffiths works in welfare rights. He struggles with the difficulty in his language, in a voice that combines or mixes, sometimes very uncomfortably, generalising statement and highly inventive metaphor. Thus he can speak of sensing "an odour of fascism/round a lack of generosity",[35] and produce mixed metaphors such as "The patter of bombs scars its thread in the walls",[36] (which, I have to admit, means little to me). The difficulty may be seen more clearly in 'Shrinking horizon',[37] which begins: "In a public darkness/private stars glimmer behind a curtain", and states, two verses later: "They are closing the children's wards,/they are breaking up the future". But what may seem impatience to speak out on the poet's part, without sufficient care for the construction of meaning, is really violent unrest, the anxious rage of a gifted poet in circumstances in which he cannot trust his gift. 'Guardianship'[38] states the reason:

> It is easy to see the provision
> of any order as a saving grace,
> my desk as a liner in savage lightless seas,
> shedding the reassurance of its cabins' trim
> on the gaping, clashing rooves of the waves,
> cherishing the machinery,
> the possible,
> for want of another principle.

The "airs" of his poetry threaten to be "a saving grace", a form of personal salvation, excluding the public chaos in which he lives, the society without a principle of common purpose or social justice. It is evident, too, that Steve Griffiths feels as guilty as a social worker tempted to hide behind "the machinery" of office, as he does as a poet escaping by "the machinery" of the poem. It is impossible to doubt his sincerity, yet there are occasions when the extremity of the all-pervading guilt seems an indulgence, indeed, another form of escape, and when this produces what I interpret as a compensatory fascination with anti-social violence, as in 'Watching riot', I think he is seeing and writing superficially.

Steve Griffiths feels trapped, then, not only because "the horizon's cemented in, though flawed",[39] but because he is conscious of being a bystander and an observer, even, as an educated man, an exploiter of other people's misery. In 'Writing room'[40] he says:

> I am a child at the window
> who looks out on puddles and shoppers
> who look back.
>
> From another room
> the peaceable kingdom gazes out impassively,
> the ghost in the double exposure.
>
> Sensitive, its gaze in its own domain.
> Unresponsive as a lord in an old photograph,
> with his tiger.

There could hardly be a more extreme, (or more strained), inversion of the traditional order of visionary art, which, instead of bringing the savage world together in peace and harmony, is both locked in its privacy, and a predator on what it excludes. In Anglesey, the poet's sense of being in a shared world, however difficult his relationship to it, prevented this from happening. But *Civilised Airs*, in its political poems, is a book of guilt and social alienation, and of refusal to escape from the predicament in a poetry of personal order. It is a book in which the poet places himself in what he apprehends as the general condition, and refuses to imagine a private escape from the public fate. This is a direction in which George Oppen also felt compelled to develop, and there are not many other ways which are as honourable now. Like the society, the poetry is under enormous strain. Steve Griffiths seeks a principle of order and connection in disorder and disconnection, and breaks conventions of seeing and feeling and writing which he feels belong to an old, false harmony between poet and society.

6

John Davies was born and brought up in industrial south Wales, but now lives and teaches at Prestatyn on the north Wales coast. He had already had a period of teaching in North America, in Michigan, before some of the poems in his first book, *At the Edge of Town* (1981), were written, and since then he has taught for a time in Washington. His experiences of Wales and America are complementary rather than opposite, and in both places he is frequently "at home but reaching/at last for what's new".[41] He is more balanced than divided between being settled and the desire to travel, but his sense of 'here', whether in north or south Wales or in America, always depends to some extent on his knowledge of 'elsewhere'.

John Davies emerges from his first book as a poet influenced by Philip Larkin, but with a strong, independent mind; a wry, questioning, self-conscious poet, aware of the distance between people but celebrating occasions when, as in 'Picture Time',[42] "ex-islands now become the main". He celebrates family love and order, and is acutely aware of their vulnerability. Like Robert Minhinnick, he is haunted by what he calls, in 'Downstairs',[43] "life's other life". He is conscious of social ills and obligations, but without the bitterness of hard-edged political anger, with a tendency to caricature its objects, of Mike Jenkins and Steve Griffiths. Writing of lives "at the edge of town", in suburban coastal north Wales, John Davies is tolerant and compassionate, his main difference in attitude from Philip Larkin being the instinctive, (or culturally ingrained), democratic spirit with which he places himself on a level with those around him. For example, he does not scorn a neighbour's "rustic dream",[44] built with such things as garden gnomes and elves and a concrete pond, but recognises that fulfilment of vision eludes them both. His 'Sunny Prestatyn'[45] is quite without either Philip Larkin's tourist's eye view or R.S. Thomas's hatred of visitors and newcomers, (which became almost a standard emotion of Anglo-Welsh poetry in the 1960s amd '70s). For John Davies, the retired people, "detached, with no shared memory", "are us writ large". His sympathy is with the shy and unnoticed, with "small things half-visible/and quiet",[46] like the squirrel at the zoo. He accepts with fond amusement the absurdities and small contentments of surburban life, recognising the affinities between his dreams and failures and partial successes and those of others. In this context, his use of a neighbourly, familial "we" in a number of poems is particularly significant. Again, it has something in common with Larkin's, but is more intimate, and more democratic. In a recent poem, 'The visitor's book',[47] he writes: "Why can't poems be clearer? This one/of yours' — Even now my mother makes me jump". This is only one particularly strong piece of the widespread evidence that John Davies's "we" includes specific people — his family and the 'people' to whom they belong — and that he writes to be understood by them. Not always with complete success or without anxiety, of course, but always with respect for their understanding. Indeed, he is an accessible, even sometimes a genuinely 'popular', poet; but he is also formally inventive, complex, with rich verbal resources. This suggests to me that his family relationships, rather like Alun Lewis's, and true to a pattern that is not uncommon in south Wales, guarantee him a large measure of freedom without fear of being misunderstood in his poetry.

John Davies reserves his anger and his witty satire for those he regards as bogus and pretentious. It is important to understand, I think, that his notorious 'How to Write Anglo-Welsh Poetry',[48] (a good poem for which he is in danger of becoming well-known especially outside Wales for the wrong reasons), is part of his necessary attempt to clear the ground around him in order to make space for the reality he perceives and values, and which he believes, not without justification, that Anglo-Welsh poetry of the preceding period did not. To show the present, he has to clear away such traditional Anglo-Welsh poetic props as "myth" and "exile, defeat, hills". However, the poem is in fact an offensive on behalf of Anglo-Welshness, of the life John Davies knows in north and south Wales, against those who apologize for "being Anglo-*any*thing". As he says in 'Country Quest (2)':[49] "I'm tired of the old nostalgia game", and:

> We are going to have to take what's here
> to stay, make less of that tempting blur,
> our dream-past. And to accept what is new
> as something most have travelled to —

This means celebrating, not just "the doors of caravans" flung wide in Spring, but people like Mr. Dyas, a widower, old and blind, whose voice is "a torch in our own small/dark, and that upright walk an advance/into symbol".[50]

Always a poet with a good sense of rhythm, John Davies has, at times, a surprising, almost mystical, lyricism. This appears in 'Another Kind' in *At the Edge of Town* but is generally more evident in the poems in *The Silence in the Park* (1982), where he sometimes, as in 'Mist' and 'Winter', transforms things imaginatively instead of representing their appearances. For example:

> the bandstand
>
> its worn loudspeakers
> are broadcasting snow   more snow
>   notes falling
>   to faint applause of trees
>
>   the lawns listen
>   muffled in white[51]

The book is the work of a delicate, praising poet, who experiences joy in family life and in work, and who is more than ever aware of vulnerability and the passage of time. He is tentative, with a sense of mystery, and his humanism, as in *At the Edge of Town*, is based on a sense of what is actually possible within the limitations of human life. As he says in 'A letter',[52] a poem addressed to a poet friend who is evidently a 'confessional' extremist:

> I've glimpsed that land
> where only self's the mystery, not words, not sand,
>
> and would not want to return though you swear
> nevada would be mine if I'd learn to fly a needle there.

> But from reflected heat I learn my own temperature.
> This light cooling through trees that moistly stir,
>
> and which seems not always sharp or new, must go
> to make metaphors framing what I but half-know
>
> not just about myself till I gradually see it clear.

Having cleared his space by rejecting Anglo-Welsh stereotypes and the pressure to conform, John Davies in *The Silence in the Park* is writing a poetry of relationships and experience that is true to himself and to this aim.

The same may be said even more emphatically of *The Visitor's Book* (1985), which in my view is one of the most considerable books of poetry by any Anglo-Welsh poet in many years. Here, he is a visitor to Cymmer Afan and Port Talbot, the places of his birth and upbringing, and to places in Washington. Characteristically, although a number of poems set in Wales and America depict him as a man who is driving through, he is less unsettled in either country than this might suggest. In south Wales he has the unease of an inheritor not quite sure what he has inherited. As he says in 'The voice box':[53] "Nor am I like my father:/knowing just where he was, he felt no lack/ of road where mine gives out — and Well, he'd say,/just where d'you think you're going anyway?" Yet his way of seeing the valley, its history, people and things, which were his father's, has a confident intimacy which shows that it is more his than he claims. It is distance, though, as well as intimacy, that enables him to see place, as the last verses of 'In Port Talbot'[54] show:

> Look out on winter's thin streets. See how steel
> lights up the whole town still. Although it shivers now
> in November dreaming of steel's breaking point, its people –
> kept from clean air but not each other — could tell how
> common purpose, gathering, runs strongest
> on hardest ground. As here where the land turned
> overnight to metal, where smoke blooms in the window.
>
> And when at last shared work's vibrations cease,
> sharing itself will fade (as in the mining villages nearby)
> with Keir Hardie's dream, with Bethanias long since ghosts,
> down history's shaft. Difference and indifference will untie
> taut bonds of work that cramp yet forged here a community;
> then old South Wales will have to start a New. Meanwhile
> reverberations still, slow leavings, long goodbye.

Here and in north Wales, in 'New spaces, Clwyd', he sees the human cost of urban and industrial dereliction, but he has, too, a sense of the 'New', which, if it has no basis in political faith, derives from his experience and observation of everyday human transformations of hostile circumstance. This is equally true of his perception of the recent history of the Indians in America, and in 'The white buffalo', the finest achievement in the book, the balance between distance and belonging, detachment and intimacy, in his Welsh experience relates subtly to his view of both white settlers and Indians. The sequence ends on the following note:

> This singing in another tongue old anthems
> in a shared redoubt, I've no part in.
> But am not apart. I have been here before
> elsewhere, just visiting from a century
> aging faster than time that has said no
> to so much now there's just money,
> as though inside might be someone or
> something I'd half-known and lost.[55]

The voice, easy, intimate, yet generalising, with a quiet sad lyricism, owes something to the recent American poetry John Davies admires, most notably Richard Hugo's, but it is unmistakably his own, as he responds with his particular Welsh sensibility to the old in the new.

To have no part in "a shared redoubt", yet to be "not apart": this is a paradox suffered, in different degrees, by all of the poets whose work I have discussed in this essay. It has not been my purpose — either out of presumption or folly — to define what is Welsh or Anglo-Welsh, but to examine the responses to the critical historical present of five young poets from different parts of Wales. In an area in which much is dark, it is clear to me that each poet derives values from Welsh communal life — values forming an inheritance, which is known as intimately as a person may know his closest kin – and brings them to bear on a society whose governing powers are intent on their devastation. The voices are, in that sense, 'resistant' — they are, in Emyr Humphreys's words, "defending a realm under siege". Or if not a realm, then places, but places joined by the common working tradition of the people that Gwyn A. Williams invokes. The places are perceived in terms of what I have defined, in writing about an earlier generation of Anglo-Welsh poets, as the "poetry of nearness". There is, in this and in other respects, continuity between the older and younger Anglo-Welsh poets. It is also possible to perceive in some of the work of these young poets — in poems by Nigel Jenkins and Mike Jenkins and in John Davies's 'The visitor's book', for example — a feeling for the Welsh language which echoes that of the previous generation. One major difference, however, is that poets of the new movement are more tenacious of their present social reality, more inclined to defend or to wrestle with what they actually have, in places under great pressure or already partially devastated, and to resist the judgement of 'traditional' Welshness, as well as the condescension or indifference of English centralism.

Notes

1. *The Taliesin Tradition* (1983), pp. 5-6.
2. *Ibid.*, pp. 227-228.
3. "We call it the literary tradition of Wales. It means you cannot pluck a flower of song off a headland of Dyfed in the late eighteenth century without stirring a great northern star of the sixth century." 'The Essence of Welsh Literature', *Presenting Saunders Lewis* (1973), p. 155.
4. *The Taliesin Tradition*, p. 4.
5. *Wales! Wales?* (1984), p. 165.
6. *The Country and the City* (1973), p. 197.
7. *When was Wales?* (Penguin Books), p. 304.
8. *Ibid.*, p. 305.
9. *Ibid.*, p. 165.
10. *Wales! Wales?* p. 166.
11. *Life Sentences* (1983), p. 30.
12. *A Thread in the Maze* (1978), p.13.
13. *Native Ground* (1979), p. 12.
14. 'On the Llyn Fawr Hoard in the National Museum of Wales', *The Dinosaur Park* (1985), p. 10.
15. *Life Sentences* p. 45.
16. *A Thread in the Maze* p.15.
17. *Ibid.*, p. 20.
18. *Ibid.*, p. 18.
19. *Song and Dance* (1981), p. 14.
20. *Ibid.*, p. 28.
21. *Ibid.*, p. 16.
22. 'Castration', *Ibid.*, p. 41.
23. 'Lewis Lewis on the Convict Ship', *The Common Land* (1981), p. 17.
24. *Ibid.*, p. 16.
25. *Ibid.*, p. 19.
26. *Empire of Smoke* (1983), p. 28.
27. *Ibid.*, p. 26.
28. *Ibid.*, p. 22.
29. 'Patchworks', *Anglesey Material*, p. 1.
30. 'Expectations, 3', *Ibid.*, p. 5.
31. 'Oil Terminal, 2', *Ibid.*, p. 22.
32. 'Hymns and Backward Glances, 6', *Ibid.*, p. 47.
33. 'Post-Terminal Depression', *Ibid.*, p. 24.
34. 'Suffering does for the character', *Ibid.*, pp. 17-18.
35. 'From Waterloo Bridge, ensuing dark', *Civilised Airs*, p. 29.
36. '1941' *Ibid.*, p. 36.
37. *Ibid.*, p. 34.
38. *Ibid.*, p. 41.
39. 'Children in a walled garden', Ibid.,.., p. 60.
40. *Ibid.*, p. 61.
41. 'Barns', *At the Edge of Town*, p. 21.
42. *Ibid.*, p. 13.

43. *Ibid.*, p. 25.
44. 'Country Quest (1)', *Ibid.*, p. 22.
45. *Ibid.*, p. 28.
46. 'At the Zoo', *Ibid.*, p. 30.
47. *The Visitor's Book* (1985), p. 12.
48. *At the Edge of Town*, p.37.
49. *Ibid.*, p. 59.
50. 'For Mr. Dyas', *Ibid.*, p. 27.
51. 'Winter', *The Silence in the Park*, p. 15.
52. *Ibid.*, pp. 20-21.
53. *The Visitor's Book*, p. 15.
54. *Ibid.*, pp.18-19.
55. *Ibid.*, p. 67.

Barbarous Reflections

I

In Guy Davenport's *The Geography of the Imagination* I value in particular the writings on Ezra Pound — especially on his "spatial sense of time" and his understanding of the meaning of Persephone for the twentieth century — and the exploration of the tradition of scientific and poetic clarity (in Agassiz, Hugh Miller, Thoreau, Ruskin, Hopkins, Ronald Johnson, and others), and its relation to the visionary tradition of Blake and the 'Ancients'.

But there is also something in Davenport that irritates me and makes me very uneasy. Or perhaps it is something *not* in him: a lack.

He is genuinely brilliant: as scholar, linguist, and above all in his talent for seeing connections. But perhaps it is just in this that something is missing too: a feeling for the meanings and morals of particular cultures, that cannot be abstracted from them and connected with apparent equivalents from other cultures, as if time were space. So my doubt focuses on Pound and on other Modernists (especially James Joyce) as well.

Guy Davenport's quick intelligence sometimes reaches beyond meaning into emptiness — when for example he claims to have 'understood' Treblinka and Buchenwald, as if easy words about the unspeakable didn't betray terrible presumption. As Czeslaw Milosz says, there are times when it is better to stammer. This instance arises from Davenport's light-handed treatment of Pound's anti-Semitism, which in turn shows a moral irresponsibility that's all the more disturbing in a critic who values *attention* above all.

"Eclectic religion": the phrase brings much of the problem to a focus. We can get the impression from reading Pound that we know something in depth of other cultures and religions. And indeed Pound does preserve, and makes connections. At the same time, though, he *isolates*, and though what he isolates is, often, living voices, they are abstracted from the whole order which gives them meaning only because they belong to it. There is then a further process of abstraction when the scholar, who is Pound's true reader, pursues the knowledge in the poems as an end in itself. Or if not as an end, the eclecticism is a method of treating religion and culture *aesthetically*. I am uneasy because I sometimes feel that Davenport's brilliant range is over a void: that he can take from past and present what he wants and leave what he doesn't. Pound's choice was, after all, his life: he took or left what he wanted to, and in doing so he built a 'world'. Now, it seems, there are people living in it, without Pound's necessity.... This, perhaps, is always a critic's danger, as evident in Leavis's relationship with Lawrence as in the Poundians: they enter the house, they inhabit it, they show its construction and every corner to others, but there seems to be no inner pressure to make something for themselves — (in Davenport's case, I speak of his apparent lack of pressure to *question* Pound, not of his fiction and poetry, which I don't know) — the artist's inner pressure which is intimately related to his sense of the challenge of being alive *now*, of being asked eternal questions, but immediately, and in terms of the history he has to live. However bookish he may be, the artist feels and responds to this pressure; he cannot live in a house of literature as an academic critic may — given the authority literature has been granted since Matthew Arnold, together with the rise of academic criticism as a profession.

Davenport sees brilliantly; what he doesn't see is the Modernist conventions determining his seeing. I realize that my irritation comes also from feeling close affinities with him in some respects, and then being disappointed that his fine knowledge of the tradition of *seeing* shouldn't have given him a more independent view of the most self-conscious but least self-questioning Modernist methods.

2

Perhaps our language is all we have to understand with, and we articulate in words what we can of our feelings and instincts — all the non-verbal intuitions and forms of communication that reach deeper than we can say. So, the more I put into words, the greater my sense of failure, from the correspondingly greater awareness that it's impossible to capture even the life that we ourselves live, let alone the lives of others. I can imagine a revelation that would astonish us with a familiar, yet strange vision: our lives seen as they are, from every hidden motive and remotest influence to every minutest detail, correcting our mistaken notions and distorted perceptions, completing our partial awareness. For me, the poem that works is the poem that gains a little more of this vision. Indeed all writing that is worthwhile, that exists to see, not in order to be seen, makes some gain.

The great problem is speaking of others, or analysing the self, since it's then that I'm most likely to be deceived about my motives, or, at least, to have mixed motives that I'm only partially aware of. No doubt this is why I'm most aware of the limits of my language and understanding, and recall the complete vision beyond me, after I've risked observing or analysing another person. Then, afterwards, it almost always feels like a betrayal; not an action that I want (always) to undo, by destroying what I've written, but an action for which I need forgiveness. And in a way, writing as I do, I feel this is true of all my words, because each is a kind of judgement (even of what to see at any time in any place) and must therefore submit to be judged.

Since language belongs to the community of us all, living and dead, I believe that at each instant we are either wasting words, or using them to slight or destroy, or partially realising the community to which we belong, mostly, unseeing. Words among us all are either gain or loss.

3

So far in rereading John Cowper Powys, I have found (after a shaky start with *Maiden Castle*) that my admiration and gratitude are greater than ever. For *Weymouth Sands* above all, at this stage; which is much funnier, as well as deeper and more interesting, than I remember. In fact, I can see that in my concern to define the *underlying* poetic structure of the novels, when I wrote my study of them, I was selective in what I saw and what I enjoyed, and made the books (and the man) less than they are. At the same time, particularly in rereading *Autobiography*, I'm even more inclined to question him, especially about his *escape* from class and the historical present. I find him as liberating as ever, in the generosity he shows, and stimulates in others, and in the enjoyment he shares, but I press more on what his "life-illusion" obscures and evades. I have read *Autobiography* in conjunction with his letters to Llewelyn, mainly to compare two versions of the same events, and the equilibrium of the later, cunningly constructed, book with much rawer, more confused, immediate feelings. (*After my Fashion*, with its rawness and exposure, also suggested this.) But if I set out with some critical disinterest and curiosity, the effect on me has been personal, and mixed.

Powys reconfirms my belief in the generosity of great art. For me, though, depth involves something more historical, more social, even, in a way, more personal, than it did for him, and it is less 'romantic', less to do with an imagination, supposedly independent of social and historical forces, that can create and destroy 'reality'. I approach him with what I have come, through living and writing, to see of the world, and with what reading George Oppen in particular has strengthened and developed. Consequently I couldn't now speak of 'reality' as Powys does, with a kind of careless — if exultant — confidence in his imaginative mastery of it. I feel, too strongly, something *irreducible*, a hardness and impenetrability in things, and, closely associated with this, a sense of being *under judgement*, so that compared with great realists, like Kierkegaard or Simone Weil or Oppen, Powys's philosophy seems to me, when I look for its foundation, rootless, unreal; or it seems at best a psychology, or psycho-sensuality, that may be very helpful to certain individuals (as it has been to me), but, when compared to the Christianity which it partly exploits and partly replaces, is neither a philosophy nor a religion. But for all that, Powys's generosity, with its embrace of childishness and immaturity and abnormality, is an intelligent as well as affectionate acceptance, which well understands the trickiness of terms like 'mature' and 'normal'. For if I'm right in thinking his philosophy rootless, what he gives is the sympathy and understanding and abundant vitality of a living man — it is the self he gives that is so large, the self and its capacity for understanding and accepting others, and for enduring suffering too. And for all I've said about 'reality' his fictional world is truer to real mystery, the mystery of nature and of people's lives, than anything that a Leavisite or Marxist could produce. Our dominant academic methods would make short work with Powys; but that's a good example of what makes them short of the intelligence and imagination that a generous spirit is capable of.

4

If I, like Richard Jefferies, were ever to write the story of my heart, I think it would be this: the spirit trapped in the self, mine, but not mine alone, rather the common desire to live outward, communicating naturally at a deep level with others, giving oneself to a life in common; the desire constantly frustrated, turning the mind in upon itself, destructively in depression, despair and madness, positively in creative work in which others too may find a kind of release, but most often negatively, in fantasies, minor neuroses, jealousies, suspicions, twists and turns of the self. It would be a story about how the mind that can live fully only in light sinks again and again into darkness; how clay in the shaping hand crumbles, and the image is monstrous; how the eye of love wakes momentarily, and sleeps again. It would be a story of desire to live in the open, the world a meeting-place, and instead, of inhabiting a cramped, ill-lit, subjective space. It would not be an abstract story, but the story of a life and a time; and it would be more than that. And, of course, it would be a story that I don't fully know or understand, and that still may be changed beyond my conception!

My story too would rise from prehistoric barrows and Downs, and touch grassblade and sea and stars. But it would not be *more* about the future than the past. It would not be about the ideal, or abstracted spirits; it would be about particular real people and places and things. It would be about trying not to lose anything of the good we have been given, but to carry it *through*. It too would be about the Now — but our lives are in constant movement; it is only the transfigured moment that can both live, with the momentum of time and change, and 'stand' eternally. Jefferies abstracted his soul from his life and his world; in pursuing the ideal, he rejected everything that is human — all philosophies and religions, and, by implication, all past and present human lives. My story would be about desiring that none is ever lost, and that our common world embrace the living, dead, and unborn. Light would pick out now this, now that, and the darkness of partial vision sweep over it, as shadows chase light from the Downs. But my prayer would be that what I can see only darkly should be seen and known and cared for by a love greater than I can conceive.

5

Walter Benjamin's "angel of history":

> His face is turned toward the past. Where we perceive a chain of events, he sees one single catastrophe which keeps piling wreckage upon wreckage and hurls it in front of his feet. The angel would like to stay, awaken the dead, and make whole what has been smashed. But a storm is blowing from Paradise; it has got caught in his wings with such violence that the angel can no longer close them. This storm irresistably propels him into the future to which his back is turned, while the pile of debris before him grows skyward. This storm is what we call progress.
> ('Theses on the Philosophy of History', *Illuminations*)

More prosaically, E.H. Carr in *What is History?* says: "The absolute in history... is something towards which we move". He calls this, "the secular truth behind the religious myth that the meaning of history will be revealed in the Day of Judgement". "It is this sense of direction in history which alone enables us to order and interpret the events of the past." Benjamin is more eloquent, more *poetic*, in his conversion of religious into secular terms: "only a redeemed mankind receives the fullness of its past". "The Messiah comes not only as the redeemer, he comes as the subduer of Antichrist. Only that historian will have the gift of fanning the spark of hope in the past who is firmly convinced that *even the dead* will not be safe from the enemy if he wins."

To say the least, this makes me feel obscurely uneasy. Despite Benjamin's concern for the dead, I feel that when past and present are made to depend on the future for their meaning, then each particular life is somehow robbed of significance and integrity, robbed of the absolute seriousness which is the right of every one. Even if we are all responsible to the future — as I believe we are — the meaning of each is what he is and does *now*.

What *is* progress? It is possible to believe in material betterment — in health, housing, welfare generally — without believing in progress. Not just in the sense that the belief has become increasingly difficult to hold since 1914 either. No, but rather in the sense that it *always* robs the human being of the possiblity of knowing and living the truth — because the truth belongs only to a future state of mankind. Replace God with History in the seat of

Judgement and man is no longer each particular being, with a soul, but the abstraction, mankind. The irony is, that Marxist historians, to whom we owe so much for retrieving 'the people' from oblivion, also rob their lives of what to them often was, (and perhaps eternally is), their greatest seriousness.

Benjamin's image of the angel of history is magnificent; but I distrust it. To begin with, he has stolen his terms from Judaism and Christianity, for which angel and Paradise have other meanings. By this means, he has validated his secular vision. But when belief in progress fails, the image falls to pieces, leaving a helpless being — a projection of the human imagination — unable either to turn from history as a spectacle of horror, or to offer any comfort to its victims. The historical mind that believes neither in progress nor in redemption will be fixed in the angel's gaze, and driven into the future by a storm that does not blow from Paradise.

Benjamin sees desperately, but he sees with the hope of the Enlightenment, the rational faith in progress represented for him by the communist future. The world in the West is darker now than it was before the Second World War, not only because of the terrible things that have been done, but because the hope that they will at least lead to a just future is dead. Not dead for all, of course; perhaps absolutely dead only for the cynical or completely disillusioned, since a juster social order and saner international relations are certainly possible. But the idea is dead that we can somehow understand, let alone justify, all the suffering; while the action of evil in progressive and reactionary forces alike, in the human beings who bear them, gives a certain complacency to Benjamin's angel, wings violently held open by a storm blowing from Paradise. No philosophy or metaphor or image can comprehend suffering and evil; these are inextricably part of the history we are in, the history that is in us, irrespective of whether we suffer materially, or whether we commit visibly evil acts. We are blind to so much that we are part of, we can rarely see much of what we are living and what we are making. With imagination, historian and poet may see something — the ground we are moving over in a flash of light, a stretch of the past fitfully illuminated — but I don't think they will see anything unless they know that their implication in what they are looking at makes them partially sighted, and that they too, like their human subjects, are under a judgement that no man can make. It isn't possible to substitute "secular truth" for "religious myth", Progress or History for God, because the former is always a human measure, and therefore can never be absolute. Stealing the religious myth in order to give the human measure a semblance of the absolute makes man a tyrant, with unlimited scope for his cruelty and arrogance, for shaping the human material according to his idea. This is not a justification for political quietism. We are in history and have to struggle for the common good against destructive individualistic and collective powers, *and* for excellence — for genius, and the creative potential of every human being — against the weight of complacent mediocrity. But we have in struggling to know ourselves subject to the absolute, not its measure.

J.G. Hamann, in the eighteenth century, saw the field of history as Ezekiel's valley of dry bones, which only the prophet could animate. Having covered them with veins and flesh and skin, they are still without breath, "till the prophet prophesies to the wind and the word of the Lord speaks to the wind". It is not a storm blowing from the future that restores the dead to life, it is the word of God spoken to each — to the figures we read about in history books, and the scattered teeth and bone splinters of labourers buried in clay and soldiers in ancient battlefields and modern cemeteries; every one "unknown to history". How should Utopia ever find a place for them? — by commemorating the countless unsung heroes? or by a metaphysical theory by which every victim gains retrospective meaning from the just society to which his fate has contributed, as all destroyed in the class struggle nevertheless contribute to the final victory of the proletariat? I have seen communist monuments; they are grand and impressive. If their grandeur and representations of the heroic ideal are hideous, the aesthetic judgement is merely impertinent. It is the intention that counts; nothing could be too grand that commemorates those who died for the common good. Seen truly, the land of every country is a living monument to the humblest man, woman, and child who tilled it; so are towns, villages and workplaces to those who built and worked in them. No: it is the selectivity of all human memory that utterly disqualifies man from being the absolute judge. For one thing, there are countless lives of which we know nothing. How could it be otherwise, when we learn to love, and it isn't without effort that I really know even those dearest to me? To the individual mind, mankind alive at this moment, let alone all mankind from the beginning of time, can be no more than an overwhelming *idea*. For another thing, every person, and every regime, is biased, seeing the 'good' and the 'bad' from a certain point of view, and nothing that is outside it.

Even with imagination, much of the history of our own time remains a field of bones, even the particular history we live, and most human beings will experience times when they are no more than scattered dry bones to themselves. We are so many disarticulate skeletons. Without "the religious myth" we stumble blindly through history, we are scattered in our own lives, the words we think our own are a stale breath, common but without the spirit to open and renew us for one another, and to restore the dead. Only hope and faith may conceive what we cannot think or imagine in living detail: resurrection of the dead, restoration to each of unique being, revelation of its meaning, redemption. "The secular truth" is wreckage piled on wreckage, field of bones under field of bones.

6

John Bayley, in *The New York Review of Books*, quotes Marina Tsvetayeva:

> No language is the mother tongue. Writing poetry is rewriting it.... A poet may write in French; he cannot be a French poet. That's ludicrous.... The reason one becomes a poet... is to avoid being French, Russian etc., in order to be everything.... Yet every language has something that belongs to it alone, that *is* it.

Bayley remarks, of Tsvetayeva, Rilke and Pasternak: "The idea of all poetry as not national, but always translation into a higher medium, is true for all three poets".

Alain Finkielkraut, in 'What is Europe?' (in the same issue of *NYRB*), describes two ideas of Europe:

1. Oswald Spengler's 'culture', defined "according to the Romantic tradition born in Germany with Herder, as a unique spirit, a specific character, a soul, a *Geist*, which spreads throughout all the activities of a given community". In the words of the 19th century French critic, Hippolyte Taine: "The more an artist is perfect, the more he is national".

2. Julien Benda's "autonomy of the spirit", by which artist and thinker transcend their particular contexts. "If you answer that you do not believe in the autonomy of the spirit, that your spirit cannot be anything else than an aspect of your being, then I say to you that you will never construct Europe. Because there is not such a thing as a European being!" (Julien Benda)

Finkielkraut says the idea of Europe has been discredited since the Second World War by two things: Hitler (Sartre said that in the word 'Europe', "you can hear the boots of Nazi Germany"), and decolonization and the view of Europe, among European intellectuals as well as in former colonies, as an imperial force.

I suppose he would see the following as extremists on Spengler's side: Mircea Eliade, in his belief that "the mystical experience of autochthony, the profound feeling of having come from the soil, of having been born of Earth", still lingers among Europeans today, who feel themselves "*people of the place*", with "a feeling of cosmic relatedness deeper than that of familial and ancestral solidarity" (*Myths, Dreams and Mysteries*); George Eliot, with her homelier accent, who said: "We could never have loved the earth so well if we had had no childhood in it", and called the familiar things of childhood "the mother tongue of our imagination" (*The Mill on the Floss*, Chapter 5); D.H. Lawrence, for whom "the sprit of place is a great reality" ('The Spirit of Place').

Alain Finkielkraut writes strongly in favour of Julien Benda's idea, and discredits the opposing idea by identifying it with Spengler. The essay (originally a lecture) is clear and useful because it is clear. Yet clarity of definition frequently does violence to actual experience. I wonder how many writers and thinkers who have upheld the humanist values of "the autonomy of the spirit" have actually felt that they are Europeans rather than French or German or Polish etc. It seems to me more likely that most people who think of themselves as Europeans, and most who have so thought of themselves in the past, feel themselves to belong first to one nation or territory. In any case, what would Europe be without Italy or France or the Netherlands? (What was it before they existed?) What would Europe be if not felt and conceived through the experience of particular peoples and their interaction? It may be that Julien Benda's question is more subtle than the context in which it is quoted suggests. But I can't imagine an autonomous spirit constructing anything, let alone a great historical construct like Europe. How can we know our spirit apart from our being? Where if not from being would spirit get things to construct with? It seems to me that we need both ideas, and that ideally they balance each other, with national culture giving substance to spirit, while spirit, imbued with ideas such as freedom, justice, and co-operation, which do indeed transcend particular contexts, converts the dark side of nationalism. Yet even as I write this, and especially 'ideally', I realize that history is always actual experience, and remember something of what European history has been. But hasn't it been *at best* an intersection or crossing — so to speak — of particular cultures and transcendent values, as when Christianity penetrated pagan societies, or Classical thought re-entered the different literatures of medieval Europe? Shakespeare can no more be conceived in an English language closed to everything outside England than without the English language. Indeed, his Englishness is commonly overemphasised at the expense of what he owed to Europe and beyond. The same may be said of Dante and his culture and tongue, though in his case it may be the universality that is more commonly overemphasised. But what does this prove? What I'm showing myself is that spirit and being work together to form identity.

"The reason one becomes a poet ... is to avoid being French, Russian etc, in order to be everything." My strong attachment to "the mother tongue of our imagination" initially made it difficult for me to understand what Marina Tsvetayeva was saying. Here, though, is another paradox. Whatever the reasons for her holding such an idea may be, whatever the elevated sense of the poet's calling, and the agony of being Russian at that time, it seems clear that we owe the survival of certain essential national things to writers and thinkers who strove to transcend nationality. Has there been a single great writer or thinker who thought of him/her self as *exclusively* Russian, English, German etc?

7

No English poet has had the experience of a Paul Celan, driven to sing songs "on the other side of human kind". Yet things are fundamentally more extreme for the English than appears on the surface.

The crowded island is a country of inner 'worlds', a society of isolated selves, driven inwards, not just scared of exposure, but unable to stand in the open because there is no meeting-place. When human communication continues only on the surface, and the need for a deep common purpose is frustrated, the mind becomes a cave haunted by shadows.

8

When "the human essence" ceases to be grounded in the sacramental materialism of Creator and Creation, I suppose there's nothing to stop it from being located in "the ensemble of the social relations" (Marx). Raymond Williams in his dry, rational way gives the irreligious view a human complexion:

> It is right to recognise that we become human individuals in terms of social process, but still individuals are unique, through a particular heredity expressed in a particular history. And the point about this uniqueness is that it is creative as well as created: new forms can flow from this particular form.
>
> (*The Long Revolution*)

"Still individuals are unique" — but not when the substance of the self has been deconstructed into the historical, psychological, and linguistic forces which supposedly construct it. And what is there to prevent this from happening if social existence determines consciousness? Doesn't the deconstruction logically follow that?

The 'new' thought seems, in the main, to be left-wing in its political stance or implications. But insofar as it is anti-humanist, what I don't understand is why one form of social organization should be better than another. An atomised and competitive individualism can only be considered bad against an idea of man's wholeness: that we need each other and can only be truly ourselves in a common world. It is one thing to destroy a false image of the ego, and quite another to deny all possibility of authentic individual being. Who is there for a thorough-going deconstructionist actually to love? and who is to do the loving? On the other hand, if we are clever enough to see how 'individuals' are constructed, why shouldn't we play god in the matter of their re-construction?

9

> For such people, like so many beasts, have fallen into the custom of each man thinking only of his own private interests and have reached the extreme of delicacy, or better of pride, in which like wild animals they bristle and lash out at the slightest displeasure. Thus in the midst of their greatest festivities, though physically thronging together, they live like wild beasts in a deep solitude of spirit and will, scarcely any two being able to agree since each follows his own pleasure and caprice. By reason of all this, providence decrees that, through obstinate factions and desperate civil wars, they shall turn their cities into forests and the forests into dens and lairs of men. In this way, through long centuries of barbarism, rust will consume the misbegotten subtleties of malicious wits, that have turned them into beasts made more inhuman by the barbarism of reflection than the first men had been made by the barbarism of sense.
> (Giambattista Vico, *New Science*)

I came on this passage after destroying what I'd written in recent days, first on critical theory, in response to the issue of *PN Review* on the subject, which made me see that I have to examine and clarify my critical values, and secondly on Philip Larkin following his death. I saw that what I had written was false, and false mainly on account of its detachment. Thus in writing about Larkin, and beginning with the things that move me in his poetry, I soon abandoned the man and his work to pursue what he 'represented' — which is precisely what the criticism I most suspect does, i.e. abstract intellect from the critic's humanity and use it with the instrument of theory to reduce author and work to their socio-historical 'significance'. Sickened by the falsity of my writing, but still preoccupied by the central themes, I could hardly have found words more apt than Vico's.

In the first place, they remind me sharply that I'm subject to the very "barbarism of reflection" which, in different terms, I've often tried to analyse in English social life, especially among the privileged and, more narrowly, writers and critics. And in the second place, living "like wild beasts in a deep solitude of spirit and will" is a piercing description of the condition I've come to see and feel ever more intensely.

If I can't speak as a man of a fellow man or woman, which means speaking from perplexity and division as well as conviction and knowledge, I should not speak at all. This doesn't mean that I want to kick away all theory as a ladder to an overview; only the overview has to be part of the larger relationship between myself as critic and the work, and to apply equally to both.

When Stan Smith, in ' "A language not to be betrayed": Language, Class and History in the work of Edward Thomas', writes of Edward Thomas (in his words) as a "superfluous man", representative of a liberal individualism faced with the prospect of redundancy, I recognise a more intellectually rigorous diagnosis than my different treatment of the subject in 'The Sad Passion'. And at the same time I feel curiously disoriented, even very slightly dizzy, because something is missing. The absence is that of Stan Smith himself from the argument. He is there as an incisive intellect acting on a critical theory, but not as a perplexed and feeling human being. Presumably he is not perplexed; for him, the Marxist theory represents the truth, and perplexity or doubt, even certain feelings and above all any sense of *mystery*, are merely confessions of failure to see the truth, or mystifications which bear it out. I concede a lot to Smith and the few who are as skilful as he is at using this kind of criticism, and I learn useful things from them. What I do not concede is the ability to penetrate the fundamental reality of either literature *or* history. They skilfully open up things and show how certain processes work, but the actuality of person, work of art, or historical time escapes them. As it escapes us all, but I believe less escapes if we bring our full humanity to the act of understanding.

And the more of ourselves we bring to meet another — for I don't make a fundamental distinction between the attentiveness we owe another person and the attentiveness we owe their work — the more we have to recognise the shared mystery of being human. This isn't an excuse for suppressing oppositions and for adopting an all-accepting 'generosity', as though viciousness and incompetence alike were harmless frailties, and differences of principle and conviction didn't really matter. It is a recognition that the 'dark' in which we partly move is the very mystery making the ground firmer under our feet and helping us to see and feel as men and women, because without it we are not fully human, but ghostly intellects.

The Marxist impulse is generous — at least, it is generous to the oppressed and to the future. And Marxism would diagnose the "barbarism of reflection" as alienation. But it is my feeling that the absence of critical theorists as real persons — and not all are equally absent — increases the isolation of people in separate cells that characterises much of contemporary English (and of course, not only English) intellectual life. This on one hand, and on the other our dreaming of worlds or Englands we can actually bear to live with or even celebrate and love — as I have dreamed, and still dream. For me, the task is to recognise the dream, know its negative and positive elements, and always submit it to the test of reality; and, in concerning myself with other people's work, to meet it on the shared ground even when we are opposed to one another, instead of shooting high into the clearer air of theory, to look down on benighted and deviant strugglers below.

Of course criticism is an act of mind — even when, like poetry, it has to call on the body's knowledge — but of mind alive with feeling and imaginative sympathy, with a moral sense applied first and always to the self, with historical imagination, patience, and the various skills which make a good reader. This is the human mind; mind as critical intellect alone is an instrument of barbarous reflection.

10

Suddenly, a few days after recent, fairly confident speculations, I thought: but suppose there really is no substantial self? The truth is, I'm not sure. For me, the original powerful sense of unique identity which every being and thing has, which was my first and most fundamental conviction — it was what I *saw* as a boy, it is what I *see* now — conflicts with the equally strong sense I have developed, of the relationships — ancestral, cultural, historical, personal — that shape us, and in and through which we live. It may be that, fundamentally, there are no grounds of conflict; but I move in feeling between the extremes, and have still to reach the understanding that will enable me to argue coherently, and with complete conviction, against ideas of determinism and deconstruction. Yet, perhaps the only understanding of this that can be reached is *faith*: faith in the other, the uniqueness and substantiality of this being, even though at the same time perceiving structures and relationships — some of which the subject (assuming a dead author) could not have seen — without which his or her life would have been different. And if these are channels of the individual spirit, now damming, now deflecting or directing it, what spirit can have an existence independent of the life? Yet we do see spirits deformed by a wrong life, trapped by circumstances, misdirected by bad choices, and being destroyed, or sometimes at last coming out clear.

In my son's head and bearing I have recently seen characteristics of my father in his younger days, and in his face, especially his mouth, and sometimes in his attitudes and emotions, I see a lot of his mother. Yet I have known him since the moment of birth, and there was never a time when he was not a completely distinct individual, himself, before he could talk, as he would have been whatever our circumstances, and if he had been given another name. And as he grows the distinctness develops — the lives of others show in him, his response to circumstances affects him, but he becomes more fully his original self. I can't prove anything, but I feel that if we don't stand on this ground — of the selves we must win from all that would express them falsely and suck their blood — we will not be able to make anything with love.

11

Ernst Fischer, in *The Necessity of Art*, domesticates Walter Benjamin's angel of history in a simpler form of Marxist optimism. He adds to it a second face by which artists like Mayakovsky and Brecht, who have committed themselves to the workers' cause, can see the new world which the working class is building. His words admit the difficulties, but are optimistic, and identify hope with a future society. To me, this is complacent, monstrous. What has hope to do with a future society or humanity or mankind, if it relegates countless numbers of people, past, present and future, to what Gwyn A. Williams calls "the dustbins of history"? Hope in this context is not for every one, it belongs exclusively to the victory of the working class. Even in that sense it loses meaning, since the communists have hewn their bloodstained social order out of masses of human flesh, and maintain it with oppression.

Significantly, Fischer's book is good on the social nature of the 'I', on alienation and the difficulties of the artist under capitalism, but vacuous in its account of socialist advantages. It is interesting to note that although he praises Mayakovsky on several occasions, he never actually quotes him, while he mentions Pasternak (as author of *Dr Zhivago*) only once in passing, and doesn't even mention any of the other great poets silenced, exiled or killed by Stalin or East European communism. It is also interesting to read an account of man's social and artistic origins and development that says almost nothing about religion. Yet when he talks about the 'I' separating itself from the chorus, or the ineradicable social content of even the most alienated 'I', I respond positively to what he has to say. His humanist principles and sentiments appeal to me too. But what in practice is a humanism which, in a few words, or by what it does not say, dismisses countless people to oblivion or a secular hell?

Karl Löwith's *Meaning in History* is of a different intellectual order. It is also the most extreme denial I have read of historical progress. "What the Gospels proclaim is never future improvements in our earthly condition but the sudden coming of the Kingdom of God in contradistinction to the existing kingdom of man." Thus, according to Löwith, any social or material improvements have occurred in opposition to, or at least apart from, Christianity, so that when for example Emyr Humphreys traces Aneurin Bevan's establishment of the National Health Service back through Lloyd George's contribution to social welfare to the Christian social conscience, or passion, of nineteenth century Welsh Nonconformity, he is wrong. Or rather he may be right, only it is wrong to describe *any* worldly improvement as 'Christian'. For as Löwith argues, a Christian *world* is a contradiction in terms.

This, I suppose, is an extreme Protestant view, according to which *all* that matters is the soul's progress towards God. Insofar as it emphasises the absolute importance of the person or individual soul, it at once restores a world of meaning — to my mind, the ground of all meaning — absent from Marxism, and perhaps also from other secular and religious philosophies. But insofar as it downgrades the importance of the social and material worlds, or indeed, completely denies their value, I revolt. It is in this respect the opposite of Nicolai Berdyaev's "Christianity is the greatest of religions because it is in the first place the religion of the Resurrection; and because it reconciles itself to neither death nor oblivion, but strives towards the resurrection of all that is truly existent" (*The Meaning of History*). Löwith seems to represent the view that man can achieve nothing with his creative will, and to project as the only value a life of prayer, turned away from the world and toward God. The view would even seem to imply that man's creativity is evil, not just potentially evil, but always practically evil in that it necessarily involves him with the world. Man makes himself at home in the world by working on its materials, creating a habitable environment for himself and making those 'gratuitous' objects in which some religious thinkers see, in David Jones's terms, his "god-shaping", and the secular see his instinct for 'beauty'. In the extreme Protestant view, this must be wrong: all art objects are 'idols', all concern with the things of the world is a distraction from God. Denial of the world is denial of the body, and vice versa. Denial of world and body is denial of art. But what kind of God is it that wants man to be all spirit and to communicate with him only inwardly, in silence or by the silent word? Doesn't God require man to use his creativity, even, as Berdyaev says, to continue the Creation?

I know nothing about continuing the Creation, but I do feel we are in the world in order to care for it and to make something worthwhile of being here, and that our making is in part what makes ourselves. On the other hand, if our worth depends on this alone, the dustbins of history will be crammed. Only God's equal concern for every soul gives man his proper worth. And exactly what one is and does — his true 'name' — isn't known on earth. I can far easier believe that the name is written on the stone mentioned in Revelation than that we can ever know who we are or who any other person truly is. And because the Marxists claim to know people's worth, not one by one but class by class, they frighten me far more than the extreme Protestant who denies the worth of man's world but gives supreme value to the human person. But neither can this help us to knowledge, because to separate the person from his or her life, and the life from history, is to create another abstraction. In Berdyaev's words, "Man is in the highest degree an historical being. He is situated in history and history is situated in him".

12

If I start with local things, that is partly because I believe we must start again with them, seeing the historical uses to which they've been put — as, for example, an idyll of 'home' abstracted from the English countryside was an imperialist creation — but then reclaiming them, starting again humbled and caring from the actual ground we occupy. In fact, however, the 'air' of Empire through which the things were perceived, has been replaced by the 'air' of America and the Cold War, so that knowing the ground of place means knowing it in this context too, indeed, in terms of all its connections with the world. But I always come back in the end to the things, the ground, the human scale of place, because the belief is rooted in me — it is ineradicable from all my thinking and feeling — that the care of people for their place, which means their active care with and for others, is the foundation of human life. Yet the grander and more emotive the words are, the harder they need to be looked at. Thus, I know that this is only one pole of the human need, and that if it is made the only one, it leads to exclusiveness, xenophobia, racism, the closed system and the closed mind. Openness is equally necessary — openness to other people and peoples, openness in the sense of exploration, adventure, going out into the world, openness to the future.

One thing I'm sure of: unless we see this as *our* world, to and for which we're responsible, we'll destroy both it and ourselves. This care is the meaning of place.

13

Gerard Manley Hopkins's words about the importance of recognition are the strongest justification of criticism I know:

> What I do regret is the loss of recognition belonging to the work itself. For as to every moral act, being right or wrong, there belongs, of the nature of things, reward or punishment, so to every form perceived by the mind belongs, of the nature of things, admiration or the reverse. And the world is full of things and events, phenomena of all sorts, that go without notice, go unwitnessed.
>   (Letter to R.W. Dixon, 13 June 1878)

But the decision of Hopkins's life, his faith as both spiritual action and structure of thought and belief, entitled him to say what I, without his faith, can say after him only with a feeling of unworthiness, and because the desire that nothing, and least of all a work of the human heart and mind, should go unnoticed is perhaps my deepest emotional spring.

Hopkins goes on:

> The only just judge, the only just literary critic, is Christ, who prizes, is proud of, and admires, more than any man, more than the receiver himself can, the gifts of his own making. And the only real good which fame and another's praise does is to convey to us, by a channel not at all above suspicion but from circumstances in this case much less to be suspected than the channel of our minds, some token of the judgement which a perfectly just, heedful, and wise mind, namely Christ's, passes upon our doings. Now such a token may be conveyed as well by one as by many.

The emphasis on justice here is not on judgement but on recognition and admiration of gifts, and on charity. And it is on our minds' imperfection, but also on their ability to act as channels for "some token" of the perfect judgement. Hopkins's terms would be derided by most critics now, and even in his lifetime, most — if they could have read it — would have thought the description of Christ as "the only just literary critic" ludicrous and fanatic — which, out of context, it is. But of course, it would be merely mischievous to pretend that Hopkins visualizes Christ as a book reviewer! For Hopkins, all judgement rests ultimately with the absolute: Christ, who is the fount of all true love and justice. And this is Hopkins's difference from most modern thinkers. For him, all gifts relate to Christ the giver. Christ is ground of man and his works, since man is an image of the divine. The integrity of person and work expresses this relationship, and it is their ultimate worth and seriousness that they are subject to judgement. But Hopkins, at this moment, isn't thinking of the Law, he is thinking of Love, of God who sees and cares for all, who values all.... I can't use his terms as he does — they can't be used except on the basis of his absolute belief — but what he implies about the critic as one who can recognise the work, and whose mind is an imperfect channel which may nevertheless give some expression of the perfect judgement, appeals strongly to my emotional conviction.

14

I know that I am not a systematic thinker, capable of logically thinking through all that is implicit in my 'exploratory' criticism, and of defining it systematically as a method in opposition to other methods. Yet I want now to be as clear about it as I can, even if that means isolating emotional attitudes, which employ religious and historicist ideas, as well as opposing them to each other, but without a firm metaphysical or materialist ground. My criticism wouldn't be exploratory if I knew what I was going to find before I set out; and perhaps if I set out with a system I'd find only what it led me to. It would be absurd though, to imagine that I begin with *nothing*, and only honest to say what my values are.

While I think "the death of the author" has meant, generally, not the birth of the reader, as Roland Barthes claimed, but the liberation of the critical theorist at the expense of the 'text', I'm not hostile to all structuralist or post-structuralist ideas, (nor is my knowledge of them anything like comprehensive). Insofar as they affirm the desirability of knowing the *history* of any thing and any one, including the knower, I welcome their emphasis. I note, however, that I usually turn the idea back on the critic first, so that when for example Christopher Norris claims for theory "the power to demystify aesthetics precisely by revealing its textual blind-spots and its covert dependence on simplified and question-begging models of thought and perception" (*PN Review*, 48), I think of theory having the power to reveal the reasons for the theorist's fear of mystery and dependence on modern thought-systems, such as Marxism and Freudianism, with dogmas of the author's social and unconscious blindness. I want to defend the integrity of the literary work, but this doesn't mean its perfection or infallibility. It means admitting blind-spots and unconscious limitations of thought and perception; all, in fact, that makes the author human, not just a mind operating as the instrument of an abstract intellectual system. The reader, at least equally limited in his humanness, knows the work isn't God or a product of His mind, but enjoys and learns from a fellow being's creation, the kind of order it achieves and the degree of meaning, against the ugliness, disorder and confusion rife in society and his own unconcentrated mind. But the professional theorist, safe in his enlightened position from the author's struggle with form and meaning, refuses to enter into dialogue with the work, but uses it to reveal the author's darkened sight. In effect, the refusal of relationship is the denial of humanity, both his own and the author's.

Of course all interpretations are partial, situational, relative; of course we can't now talk confidently about the critic's power "to see the object as in itself it really is", as Matthew Arnold did. Yet surely there's a dishonest slide from this to denying the work's integrity as a made thing — an object independent of the mind that created it, but bearing the imprint of that mind, and existing more fully in the mind that is attentive to it than in the mind glancing off or over it, or wanting to use it for an ulterior purpose. The fuller existence, of the work in the mind of the reader who knows that its fullness is beyond him, is what the exploratory approach seeks to know, and its principal aids are patience and attentiveness and imaginative sympathy.

In my experience, the main ulterior purpose of criticism is the desire to talk about the work, either to display one's cleverness or to use it to support a theory, but in either case radically diluting and even distorting it. In institutions where literature is taught, it is common to find good talkers, but rare to find good *readers*. Reading, whether aloud or carefully in the mind, means *hearing*, attending to the work as an object, giving oneself to it sympathetically. It requires a kind of love — love as Martin Buber defines it: the opposite of the "life of monologue", which is "never aware of the other as something that is absolutely not himself and at the same time with which he nevertheless communicates" (*Between Man and Man*). In Buber's terms, criticism is a relationship, which occurs in his *between*: "We do not find meaning lying in things nor do we put it into things, but between us and things it can happen". The sense of awe is similar to Heidegger's, but the relationship is active, quite without the *passive* listening, (which Terry Eagleton, in *Literary Theory*, calls "an astonishing cringing before the mystery of Being", and which, according to an English commentator quoted by Eagleton — apparently unembarrassed by patrician condescension —

"bears all the marks of a 'stupified peasant' ").

The ground of Buber's philosophy is metaphysical. For him, "the essential is... that we should 'see things in God', the things themselves"; which is a foundation Arnold's "the object as in itself it really is" lacks. Simone Weil's idea of attentiveness, too, is religious: "Above all our thought should be empty, waiting, not seeking anything, but ready to receive in its naked truth the object which is to penetrate it". The title of the essay from which this comes couldn't be more candid: 'Reflections on the Right Use of School Studies with a view to the Love of God'. For her, "the development of the faculty of attention forms the real object and almost the sole interest of studies".

George Oppen, without being theological, is nevertheless speaking a similar language when he talks about being "concerned with the substantive, with the subject of the sentence, with what we are talking about, and not rushing over the subject-matter in order to make a comment about it". This is how a man talks who has lived and worked with people in the world, who knows that people, world, and things are irreducibly present, to be met as they are in relationship, even when the aim is social or political change, for if they are not, the individual destroys himself and may harm or destroy others with his illusions. But perhaps Oppen's faith in the substantive is a theology: the faith that the deer in the woods really are there. The world is there; we are in it, and it is in us, but the world is not identical with us; our words name it, it is not our linguistic construct... (How far we have fallen from belief that makes the world our home, to be struck with awe that it exists!) The poem is an act of care for "the subject of the sentence"; criticism, with the poem as its subject, should be no less.

Simone Weil's attentiveness, Martin Buber's 'other' and 'between', George Oppen's concern for the substantive: these are the modern ideas that have most influenced me, and on which I base my conviction that criticism is first and last a relationship between human subjects. No doubt their influence is due to the philosophical support they give to my first and strongest emotional perception — the mystery of the unique presence of every being and thing. Such integral being is of course what deconstruction deconstructs, at least to its own satisfaction, and the whole weight of modern historicist, linguistic and psychological theory is against it. After my reading at Aberystwyth, Laurel Brake said that my talk about 'reality' disturbed her, because, in contrast to modern ideas about the way in which our minds construct reality, I seemed to be invoking belief in authority. I denied that this had anything to do with authoritarian politics, and said that I was aware of the modern ideas, and sceptical of them. I might also have said that I couldn't live with the belief that we, mankind, construct all meaning, and therefore without awe at a power and an order greater than ourselves. So I suppose *presence* is a kind of authority; it requires respect from a self-respecting mind; it is a place in which the mind is not to play at random, but to meet what is there; it is, for example, both Bishop Berkeley and the world he is in, though his back is turned to most of it.

Martin Buber, Simone Weil, George Oppen, all had the ancient Jewish reverence for the not-self; and that would count heavily against them among ardent demystifiers, even if none of them could be described as a stupefied peasant. It is true, of course, that neither Martin Buber nor Simone Weil was talking about literary criticism, although it is obviously an important opportunity for dialogue and attention. When I first started to write criticism, partly in response to academic pressure, partly from conviction and inclination, the only justification I could find *for myself* — I have never considered it a general rule — was to explore good but unjustly neglected work, with a view to helping to make it better known. Later, I came consciously to value patience and attentiveness, but they were implicit, from the beginning, in my sense of the work as a presence needing to be approached with care. Actually, I don't believe the author is ever dead, even when dead in fact. I believe the work is a kind of living thing, not 'organic' or an essence or ghostly shadow of its author, but a creation of the unique human being, blind and unconscious in some ways as we all are, but with the gift of self transcendence which, mysteriously, establishes the self beyond its accidents. It is the deepest mind, as well as blind-spots and limitations of thought and vision, that lives on in the work. The presence is distinctly, uniquely, human; it is personal as well as historical. But once removed from experience, once abstracted from a living relationship, once no longer listened to or heard, anything can be dismantled, to prove there is no-one and nothing inside.

15

A friend, who is a distinguished academic and critic, spoke in a recent letter of "the glorious redeeming power of the human imagination and individual spirit". In an academic context — even to my mind, made circumspect by academic discourse — the words do of course have an archaic sound. Indeed it would be difficult to use them in such a context without being scorned as a romantic and sentimentalist, and no doubt a bourgeois liberal humanist as well. But they are true: true for the person who, like my friend, cares deeply for literature, and has suffered so that he no longer has time for what doesn't really matter; true for serious writers, who write partly because they have found that power in books, and felt it to be the only power worth having, and in individual people, and felt that to honour it is the one thing necessary. It is less likely that the words would be true for all, or many, students of literature, and, plainly, they are irrelevant for most contemporary critical theorists. The reason for this is, I think, that the power which the critical mind — the mind that has suppressed the creative faculty — most desires is power over others: power to win arguments, power to *master* the text, by gaining a position of superior knowledge over it, power to assert the intellect and the self, power in the struggle for professional advancement. The mind in this state feels no need of redemption of any kind, and scorns 'imagination' and 'spirit' as inferior rivals. It is also a fact that the political impotence, which many of us feel acutely now, makes power over the text the only power available. Add this to retrospective anger against the hierarchical values embodied, in one form or another, in most works of 'the great tradition', and there is a recipe for hatred of literature, which is not uncommon among academics and literary intellectuals. The positive movement in a situation of great spiritual danger is towards rescuing and developing alternative — democratic, radical, non-individualistic — traditions. But if I don't emphasise this now, or the fine lecturers and teachers known to me, who are exceptions to all that I am criticising here, that is because I feel the spiritual danger has been hardly recognised, and is largely ignored in the contention between different critical theories and ideas of English Studies. The critical mind has a terrible capacity for destruction. It can destroy the self, too — paranoia born of the power struggle, on which the self stakes itself, is a common academic and intellectual disease. It is an even greater tragedy when generosity and compassion, dammed up in the social world, can only energize hatred in the struggle for power over words and ideas in the world of the intellect. But to affirm the existence of "the glorious redeeming power of the human imagination and individual spirit" is not to deny the validity, even the necessity, of critical and historical methods, let alone to justify a return to belletristic impressionism. It is to affirm that literary studies should be concerned primarily with learning how to receive from literature a great gift — a gift not only of imaginative enlargement but of sensitive critical thought; learning how to listen and hear, which requires at least as much discipline and skill, of a different kind, as brilliant theoretical talk.

16

Poetry too can be a destroyer. Again it is the desire for power that kills: the use of a gift to promote and assert the separated self. Under communism, the State kills or silences poets. Under capitalism, they destroy themselves.

17

Detachment in order to gain a critical or historical overview of a writer or work is a valuable part of the critical relationship. I know, however, that there are vantage-points beyond my reach, or which I have to refuse. Terry Eagleton envisages the possibility of "a deep enough transformation of our history", by which we may produce a society in which "Shakespeare would be no more valuable than much present-day graffiti", and says that, "though many people would consider such a condition tragically impoverished, it seems to me dogmatic not to entertain the possibility that it might arise rather from a general human enrichment" (*Literary Theory*). That is a height above the known world to which I cannot reach.

Christopher Norris writes of the conservative idea of tradition, from Burke to T.S. Eliot and beyond: "What had to be resisted at all costs was the idea that thought could get a critical vantage-point outside the given context of values and assumptions that made up the national culture" (*PN Review*, 48). Of course, it isn't difficult to detach oneself from *that* idea of tradition; but how stand outside the "national culture"? How rise above all the ideas, influences, and feelings associated with people, places, the land and its history; all the vital cross-currents, all the mixed contradictory things, that shape a human identity? "Given context", "values and assumptions", "national culture", are in this sentence only abstract words. With thought at this height above its subject, all actual being dies, all substance is emptied out. Authors die together with nations and every actual human being and work. The mind is a spectral eagle looking down on what appears to be the structures of a baseless earth.

18

Anger and shame, too, have been among my motives as a critic. At what Emyr Humphreys calls "that touch of iconoclastic arrogance ... the hallmark of readability in English criticism" (*The Taliesin Tradition*). It is a *class* tone: superior, amused, dismissive. Examples, of varying degrees of offensiveness, may be heard in every issue of English literary journals and in the review pages of newspapers. It may be heard widely in Britain, but needs metropolitan smugness to perfect it. My favourite example occurs in *Poetry Today* 1960-1973 (published for the British Council), in which Anthony Thwaite, having more or less dismissed John Ormond, Roland Mathias, and other Anglo-Welsh poets, says: "The difficulty of the Welsh language may be hiding from non-Welsh readers the best poetry being written in Wales, but one rather doubts it".

But critical passion also requires some arrogance. Because it is a passion for justice, and therefore implies that the critic trusts his judgement, often in opposition to the judgement of others. Thus, when James A. Davies, writing (in *Planet* 55) of the Welsh Joint Education Committee A-Level syllabus says of "English literature's finest achievements", "we all know what they are", I violently dissent.

Of course "we" don't know; literary history proves, over and over again, the temporary, and sometimes long-lasting, triumph of superficial fashions, and the neglect or underestimation of great writers. Only consider the eighteenth century attitude towards the Metaphysical poets, or, for that matter, Shakespeare; or the Modernist bias against Milton, and against the Romantics and Victorians; or the history of Clare's reputation, or Blake's, or Hopkins's, or Ivor Gurney's, or John Cowper Powys's.... Literary history proves, over and over again, the extremely selective vision of every dominant 'we' in the fields of literature and education. In only twenty years, I have seen the reigns of three metropolitan poetry establishments, each of which has promoted some poets of worth — Ted Hughes and Philip Larkin for example — and all of which have either ignored, or subtly downgraded, poets such as Basil Bunting, David Jones, Hugh MacDiarmid, Charles Tomlinson, Roy Fisher, John Riley, and, of course, all writing on the far side of Offa's Dyke. Then there are various 'undergrounds', usually places where some vital work is done. What depresses me, though, is the mutual exclusiveness of all groups, whether undergrounds or establishments, in a small country where few people read contemporary verse anyway: the fragmented specialisms which poetry, expressing our general social condition, now is. This is one reason why I write criticism from one neglected corner of the field, but not exclusively from there, though I know that much escapes me. I shall never forget that I knew almost nothing of one of the finest poets of my generation, John Riley, until after his death. Others were less ignorant. But it is still possible in Britain for good poets to live and die virtually unnoticed. In recent years, the promotion of poetry — in effect, of one narrow convention — has made the situation worse.

I think three things justify, or at least excuse, the arrogance which seems inseparable from critical judgement: (1) A passion for justice. (2) Concentration on the work itself. (3) A desire to seek recognition for the work or writer, rather than publicity for oneself.

19

It isn't only with deliberate cruelty or anger that we kill with words, but with everyday sentences, written or spoken, in which a person is reduced to a reputation, a rumour, an image, a name. Even when speaking or writing about others sensitively, with care and knowledge, the reality escapes. But how best remember, and act on the knowledge? By keeping a sense of the difficulty and complexity of knowing ourselves within the forces acting upon us — the history we are in, family, nation, all our complicated and sometimes contradictory attachments. By realising that countless words slide over us without touching us; that we have an unrecognisable sub-life, encapsulated in theories, statistics, other people's careless thoughts. Real thought is difficult: it refuses to slide over the particular, to empty out the substance of a life by casually naming it. I know we can't think without categories, theories, abstractions; but thought means nothing if we begin by emptying out what we best know and love, the mystery of personal being in those dear to us, and the irreducibility of the world we share with them. If only in naming others, in mastering them in sentences or images, we catch the eye looking out of the world, out of history, and look back conscious that we too are in a world pressing upon us, enabling and disabling our being and sight. Thought that wants to apprehend reality must proceed by breaking as well as making images, by complicating as well as clarifying perceptions, and always in the knowledge that success is measured in degrees of failure.

20

The poetry of our time that really matters has been or is being written by people who have had forced upon them, without accepting or enjoying it, the experience described by Walter Pater at the end of *The Renaissance*:

> Experience, already reduced to a group of impressions, is ringed round for each one of us by that thick wall of personality through which no real voice has ever pierced on its way to us, or from us to that which we can only conjecture to be without. Every one of those impressions is the impression of the individual in his isolation, each mind keeping as a solitary prisoner its own dream of a world.

In this poetry, there is a struggle to see the terrible failure of human relationships and self-images in Western society, and discover alternatives. Pressed into the imprisoning dream as many of us are — with differences between the societies of Britain and America, for example, and with differences within both, but with a general pressure — the poets have begun by recognising and knowing the forces producing the dream, instead of by 'expressing' it blindly, and have tried, more or less successfully in different cases, to break out. It is in this context, too, that I am beginning to enlarge the idea that sees connections among many artists who may be unaware of each other, and feel completely isolated. I understand better now that all thinking is the perception of connections among what we at first think isolated phenomena, and that we develop by seeing them in ever greater depth and extent, but that the whole pattern, with its changes and permanent features, will always be beyond us. With patience, a person will see more in a lifetime; people working together in mutual goodwill could see much to benefit us all. But nothing is seen without patience and care, or with slogans and lies. Every clod of earth is a world of abundant, flowering life. Mind is an equivalent mystery in that we do not know what it is, and a greater mystery in that we do not know what it is capable of. And if mind does not work with an equivalent sensitivity, patience and persistence, if it reacts violently to its problems, it will not only see nothing but be the most dangerous instrument of our blindness.

Acknowledgements

'Jeffrey Wainwright' was first published in *PN Review*, 46, ed. Michael Schmidt, 1985.

'Mary Casey: The Poetry of Aloneness' was first published in *Agenda* Vol. 22, Nos. 3-4, ed. William Cookson and Peter Dale, Autumn-Winter 1984/85.

'Seeing the World: The Poetry of George Oppen' was first published in *PN Review*, 41, ed. Michael Schmidt, 1984. It was republished in *Not Comforts/ /But Vision*: Essays on the Poetry of George Oppen, Interim Press, 1985.

'"The Boundaries of our Distances": George Oppen's "Of Being Numerous"' was first published in *Ironwood* 26, George Oppen: A Special Issue, ed. Michael Cuddihy, (Arizona), 1985.

'Crossings and Turns: The Poetry of John Matthias' was first published in *Poetry Wales* Vol. 20, No. 4, ed. Cary Archard, 1985.

'John Ormond: The Accessible Song' was first published in *The Anglo-Welsh Review* Vol. 23, No. 51, ed. Roland Mathias and Gillian Clarke, 1974.

'The Poetry of Anthony Conran' was first published in *The Anglo-Welsh Review* Vol. 25, No. 54, ed. Roland Mathias and Gillian Clarke, 1975.

The review of John Tripp's *Collected Poems 1958-78* first appeared in *The Anglo-Welsh Review*, No. 65, ed. Gillian Clarke and Tony Bianchi, 1979.

'R.S. Thomas: Prytherch and After' incorporates material from reviews of *H'm* and *Frequencies* published in *Poetry Wales* and *Llais Llyfrau* respectively.

'Roland Mathias: ":The Strong Remembered Words"' was first published in *Poetry Wales* Vol. 21, No. 1, ed. Cary Archard, 1985.

'"A Big Sea Running in a Shell": The Poetry of Gillian Clarke' was first published in *PN Review* 50, ed. Michael Schmidt, 1986.

'The Presence of the Past' and 'The Poetry of Nearness: Anglo-Welsh Poetry in the 1960s' both grew from lectures, which were given, respectively, at the Rijksuniversiteit, Groningen, and the Academi Gymraeg Conference at Aberystwyth, in 1985.

Quotation from the works of David Jones and T.S. Eliot is made by permission of Faber & Faber Ltd; from Basil Bunting by permission of Oxford University Press; from Geoffrey Hill by permission of André Deutsch Ltd.; from George Oppen by permission of New Directions Publishing Corporation (*Collected Poems*. Copyright © 1960, 1961, 1962, 1963, 1964, 1965, 1966, 1967, 1972, 1974, 1975 by George Oppen); from John Matthias by permission of Anvil Press Poetry; from Roland Mathias, Anthony Conran, Raymond Garlick, and Harri Webb by permission of Gomer Press; from Emyr Humphreys by permission of Gee & Son (Denbigh) Ltd.; from *Native Ground* by Robert Minhinnick and from John Tripp by permission of Christopher Davies Ltd.

Index

(n = note)

Abse, Dannie 177
Ackroyd, Peter 49, 57n
Agassiz, Louis 199
Aneirin 15, 19, 20, 21
Anstey, Sandra 140n
Archard, Cary 147
Aristotle 21, 22, 138
Arnold, Matthew 71, 200, 216, 217
Ascherson, Neal 28, 29
Auden, W.H. 12, 99

Barrell, John 27
Barthes, Roland 215
Bayley, John 206
Bellerby, Frances 44
Benda, Julien 206, 207
Benjamin, Walter 26, 203-04, 211
Berdyaev, Nicolai 212-13
Berkeley, George 218
Berryman, John 99
Bevan, Aneirin 212
Bidgood, Ruth 168-71
Blackstone, William 24
Blake, William 11, 13, 16, 22, 24, 25, 59, 74, 158, 159, 187, 188, 199, 221
Blunden, Edmund 157
Blythe, Ronald, 96n
Borrow, George, 167
Bourget, P.C.J. 167, 168
Bradley, F.H. 51
Brake, Laurel 217
Brecht, Bertolt 211
Britten, Benjamin 29
Brontë, Emily, 38, 42, 44

Browning, Robert 143
Buber, Martin 62, 216-18
Bull, John 27
Bunting, Basil 9, 12, 18-21, 22, 23, 24, 28, 30, 173, 221
Burke, Edmund 220

Carr, E.H. 203
Casey, Mary 37-45, 155
Celan, Paul 208
Chadwick, Owen 167
Clare, John 221
Clarke, Gillian 151-55, 168
Coleridge, S.T. 11, 21, 22, 24, 25, 27, 33
Collingwood, R.G. 22
Conrad, Joseph 48, 123
Conran, Anthony 7, 114-22, 127, 156, 160, 161, 164, 168, 172
Crabbe, George 22
Crawshay, Richard 188
Croce, Benedetto 51

Dafydd ap Gwilym 149, 155, 162
Dante Alighieri 91, 207
Davenport, Guy 199-200
Davies, James A. 221
Davies, John 181, 192-96
Davies, Idris 124, 126, 156, 176, 180
Davies of Hereford, John 101
Delius, F. 159
Dembo, L.S. 72n, 75, 76, 95n, 96n
Descartes, René 90
Dixon, R.W., 214
Donne, John 51, 71
Dorn, Ed 97
Du Plessis, Rachel Blau 75

Eagleton, Terry 216, 220
Eliade, Mircea 206
Eliot, Andrew 47
Eliot, George 206
Eliot, T.S. 9, 10, 11, 15, 21, 25, 27, 28, 37, 38, 42, 46-57, 69, 90, 91, 97, 99, 100, 115, 124, 134, 157, 162, 174, 220
Elyot, Thomas 55
Emerson, R.W. 61, 81, 97
Emrys, Dewi 124, 126
Evans, Caradoc 126, 128
Ezekiel 54, 205

Finkielkraut, Alain 206
Fischer, Ernst 211, 212
Fisher, Roy 173, 212, 221
Forster, E.M. 186
Frazer, J.S. 51
Freud, Sigmund 51, 216

Garlick, Raymond 156, 157, 160, 161, 162, 167, 170, 177
Gaudier-Brzeska, Henri 72, 89, 96
Geoffrey of Monmouth 179
Giraldus Cambrensis 159
Gissing, George 182
Graham, W.S. 137
Graves, Robert 115
Greene, Graham 124
Griffiths, Steve 185, 186, 189-92, 193
Gurney, Ivor 10, 29, 221
Gwenallt (D. Gwenallt Jones) 127, 160

H.D. (Hilda Doolittle) 51
Hamann, J.G. 205
Hardy, Thomas 10, 26, 71, 93, 109, 146, 157
Harrison, Tony 11, 30, 33
Hatlen, Burton 72n, 95n, 96n
Hazlitt, William 89, 96n
Heaney, Seamus 11, 12, 13, 26, 30, 103, 152, 154, 181, 183
Heath, Edward 26
Heidegger, Martin 62, 78, 81, 82n, 83, 89, 90, 174, 216
Herbert, George 134
Herder, Gottfried 206

Hill, Geoffrey 9, 10, 11, 22-28, 30, 31n, 33, 50, 101, 103, 124, 137, 147, 173
Hitler, Adolf 89, 206
Homer 9, 17, 38, 49, 151
Hopkins, Gerard Manley 143, 199, 214-15, 221
Horovitz, Frances 154
Housman, A.E. 30
Hughes, Ted 10, 11, 126, 133, 152, 185, 221
Hugo, Richard 196
Huizinga, Johan 103
Hulme, T.E. 51, 89, 90, 96n, 155
Humphreys, Emyr 145, 146, 147, 149, 158, 160, 166-67, 177-78, 179, 180, 196, 212, 220

Iolo Morganwg 180

James, Henry 97
Jefferies, Richard 202
Jenkins, Mike 182, 185, 186-89, 193, 196
Jenkins, Nigel 181, 184-86, 188, 196
Jenkins, Randal 108
Johnson, Ronald 97, 102, 159-60, 164, 199
Jones, Bobi 171
Jones, David 9, 10, 11, 12, 13-18, 19, 21, 22, 23, 24, 28, 29, 30, 37, 40, 50, 98, 99, 101, 103, 105, 109, 114, 126, 135, 136, 149, 156, 157, 158, 160, 162, 167, 168, 172, 173, 174, 176, 213, 221
Jones, Glyn 124, 156, 160, 173, 176, 177, 180
Jones, J.R. 28, 173
Jones Peter 51, 96n
Jones, T. Harri 168
Joyce, James 10, 199
Jung, C.G. 51

Kavanagh, Patrick 148, 173, 176
Keats, John 22, 44, 152, 153
Kierkegaard, Søren 62, 82, 88, 94, 96n, 134, 138, 201
Kilvert, Francis 159
Kipling, Rudyard 11, 30
Kyffin, Morris 161

Index

Larkin, Philip 11, 193, 209, 221
Lawrence, D.H. 12, 13, 29, 38, 120, 152, 155, 200, 206
Leavis, F.R. 200, 202
Lenin, V.I. 103
Lewis, Alun 168, 193
Lewis, Lewis 187
Lewis, Saunders 15, 149, 160, 173, 174, 176, 178
Lifton, Robert Jay 56
Lloyd George, David 212
Lock, Charles 37, 40, 43, 44, 155
Lowell, Robert 99, 183
Löwith, Karl 212, 213
Lowrie, Walter, 96n

MacDiarmid, Hugh 221
Mandel, Tom 72n, 95n, 96n
Maritain, Jacques 58, 66, 76, 90
Martin, David 29, 30
Marx, Karl 103, 167, 203, 204, 208, 210, 211, 213, 216
Mathias, Roland 101, 124, 141-50, 156, 164-66, 167, 171, 172, 177, 220
Matthias, John 97-105
Mayakovsky, Vladimir 167, 211, 212
Melville, Herman 81
Miller, Hugh 199
Milosz, Czeslaw 199
Milton, John 78, 144, 221
Minhinnick, Robert 180-84, 193
Monroe, Harriet 58

Nairn, Tom 30
Norris, Christopher 215-16, 220
Norris, Leslie 156, 163-64

Olson, Charles 98, 99, 175
Oppen, George 33, 58-72, 73-96, 190, 192, 201, 217, 218
Oppen, Mary 65, 71, 83, 84, 96n
Ormond, John 7, 106-13, 156, 168-69, 220
Owen, Johnny 182
Owen, Wilfred 11, 22, 129, 188

Pacey, Philip 186
Pasternak, Boris 206, 212

Pater, Walter 222
Pevsner, Nikolaus 25
Pindar 38
Pinsky, Robert 97, 105
Plath, Sylvia 99, 183, 184
Plato 23, 27, 138
Plotinus 42, 43
Pope, Jessie 22
Pound, Ezra 10, 38, 42, 46, 51, 52, 68, 72, 89, 90, 96, 97, 98, 99, 158, 174, 186, 199, 200
Powell, Enoch 30
Powys, John Cowper 27, 28, 31, 32, 38, 201-02, 221
Powys, Llewelyn 38, 201
Powys, T.F. 38

Raleigh, Walter 11
Ranke, L. von 22
Reznikoff, Charles 64, 65, 66, 72, 87
Rhys, Keidrych 157
Riley, John 221
Rilke, R.M. 206
Rousseau, J.J. 167
Rözewicz, Tadeusz 33
Ruskin, John 199

Samuel, Raphael 30
Sappho 38
Sartre, J.P. 29, 206
Seneca 54
Sassoon, Siegfried 11
Shakespeare, William 23, 48, 50, 68, 89, 154, 207, 220, 221
Sidney, Philip 21-22
Sisson, C.H. 24, 137
Smith, Dai 178, 180
Smith, Stan 209-10
Snyder, Gary 186
Spengler, Oswald 206
Stalin, Joseph 212
Steiner, George 89, 96
Stephens, Meic 157, 171
Stevens, Wallace 100
Stevenson, Anne 143, 165
Swift, Jonathan 135

Taine, Hippolyte 206

Taliesin 19, 20, 21, 178
Tennyson, Alfred Lord 13
Tertullian 83
Thatcher, Margaret 104
Thomas, Dylan 107, 123, 124, 150, 160, 163, 169
Thomas, Edward 10, 29, 38, 134, 156, 163, 168, 169, 171, 209
Thomas, Ned 160
Thomas, R.S. 44, 124, 128-40, 145, 147, 154, 156, 157, 158, 160, 169, 170, 175, 176, 177, 179, 185, 193
Thoreau, H.D. 61, 81, 199
Thwaite, Anthony 220
Thompson, E.P. 30, 33
Tolkien, J.R.R. 159
Tomlinson, Charles 63, 72, 221
Torrance, Chris 186
Traherne, Thomas 165
Tripp, John 7, 123-27, 158, 160, 173
Tsvetayeva, Marina 206, 207

Vaughan, Henry 145, 159
Vico, Giambattista 209
Virgil 17

Wainwright, Jeffrey 30, 33-36

Watkins, Vernon 109, 124, 156, 164, 168, 169, 173
Webb, Harri 160, 161-62, 177
Weil, Simone 63, 64, 72, 201, 217, 218
Weston, Jessie L. 51
White, Gilbert 175
Whitehead, A.N. 51
Whitman, Walt 47, 61, 67, 81, 90, 167
Williams, Gwyn 126, 160
Williams, Gwyn A. 178-79, 180, 187, 196, 212
Williams, John Stuart 157
Williams, Raymond 28, 30, 179, 208
Williams, Waldo 160, 164, 167, 180
Williams, William Carlos 46, 47, 51, 57, 64, 65, 66, 67, 72, 98, 99, 158, 173
Williams Parry, R. 117
Wilson, Edmund 50
Wordsworth, William 11, 71, 87, 114, 128, 144, 171, 172
Wyatt, Thomas 38, 71

Yeats, W.B. 10, 70, 180

Zukofsky, Louis 18, 58, 66, 72